The Path of
Speech Technologies
in Computer Assisted
Language Learning

Routledge Studies in Computer Assisted Language Learning

EDITED BY CAROL CHAPPELLE

The Path of Speech Technologies in Computer Assisted Language Learning

From Research Toward Practice

Edited by

V. Melissa Holland

and

F. Pete Fisher

Routledge
Taylor & Francis Group

New York   London

First published 2008
by Routledge
711 third Avenue, New York, NY 10017

Simultaneously published in the United Kingdom
by Routledge
2 Park Square, Milton Park, Abingdon, Oxfordshire OX14 4RN

Routledge is an imprint of the Taylor & Francis Group, an informa business

First issued in paperback 2012

Typeset in 10 point Sabon Roman by IBT Global.

Library of Congress Cataloging in Publication Data
The path of speech technologies in computer assisted language learning : from research toward practice / edited by V. Melissa Holland and F. Pete Fisher.
p. cm. — (Routledge studies in computer assisted language learning ; 4)
Includes bibliographical references and index.
ISBN 978-0-415-96076-2 (hardback : alk. paper)
1. Language and languages—Computer-assisted instruction. 2. Speech—Data processing. I. Holland, V. Melissa. II. Fisher, F. Pete.

P53.28.P38 2008
418.0078'5--dc22   2007024389

ISBN13: 978-0-415-96076-2 (hbk)
ISBN13: 978-0-415-54300-2 (pbk)

Contents

List of Figures

Chapter 9

Chapter 10

List of Tables

Chapter 7

Chapter 8

Chapter 9

Chapter 10

1 The Path of Speech Technologies in CALL

Tracking the Science

V. Melissa Holland and F. Pete Fisher

ORGANIZING THE BOOK: REFLECTING THE FIELD

Stages of CALL Science

We designed this book to show the range of speech technologies in computer-assisted language learning (CALL) in the United States and Europe. While that range can be described on many dimensions, our original idea was to present work in three basic pillars of speech technology relevant to CALL: recognition, synthesis, and visualization. Research in these pillars leads to computer applications that, potentially, listen to learners speak (speech recognition), talk flexibly to them (speech synthesis), and display pictures of their speaking difficulties (visualization of the speech signal).

Yet, as we reviewed work in speech technologies for CALL, we were led to a new organization, one that suggests the relative maturity of the work in each pillar and that is more meaningful for viewing CALL as a scientific endeavor (acknowledging Davies, 2001). This organization reflects how science progresses from theoretical research through experimentation and development to test and evaluation, as schematized in Figure 1.1. We then shaped the book to reflect the paradigmatic path of CALL science more than to show the comprehensive uses of speech technologies in CALL. As instructional science, CALL starts from foundations of theory and research (e.g., second language acquisition, linguistics), moves to analyzing learner needs to give a focus for instruction, adapts core technologies (in this case, speech technologies) to those needs through experimentation, develops prototypes that integrate the adapted technologies, and, finally, evaluates those prototypes to inform refinements and extend the base of knowledge about CALL. In this way, evaluation feeds back into earlier stages of the process, as seen in Figure 1.1, ultimately yielding revisions to theory. This cycling between stages reflects integrationist frameworks for CALL science from Levy (1997) to Chapelle, Compton, Kon, and Sauro (2004).

The path of CALL science also leads to practice. In fact, this book can be seen as an argument for the scientific process—for its deliberation and doubt—as the way to move speech technologies into effective language learning practice.

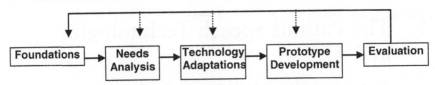

Figure 1.1 The path of speech technologies in CALL science.

Following Figure 1.1, the book is divided into sections that track the stages of CALL science. The chapters in each section are identified by author in Figure 1.2. The work covered in each chapter can be seen as representing a particular stage in a scientific progression. For example, the evaluations of an oral reading tutor described by Mostow et al. follow years of work in tapping relevant research, analyzing the needs of young readers, adapting speech recognition technology to those needs through experimentation, and developing and refining a prototype oral reading tutor. These earlier stages of the reading tutor project are well documented (Mostow et al., 1994). The same progression distinguishes the pronunciation tutors of Dalby and Kewley-Port and the automated spoken English test of Bernstein and Cheng. Signifying the culmination of long-term research and development, these systems contrast with the speech-interactive language lessons found in some commercial software, where ties to theory may be tenuous, where little research and only cursory technology adaptation precede the product, and where formative experimentation is rarely explicit or replicable. Shortcomings of speech-interactive packages in which the research path is sidestepped have been documented (Neri, Cucchiarini, Strik, & Boves, 2002; Wachowicz & Scott, 1999).

Significantly, some of the research presented in this book has transitioned into practice. Instances of these transitions will be pointed out in succeeding chapters.

Preceding each section of the book, we provide an introduction that describes how the chapters in that section fit the corresponding stage of CALL, highlights issues raised by the chapters, and references related work not contained in this book. Here, we briefly summarize each section.

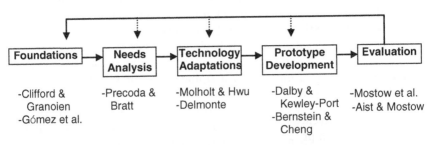

Figure 1.2 Book chapters mapped to stages of CALL science.

Sampling the Research Base

This section includes two chapters that sample the range of disciplines underlying CALL. Clifford and Granoien discuss second language pedagogical theory, the requirements it places on CALL, and its implications for employing speech-interactive CALL. Gómez et al. examine the physiological bases of speech perception and production, explaining why pronunciation is hard to teach and learn in new languages and postulating the benefits of visualization for bypassing some of the difficulties.

Analyzing Needs

The chapter by Precoda and Bratt in this section demonstrates work that ideally motivates a speech technology application: determining what is important to teach. In the context of pronunciation tutoring, the authors discuss their methodology for defining importance, how they use this methodology to prioritize pronunciation problems, and how this stage focuses the succeeding work of adapting automatic speech recognition to detect mispronunciations.

Adapting Speech Technology

This section includes two chapters on how component speech technologies are selected and adapted for second language instruction—how they are explored, tested, and shaped for CALL functions. Molholt and Hwu cover speech visualization technology for pronunciation diagnosis and instruction. Delmonte covers speech synthesis for an array of activities in an intelligent tutoring framework. The introduction to this section looks at speech recognition technology.

Developing Prototype Systems

This section treats the design and development of speech recognition-based systems following a period of experimentation to adapt the technology. Dalby and Kewley-Port address speech articulation training and Bernstein and Cheng, spoken language testing. These authors describe the assumptions and processes by which they have integrated component technologies, designed and structured exercises, and implemented and validated algorithms for scoring pronunciation and other speech skills.

Evaluating Systems

The two chapters in this section address complementary aspects of evaluating system effectiveness in real-world settings. Both chapters arise from a long-term research program in speech-interactive reading instruction. Mostow et al. present a formal assessment of a speech-interactive reading tutor compared with other forms of reading instruction; Aist and Mostow compare the effectiveness of different versions of the speech-interactive tutor varying in interface design.

Caveats

The mapping of book chapters to book schema is not as straightforward as Figure 1.2 suggests. Some of the chapters span several stages of the CALL model. For example, Gómez et al., while summarizing basic research that shows why the sounds of a second language are hard to perceive and learn, also sketch prototype designs for using visualization to teach those sounds. Similarly, Bernstein and Cheng, while describing a mature tool for assessing speaking facility, also address research bases and needs analyses. Dalby and Kewley-Port cover not only development of their articulation tutors but also evaluations in the lab demonstrating that these tutors can improve pronunciation skills. Nevertheless, the mapping in Figure 1.2 reflects our assessment of where best to place each chapter in relation to other work in the book.

Mapping Speech Recognition, Synthesis, and Visualization to Stages in CALL Science

Consider the distribution of these chapters according to the three pillars of speech technology: recognition (traditional speech-interactive CALL), visualization (spectrograms and other forms of acoustic display), and synthesis (automatically generated speech output). The chapters by Gómez et al. and by Molholt and Hwu address visualization; the chapter by Delmonte, synthesis as well as visualization; and the remaining six chapters, speech recognition as applied to pronunciation and other elements of oral skill. This distribution reflects the extent to which CALL employs each technology: A majority of the work involves speech recognition for pronunciation and related skill elements. Moreover, the speech recognition-based projects appear clustered toward the right in the model in Figure 1.1: Many have progressed through prior stages to the point of executing prototypes or evaluating systems; some projects, as we shall see (Bernstein & Cheng, Dalby & Kewley-Port, Precoda & Bratt), have spun off commercial products. By contrast, the synthesis and visualization work is newer and lies toward the left in the model. This work focuses largely on mining basic research and experimenting with component technologies. Projects at these earlier stages can pave the way for developing full prototypes and testing them with learners. We intend the organization of this book to help illuminate where recognition, synthesis, and visualization stand on the path from basic research through development and evaluation and, moreover, to suggest the readiness of each technology to move into practice.

PREVAILING CALL ISSUES: A PREVIEW

The chapters in this book bring up a range of issues, questions, and controversies in speech technology-based language learning. Here, we preview issues that are threaded throughout the volume. Further discussion of these issues appears in the introduction to each section of the book.

The Case Against Speech Technology in CALL

Pedagogical

It has been argued that using speech technology in CALL is premature. Instead of embracing speech-interactive prototypes, the language teaching community should wait for the technology to mature fully to meet the requirements of software reliability, instructional effectiveness, and communicative authenticity. The arguments may be summarized as follows:

- Automated speech recognition (ASR) makes errors so can frustrate or, worse, mislead the learner.
- Speech synthesis is not natural so furnishes a false model to the emerging learner.
- Visualization methods based on spectrograms and other acoustic displays are not meaningful for learners and for most teachers.

A moderation of the argument against ASR is voiced by Clifford and Granoien. Their chapter points out the limitations of ASR technology, which the authors suggest are often overlooked by researchers, developers, or teachers in their enthusiasm for novel and exciting methods. With the support of current pedagogical research and theory, the authors provide a framework for judging when ASR is appropriately applied so as not to overextend its technical reach.

The argument against speech synthesis is synopsized, and then answered, in the chapter by Delmonte. He offers conditions for when synthesis is a reasonable course of action, even as he rejects the extreme position that it be a primary voice for the student to hear.

The argument against teaching from acoustic displays is addressed by Gómez et al. While acknowledging the vast "semantic gap" between acoustic graphs and instructional communication, their chapter tempers the argument by describing transformations of acoustic displays hypothesized to bridge the gap. Gómez et al., like Molholt and Hwu, promote the promise of visualization but also point out the considerable research needed to develop methods that reliably use information from acoustic displays to teach articulatory distinctions.

Thus, these chapters lead to more nuanced arguments and proposals with respect to speech technology in CALL:

- ASR makes errors so it should be used for the right task and with proper constraints.
- Speech synthesis is not natural so it should be applied as a supplement, to speak text that is generated through adaptive methods that preclude prerecording of human voices.
- Visualization methods have promise and may demonstrate instructional effectiveness following a period of adaptation and user testing.

Economic

Another argument against using speech technology in CALL concerns the expense of developing and deploying speech-interactive tutors. Regarding development, some of the cost can be borne by programs outside language education, such as research in speech transcription and translation (Florian, 2002; Gauvain et al., 2005; Schultz & Kirchhoff, 2006), discussed in more detail below (the section, Speech Recognition and Future Capability). These programs, often aimed at commercial or defense needs, deliver components that are potential building blocks for CALL, such as language corpora and acoustic data in multiple languages (e.g., Mana et al., 2003; Schultz, 2002; the Linguistic Data Consortium), recognizers and synthesizers specifically targeted at multilingual speech (e.g., Tomokiyo, Black, & Lenzo, 2003), and tools to facilitate data collection, annotation, and modeling (e.g., Stolcke, 2002; Young et al., 2004). These data and tools can be leveraged for language learning, offsetting costs to CALL.

Additionally, technology can reach a point, as in the EduSpeak® product (Precoda & Bratt, this volume) and in many of the synthesis tools cited by Delmonte (this volume), where it is available from the web and may in some cases be downloaded free of charge. Examples that incorporate multilingual capability include the Festival/FestVox voice building environment (http://www.festvox.org) for developing synthetic voices and the language modeling toolkit from SRI (http://www.speech.sri.com/projects/srilm/) for constructing language models to constrain speech recognition.

Regarding deployment of speech-interactive CALL, it is true that much current work is in prototype form and thus unavailable for wide scale distribution with associated cost economies. Moreover, licenses for high-quality, well adapted speech software may not be easily affordable by the average institution. However, as speech-interactive commercial packages emerge from thorough testing and validation, the availability of high-quality speech-based CALL can be expected to increase and its cost, to decline.

The economic objection might be further mitigated by considering the benefits of speech technology in CALL. The cost of language education in the form of teacher time and classroom time, especially when consumed by low-level activities like pronunciation drills that can be offloaded to speech-interactive software, may balance the expense of developing and implementing that software. In the case of skills like reading, the indirect cost of failure to read and its cascading effect on other learning, as well as the ultimate cost of illiteracy to a society, may well outweigh the cost of developing and fielding an automated reading tutor.

Pedagogical Choices and the Need for Empirical Grounding

Clifford and Granoien (this volume) comment that CALL tends to be driven by the allure of technology more than by an understanding of how people learn. What is needed, they propose, is grounding in credible contemporary theories of second language pedagogy. The theories they point to include interactionist frameworks for language teaching (e.g., Gass, 2004; Gibbons, 2002; Kern, Ware, & Warschauer, 2004), which reflect an earlier, more general shift in cognitive and learning theory toward social constructivist and situated explanations (e.g., Brown, Collins, & Duguid, 1989). We would amend this proposal, following Anderson, Reder, and Simon's (1996) critique of situated cognition frameworks in educational research, by suggesting that CALL make additional links to theories, experimental methods, and findings from instructional science, psycholinguistics, cognitive psychology, and computer–human interface design. Ways in which work in these fields can inform CALL design have been outlined previously, for example, deciding the sequence of presentation, the frequency of repetition, and the depth of feedback (e.g., MacWhinney, 1995; Holland & Kaplan, 1995). Updates from these fields may be found in the cognitive and instructional research literature, ranging from studies of the effect of amount and pace of practice on learning and retention (Pavlik & Anderson, 2005; Peladeau, Forget, & Gagne, 2003) to investigation of text variables influencing first language vocabulary learning (Baumann, Edwards, Boland, Olejnik, & Kame'enui, 2003). Several chapters in this book tap methods and findings from these fields, including Mostow et al., whose evaluation measures come from research on the reading process; Dalby and Kewley-Port, whose tutor designs draw on research in human speech perception and production; and Bernstein and Cheng, whose assessment instrument reflects psycholinguistic models of speaking skill.

Tapping into the experimental learning sciences may counteract a tendency in CALL to lean on pedagogical assumptions that have had little empirical testing. In some of the ensuing chapters, for example, we find assumptions about the superiority of autonomous over guided learning, about the transparency of acoustic displays, and about the advantage of communicative authenticity over piecemeal practice. Many of these assumptions are accepted in the CALL community, but what they mean in application, whether they bear out in use, and how they might vary with learner type and instructional content, all need to be experimentally examined.

Evaluation and the Need for Valid Measures

Evaluation is essential for determining how to improve a CALL prototype, for deciding the readiness of a prototype to move to product, for comparing between products, and for building a knowledge base for CALL research. However, the sparseness of evaluation in CALL has been acknowledged, as have limitations of the evaluative data that are available (e.g., Zhao, 2003). The newer subfield of speech-interactive CALL presents even less assessment, and what there is, typically remains in the research lab. Clearly, laboratory evaluations are a place to start, but they leave open the question: Will prototypes scale up to use in the classroom or language lab?

Evaluations in the real world can encompass data at several levels: usability and reliability of software, attitudes and acceptance by students and teachers, and effectiveness of instruction. Whereas questionnaires and checklists have been developed to help assess attitudes and usability (e.g., Burston, 2003), assessment of instructional effectiveness is more problematic, raising questions about what to measure, how to measure it, and how to define a control group. For example, standard language proficiency measures such as the Interagency Language Roundtable (ILR) scales (http://www.govtilr.org) are likely to be insensitive to the small amount of content available in most CALL prototypes (Johnson, 2004, discusses modes of assessing language development in learners).

This book does not purport to overview or critique measures of effectiveness for speech-interactive CALL. However, several chapters (Bernstein & Cheng, Dalby & Kewley-Port, Mostow et al., Aist & Mostow) treat seriously the problem of evaluation, tracing issues in development, reliability, and validity of the metrics they use for language learning and language skill. Designs to measure learning gains are presented by Dalby and Kewley-Port and tests for validity of measures are discussed by Bernstein and Cheng. Two of the chapters—Aist and Mostow, and Mostow et al.—present longitudinal evaluations based in real classrooms. These classroom evaluations adopt measures grounded in well established instruments that have been standardized in other fields, such as the assessment of reading skill. These evaluations can be seen as models for assessing effectiveness in CALL.

Implications for Second Language Acquisition (SLA)

The prototypes described in this book have not been in use long enough to enable collection of the dense longitudinal data required to inform us about second language acquisition. Garrett (1992) originally conceived the enterprise known as CARLA (Computer-Assisted Research in Language Acquisition) in terms of text-based exercises that could yield information on grammatical errors and their evolution. Speech-based CALL also has the potential to contribute to CARLA. In particular, diagnostic pronunciation tutors such as prefigured by Precoda and Bratt (this volume) can collect spoken language data to track patterns of error and improvement in specific phonemes and thereby shed light on the acquisition of second language phonology. Data logging and tracking mechanisms must be built into the prototypes and teachers or lab directors motivated to use those mechanisms. Bernstein and Cheng's Versant method (formerly, PhonePass) for testing spoken facility in a second language (this volume) illustrates a system that records automatically generated scores—for example, on dimensions of pronunciation and fluency—which could be explored longitudinally to discover patterns of growth.

Reviewing the path of CALL science (Figure 1.1), we foresee a phase in which data collected by speech-interactive CALL feeds back into the research base on SLA—a phase in which the technology provides not only a teaching tool but also an experimental resource that strengthens the foundation for CALL. Deciding which measures are important to log, and how to combine them for testing SLA hypotheses, is a matter of some consequence and requires coordination with the SLA research community (Chapelle et al., 2004; Doughty & Long, 2003; Garrett, 1998).

Technical Issues in Automated Speech Recognition

Research in CALL takes speech technology as given and considers how best to employ and shape it for instruction. In the case of automated speech recognition, how is CALL currently exploiting the technology, and what advances in ASR might advance CALL?

Speech Recognition and Current CALL Capability

Overviews as well as detailed treatments of ASR technology are readily available (e.g., Huang, Acero, & Hon, 2001; Jelinek, 1997). In brief, speech recognizers begin by calculating a representation of the incoming acoustic signal based on sampling and extracting certain of its features. This sampling is done at very short (tens of milliseconds) time intervals, representing basic sound units. The representations for each unit are compared with models stored in the computer's memory, which correspond to phones or parts of phones. The model in memory that best fits the signal's features is a candidate for output. Next, a short sequence of basic units is compared with sequences in the computer's memory (a language model, or prediction of what sounds are likely to follow what) to find the overall best fit to that segment, which might correspond to a word or words. These best guesses by the computer are necessary because speech is inherently variable: The signal corresponding to a given word varies not only between speakers but on different occasions for the same speaker. Because ASR is an estimate, error is inevitable.

ASR errors increase with the uncertainty of an utterance, which is proportional to the number of alternative words possible in the utterance and the number of ways in which they can be sequenced (a concept formalized as *perplexity*). As computers grow in capacity, ASR can support tasks of increasing uncertainty while keeping error rates constant. Large-vocabulary continuous speech recognition, or LVCSR, can now handle vocabularies exceeding one hundred thousand words. LVCSR is the basis for today's automatic dictation systems, which permit a business or home user to dictate relatively unconstrained sentences that the computer transcribes. Although the software can be speaker-independent, it performs better after the recognizer is trained to the user's voice, attaining word recognition accuracy percentages in the high 90s. Moreover, users can immediately correct word errors as transcriptions are displayed or voiced back. These systems are available in languages with large commercial markets, such as English, French, German, Spanish, and Japanese.

What are the implications for CALL of error in speech recognition? Whereas users of dictation systems expect and can recover from recognition errors, this is not the case, arguably, for language learners. That is precisely the lesson of prior attempts to create unscripted conversational language tutors (systems such as discussed in Holland, 1999). Failing to achieve sufficient robustness to work for learners, these attempts have not progressed beyond research prototypes.

The progress toward practice has instead come from more controlled applications of ASR. One of these, as indicated earlier, is teaching or testing pronunciation and other elements of oral skill (discussed in Kim, 2006). Pronunciation scoring algorithms, adapted from speech recognition, assume a fixed spoken utterance and grade the degree to which a learner's input matches a native speaker standard for that utterance. Exercises are designed to elicit a given word or phrase by displaying it for the learner to read or voicing it for the learner to repeat. Feedback to learners is generated from the automatic scores. This application is seen in the analyses of Precoda and Bratt (this volume) and in mature products based on such analyses, for example, Eduspeak® (Franco et al., 2000), NativeAccent™ (Eskenazi, Ke, Albornoz, & Probst, 2000; http://www.carnegiespeech.com/), Versant for English™ (Bernstein & Cheng, this volume), and training aids from Communication Disorders Technology (Dalby & Kewley-Port, this volume). Additional work in adapting ASR for pronunciation training in languages ranging from Modern Standard Arabic to Korean can be found in Mote, Sethy, Silva, Narayanan, and Johnson (2004), Neri, Cucchiarini, and Strik (2001), and Kim, Wang, Peabody, and Seneff (2004).

Another controlled application of ASR in CALL is recognizing a learner's utterance from a small set of choices, which may be displayed, voiced, or implied. Multiple choice gives learners a sense of communicating while it minimizes recognition possibilities. The job of the recognizer is to find which choice is the best match to a learner's utterance. CALL software uses that determination to give feedback or to branch the dialogue or the events in the computer world. This form of speech-interactive CALL is available now, for example, in the deployed version of the Tactical Language Trainer (http://www.tacticallanguage.com/tacticaliraqi/) developed by the Information Sciences Institute (ISI) at the University of Southern California (Johnson et al., 2004).

The riskier application of ASR to "free" conversational CALL remains appealing. Instead of telling learners what to say, conversational CALL aims to let them have unscripted dialogue with the computer, a step toward linguistic immersion and in keeping with communicative language pedagogy. The idea is to limit expected utterances through tacit constraints in the task, dialogue, or interface design. Research efforts in this direction include basic work to adapt ASR algorithms for nonnative speech, such as the Spoken Conversational Interaction for Language Learning (SCILL) project at Cambridge University (Ye & Young, 2005), and experiments to marry design innovations with technology adaptations, such as the dialogue tutors by the Spoken Language Systems group at the Massachusetts Institute of Technology (Seneff, Wang, & Zhang, 2004) and the conversational agents developed for advanced virtual worlds by ISI (Traum, Swartout, Marsella, & Gratch, 2005). Robust ASR is only one ingredient of conversational CALL, which also requires natural language processing, dialogue management, and other intelligent software methods to support and maintain interaction with learners. These efforts continue to evolve but have not yet yielded practical systems. As Clifford and Granoien note in this volume, "support of unconstrained, spontaneous dialogue remains outside the realm of possibility for [speech-interactive] CALL at present."

Speech Recognition and Future CALL Capability

In addition to efforts supporting conversational CALL, other directions in ASR research have the potential to advance CALL. Here we consider developing algorithms for less commonly taught languages, modeling the speech of language learners, and analyzing prosody.

Commercial speech recognizers target languages with profitable markets, which coincide with more commonly taught languages (French, German, Spanish, English, etc.). To expand the range of languages covered by speech-interactive CALL requires development of recognition algorithms for less commonly taught languages (LCTLs), such as Tagalog and Somali. This development depends on extensive collection and annotation of speech and dialogue data in those languages to support building of acoustic models and language models.

Moreover, existing speech recognizers target native speakers—the standard user for a range of commercial applications. However, language learning applications must recognize nonnative speakers who are at different levels of proficiency. Developing this capability requires extensive collection of speech data from language learners. The challenge is twofold. First, pronunciation assessment calls for acoustic data from both native and nonnative speakers to enable construction of scoring algorithms. Also required are data on expert human scores for calibrating the automatic scores. In nonpronunciation CALL, such as multiple-choice dialogue and vocabulary tutors, ASR does not know in advance what is being said and must determine it. In that case, speech data must be collected from learners at varying skill levels so that algorithms can be trained to recognize them, even when their utterances are imperfect. In addition, data for error modeling are needed so that learner utterances falling into expected error categories can be identified by the system and the learner can be given appropriate feedback.

Therefore, a prerequisite for expanding ASR-based language learning is collecting speech data of the kind underrepresented in commercial enterprises. For the first data requirement, LCTLs, government-sponsored collection efforts are key. For example, research programs in the U.S. and Europe have begun to collect LCTL speech data to build speech transcription and speech-to-speech translation systems in support of diplomatic, defense, and humanitarian work (e.g., Gao, 2005; Messaoudi, Lamel, & Gauvain, 2004; Srinivasamurthy & Narayanan, 2003; Stallard et al., 2003; Suebvisai, Charoenpornsawat, Black, Woszczyna, & Schultz, 2005). Such efforts have led to working speech recognizers for a range of languages, such as Farsi, Thai, and Modern Standard Arabic and dialects. Boosting these efforts is research on cross-language portability methods to generalize algorithms to new languages while reducing the amount of data required to develop a specific language (Schultz, 2004; Ye & Young, 2005). Progress in portability methods is crucial for LCTLs, where preexisting speech data for developing ASR may be sparse. As translation and transcription efforts grow, aided by techniques for cross-language portability, aspects of the resulting data should serve speech-interactive CALL, enabling it to embrace new languages. Research on speech synthesis also shows progress toward portability, with methods specialized to deal with low-resource languages (Maskey, Black, & Tomokiyo, 2004).

For the second data requirement, learner speech, including typical errors and mispronunciations, data collection has begun in separate projects (e.g., Mote et al., 2004; Ehsani & Knotd, 1998; Kim et al., 2004). Arguing for a merger of such efforts, Egan and Kuhlman (1999) have advocated systematic collection and housing of data by the language education community collaborating with speech researchers. Collection and use of learner speech can be facilitated by advances in majority ASR research: for example, improved tools for data collection, annotation, and modeling; and for recognizing disfluencies in spoken utterances (Honal & Schultz, 2005). Also relevant to this requirement is research on adapting ASR algorithms for nonnative speech (Wang, Schultz, & Waibel, 2003; Ye & Young, 2005). Similarly, advances in speech synthesis, such as improving the naturalness and comprehensibility of voices (Langner & Black, 2005), could position future synthesis as a standard capability in CALL.

A third direction in ASR research with potential to advance CALL is analysis of prosody. Speech recognizers today are aimed at distinguishing segmental elements that compose words rather than suprasegmental elements that make up prosody—that is, intonation (loudness and pitch) and rhythm (duration and pauses). Yet, prosody is widely acknowledged to affect the intelligibility of learners' utterances separately from phone articulation (Celce Murcia & Goodwin, 1991), as well as to contribute independently to perception of nonnativeness (Precoda & Bratt, this volume; Dalby & Kewley-Port, this volume). Challenging the development of reliable algorithms for prosodic analysis is the enormous variation in how native speakers realize intonation and rhythm compared with how they realize phones; moreover, prosody fluctuates with semantic and pragmatic context much more than do phones. Thus, individuals uttering the same sentence can differ widely in patterns of rhythm and intonation while still being understandable and perceived as native. One way to contend with individual variation is to express prosodic measures not in absolute but in relative terms, such as the duration of one syllable compared to an adjacent one. CALL prosody prototypes have been developed on this principle to detect learners' departures from acceptable native values of given utterances, for example, work by Eskenazi et al. (2000), Delmonte and his colleagues (2000; Bacalu & Delmonte, 1999), and Komissarchik and Komissarchik (2000). Short of automatic detection of learner errors, speech visualization has been used to illustrate how specific languages differ on prosodic dimensions and how learners deviate from natives in stress and pitch patterns for particular utterances (Martin, 2005; Molholt & Hwu, this volume).

A further challenge to reliable extraction and classification of prosodic features from the speech signal is the scarcity of multilingual speech data with transcriptions marked for prosody, as needed to anchor automatic analysis. Initiatives to build such data, as well as automatic techniques to recognize prosodic features, are likely to arise from other research endeavors, such as the quest for high-accuracy speech transcription and translation.

Another aspect of the prosodic challenge is recognizing tonal distinctions in languages such as Chinese Mandarin and Vietnamese, where a change in pitch contour of a speech segment can constitute a morphemic change. Although speech-interactive CALL has not concentrated on these languages, a significant example is research by the MIT Spoken Language Systems Group to develop a Mandarin tutor that extracts pitch contours for automatic assessment of tone production (Peabody, Seneff, & Wang, 2004)—work that builds on the Mandarin speech recognizer created by MIT for dialogue-based information access (Wang et al., 2000).

CONCLUSION

The chapters in this book demonstrate the range of work in speech technology for CALL. That work encompasses the three technology pillars (speech recognition, synthesis, and visualization). It addresses both second language learning (most chapters) and first language learning (the reading tutor of Aist and Mostow). The intended learners include speech-impaired children (Dalby & Kewley-Port) as well as postsecondary adults (most chapters). Applications include both tutoring (addressed by most chapters) and testing (Bernstein & Cheng). In terms of target skill, the work extends from word pronunciation (Precoda & Bratt) to sentence syntax (Delmonte). In terms of target language, the range is from more commonly taught (Spanish, English, Italian) to less commonly taught (Mandarin Chinese and Hindi, in Molholt & Hwu). In all cases, these chapters reflect Levy's (1997) definition of CALL as inherently multidisciplinary, a point made plain in speech-interactive CALL. To integrate speech technologies into CALL takes computer scientists, engineers, psychologists, and education specialists as well as foreign language teachers. The chapter authorship in this book often reflects such a mix—for example, Dalby is an engineer while Kewley-Port is an experimental psychologist. Reinforcing the point, it has been argued that advances in the discipline of human language technology (HLT), such as natural language processing, can serve to advance CALL (Schulze, 2001) and that CALL can grow on the expanding shoulders of HLT. Speech technologies are one clear way that research in HLT can contribute to CALL research and eventually CALL practice. That this contribution must be carefully researched, scrupulously developed, and continually honed through questioning, experimentation, and evaluation, is reflected in the sum of these chapters.

NOTE ON PHONEMIC NOTATION

Phonemic symbols appear in several chapters, drawn from the International Phonetic Alphabet (IPA) or its variants, depending on the purpose and location of the author(s). Thus, notation for some phonemes varies between chapters (e.g., /ch/ and /č/ for the initial sound in "chair").

ACKNOWLEDGMENTS

We wish to recognize Philippe Delcloque of the University of Manchester, UK, for the original organizing principle of this book—the three pillars of speech technology—and for bringing into focus the emerging work on speech visualization and synthesis featured here. He is responsible for arranging the contributions in those areas by Delmonte, by Gómez et al., and by Molholt and Hwu. We also wish to recognize the CALICO Journal for publishing the first collection of U.S. research on speech recognition in CALL (Holland, 1999). Many of the contributors to that collection are included in this book, in later stages of their work. Finally, we are grateful to Gina Hall, our production specialist, who meticulously edited and formatted successive and final versions of the manuscript.

REFERENCES

Anderson, J. R., Reder, L., & Simon, H. (1996). Situated versus cognitive perspectives: Form versus substance. *Educational Researcher, 26*, 18–21.

Bacalu, C., & Delmonte, R. (1999). Prosodic modeling for syllable structures from the VESD—Venice English Syllable Database. *Proceedings of Atti IX Convegno GFS–AIA*, 147–158, Venice.

Baumann, J., Edwards, E., Boland, E., Olejnik, S., & Kame'enui, E. (2003). Vocabulary tricks: Effects of instruction in morphology and context on fifth-grade students' ability to derive and infer word meanings. *American Educational Research Journal, 40*, 447–494.

Brown, J. S., Collins, A., & Duguid, P. (1989). Situated cognition and the culture of learning. *Educational Researcher, 18*, 32–43.

Burston, J. (2003). Software selection: A primer on sources and evaluation. *CALICO Journal, 21*, 29–40.

Celce Murcia, M., & Goodwin, J. (1991). Teaching pronunciation. In M. Celce Murcia (Ed.), *Teaching English as a second language*. Boston: Heinle and Heinle.

Chapelle, C. A., Compton, L., Kon, E., & Sauro, S. (2004). Theory, research & practice in CALL: Making the links. In L. Lomicka & J. Cooke-Plagwitz (Eds.), *Teaching with technology* (pp. 189–208). Boston: Heinle and Heinle.

Davies, G. (2001). New technologies and language learning: A suitable subject for research? In A. Chambers & G. Davies (Eds.), *ICT and language learning: A European perspective*. Lisse, NL: Swets & Zeitlinger.

Delmonte, R. (2000). SLIM prosodic automatic tools for self-learning instruction. *Speech Communication, 30*, 145–166.

Doughty, C., & Long, M. H. (Eds.) (2003). *The handbook of second language acquisition*. Malden, MA: Blackwell.

Egan, K., & Kuhlman, A. (1999). Speaking: A critical skill and a challenge. *CALICO Journal, 16*, 279–291.

Ehzani, F., & Knodt, E. (1998). Speech technology in computer-aided language learning: Strengths and limitations of a new CALL paradigm. *Language Learning and Technology* [On-line], *2*, 45–60. [Retrieved on January 25, 2007, from http://llt.msu.edu/vol2num1/article3/index.html]

Eskenazi, M., Ke, Y., Albornoz, J., & Probst, K. (2000). Update on the Fluency pronunciation trainer. *Proceedings of InSTIL 2000 (Integrating Speech Technology in (Language) Learning)*, 73–76, Dundee, Scotland.

Florian, M. (2002). Enhancing the usability and performance of NESPOLE!: A real-world speech-to-speech translation system. *Proceedings of Human Language Technology (HLT 2002)*, San Diego.

Franco, H., Abrash, V., Precoda, K., Bratt, H., Rao, R., & Butzberger, J. (2000). The SRI EduSpeak system: Recognition and pronunciation scoring for language learning. *Proceedings of InSTIL 2000 (Integrating Speech Technology in (Language) Learning)*, 123–128, Dundee, Scotland.

Gao, Y. (2005). Portability challenges in developing interactive dialogue systems. *Proceedings of ICASSP05*, Philadelphia.

Garrett, N. (1992). CARLA comes to CALL. *CALL, 4*, 99–104.

Garrett, N. (1998). Where do research and practice meet? Developing a discipline. *ReCALL, 10*, 7–12.

Gass, S. (2004). Conversation analysis and input-interaction. *The Modern Language Journal, 88*, 597–602.

Gauvain, J., Adda, G., Adda-Decker, M., Allauzen, G., Gendner, V., Lamel, L., et al. (2005). Where we are in transcribing French broadcast news. *Proceedings of EUROSPEECH-INTERSPEECH 2005*, Lisbon.

Gibbons, P. (2002). *Scaffolding language, scaffolding learning: Teaching second language learners in the mainstream classroom.* Portsmouth, NH: Henemann.

Holland, V. M. (Ed.) (1999). Tutors that listen: Speech recognition for language learning. *CALICO Journal, 16*(3), 243–468. Special issue.

Holland, V. M., & Kaplan, J. (1995). Application of learning principles to the design of a second language tutor. In V. M. Holland, J. Kaplan, & M. Sams (Eds.), *Intelligent language tutors.* Hillsdale, NJ: Lawrence Erlbaum Associates.

Honal, M., & Schultz, T. (2005). Automatic disfluency removal on recognized spontaneous speech—Rapid adaptation to speaker-dependent disfluencies. *Proceedings of ICASSP 2005*, Philadelphia.

Huang, X., Acero, A., & Hon, H.-W. (2001). *Spoken language processing.* Englewood Cliffs, NJ: Prentice Hall.

Jelinek, F. (1997). *Statistical methods for speech recognition.* Cambridge, MA: MIT Press.

Johnson, M. (2004). *A philosophy of second language acquisition.* New Haven: Yale University Press.

Johnson, W. L., Marsella, S., Mote, N., Si, M., Vilhjalmsson, H., & Wu, S. (2004). Balanced perception and action in the tactical language training system. *Proceedings of the International Workshop on Autonomous Agents and Multi-Agent Systems (AAMAS WS 2004)*, New York.

Kern, R., Ware, P., & Warschauer, M. (2004). Crossing frontiers: New directions in online pedagogy and research. *Ann. Review of Applied Linguistics, 24*, 243–260.

Kim, I. (2006). Automatic speech recognition: Reliability and pedagogical implications for teaching pronunciation. *Educational Technology and Society, 9*, 322–334.

Kim, J., Wang, C., Peabody, M., & Seneff, S. (2004). An interactive pronunciation dictionary for Korean. *Proceedings of 8th International Conf. on Spoken Language Processing (ICSLP 04)*, Jeju, Korea.

Komissarchik, E., & Komissarchik, J. (2000). Application of knowledge-based speech analysis to suprasegmental pronunciation training. *Proceedings of AVIOS 2000*, San Jose, CA.

Langner, B., & Black, A. (2005). Improving the understandability of speech synthesis by modeling speech in noise. *Proceedings of* ICASSP 2005, Philadelphia.

Levy, M. (1997). Theory-driven CALL and the development process. *CALL, 10*, 41–56.

Linguistic Data Consortium (LDC). University of Pennsylvania. [Retrieved on January 23, 2006, from http://www.ldc.upenn.edu/]

MacWhinney, B. (1995). Evaluating foreign language tutoring systems. In Holland, V. M., Kaplan, J., & Sams, M. (Eds.), *Intelligent language tutors.* Mahwah, NJ: Lawrence Erlbaum Associates.

Mana, N., et al. (2003). The NESPOLE! VoIP corpora in tourism and medical domains. *Proceedings of EUROSPEECH 2003*, Geneva.

Martin, P. (2005). WinPitch LTL, un logiciel multimédia d'enseignement de la prosodie. *ALSIC, Apprentissage des Langues et Systèmes d'Information et de Communication, 8*, 95–108.

Maskey, S., Black, A., & Tomokiyo, L.M., (2004). Bootstrapping phonetic lexicons for new languages. *Proceedings of ICSLP04*, Jeju, South Korea.

Messaoudi, A., Lamel, L., & Gauvain. J. (2004). Transcription of Arabic broadcast news. *Proceedings of ICSLP 2004*, 521–524, Jeju, South Korea.

Mostow, J., Roth, S., Hauptmann, A., & Kane, M. (1994). A prototype reading coach that listens. *Proceedings of the Twelfth National Conference on Artificial Intelligence* (AAAI-94). Seattle.

Mote, N., Sethy, A., Silva, J., Narayanan, S., & Johnson, W.L. (2004). Detection and modeling of learner speech errors: The case of Arabic tactical language training for American English speakers. *Proceedings of InSTIL04*, Venice.

Neri, A., Cucchiarini, C., & Strik, H. (2001). Effective feedback on L2 pronunciation in ASR-based CALL. *Proceedings of the Workshop in CALL, Artificial Intelligence in Education Conference*, 45–48, San Antonio, TX.

Neri, A., Cucchiarini, C., Strik, H., & Boves, L. (2002). The pedagogy-technology interface in Computer Assisted Pronunciation Training. *Computer Assisted Language Learning, 15*, 441–467.

Pavlik, P., & Anderson, J. R. (2005). Practice and forgetting effects on vocabulary memory: An activation-based model of the spacing effect. *Cognitive Science, 29*, 559–586.

Peabody, M., Seneff, S., & Wang, C. (2004). Mandarin tone acquisition through typed interactions. *Proceedings of InSTIL/ICALL: NLP and Speech Technologies in Advanced Language Learning Systems*, Venice.

Peladeau, N., Forget, J., & Gagne, F. (2003). Effect of paced and unpaced instruction on skill application and retention: How much is enough? *American Educational Research Journal, 40*(3), 769–801.

Schultz, T. (2002). GlobalPhone: A multilingual speech and text database developed at Karlsruhe University. *Proceedings of Intl. Conf. on Speech and Language Processing (ICSLP02)*, Denver, CO.

Schultz, T. (2004). Towards rapid language portability of speech processing systems. *Proceedings of Conf. on Speech and Language Systems for Human Communication (SPLASH)*, Delhi, India.

Schultz, T., & Kirchhoff, K. (2006). *Multilingual speech processing*. Amsterdam: Elsevier.

Schulze, M. (2001). Human language technologies in computer-assisted language learning. In A. Chambers & G. Davies (Eds.), *ICT and language learning: A European perspective*. Lisse, NL: Swets & Zeitlinger.

Seneff, S., Wang, C., & Zhang, J (2004). Spoken conversational interaction for language learning. *Proceedings of InSTIL04*, Venice.

Srinivasamurthy, N., & Narayanan, S. (2003). Language adaptive Persian speech recognition. *Proceedings of EUROSPEECH03*, Geneva.

Stallard, D., Makhoul, J., Choi, F., Macrostie, E., Natarajan, P., Schwartz, R., et al. (2003). Design and evaluation of a limited 2-way speech translator. *Proceedings of EUROSPEECH03*, Geneva.

Stolcke, A. (2002). SRILM—An extensible language modeling toolkit. *Proceedings of Intl. Conf. Spoken Language Processing*, 901–904, Denver, CO. [Retrieved on May 22, 2007 from http://www.speech.sri.com/projects/srilm/]

Suebvisai, S., Charoenpornsawat, P., Black, A., Woszczyna, M., & Schultz, T., (2005). Thai automatic speech recognition. *Proceedings of ICASSP05*, Philadelphia.

Tomokiyo, L. M., Black, A. & Lenzo, K. (2003). Arabic in my hand: Small-footprint synthesis of Egyptian Arabic. *Proceedings of EUROSPEECH03*, Geneva.

Traum, D., Swartout, W., Marsella S., & Gratch, J. (2005). Fight, flight, or negotiate: Believable strategies for conversing under crisis. *Proceedings of 5th International Conference on Interactive Virtual Agents*, Kos, Greece.

Wachowicz, C., & Scott, B. (1999). Software that listens: It's not a question of whether, it's a question of how. *CALICO Journal, 16*, 263–278.

Wang, C., Cyphers, S., Mou, X., Polifroni, J., Seneff, S., Yi, J., & Zue, V. (2000). Muxing: A telephone-access Mandarin conversational system. *Proceedings of 4th International Conf. on Spoken Language Processing (ICSLP00)*, 715–718, Beijing.

Wang, Z., Schultz, T, & Waibel, A. (2003). Comparison of acoustic model adaptation techniques on nonnative speech. *Proceedings of ICASSP03*.

Ye, H., & Young, S. (2005). Improving speech recognition performance of beginners in spoken conversational interaction for language learning. *Proceedings of INTERSPEECH05*, Lisbon.

Young, S., Evermann, G., Kershaw, D., Moore, G., Odell, J., Ollason, D., et al. (2004). *The HTK Book (for HTK Version 3.2)*. Cambridge University Engineering Department. [Retrieved on May 22, 2007 from http://htk.eng.cam.ac.uk/]

Zhao, Y. (2003). Recent developments in technology and language learning: A literature review and meta-analysis. *CALICO Journal, 21*, 7–28.

Section I

Sampling the Research Base
Language Pedagogy, Speech Perception

INTRODUCTION: THE RANGE OF RESEARCH AND THEORY

Computer assisted language learning (CALL) builds on a range of research and theory, from linguistics to second language acquisition to pedagogy to computer–human interface. Moreover, CALL that is speech-interactive builds on research in speech perception and production as well as in acoustic engineering and physics. The research base that supports CALL might be summed up as spanning teaching, learning, and language itself. In this first section of the book, we sample the research base in two areas: pedagogical theory in the chapter by Clifford and Granoien and learning processes in the chapter by Gómez, Álvarez, Martínez, Bobadilla, Bernal, Rodellar, and Nieto.

SETTING THE STAGE FOR LATER CHAPTERS

Clifford and Granoien provide a global perspective on second language pedagogy, viewing language at the discourse level. Gómez et al. provide a local perspective on learning processes, viewing language at the phonological level. While these perspectives differ in level and scope, they are important in framing the succeeding chapters. Clifford and Granoien's holistic framework is grounded in interactionist principles that go beyond communicative language teaching to explain the development of grammatical as well as semantic competence; it is one that many researchers in language pedagogy are likely to bring to this book. Citing the functionally based proficiency guidelines of the American Council on the Teaching of Foreign Languages (ACTFL) and the Interagency Language Roundtable (ILR), their chapter shows how the succeeding chapters relate to this shared framework. Gomez et al.'s physiological framework, depicting the mechanisms of speech perception, explains why the sound discriminations of a second language are hard to hear and to produce. This explanation validates the focus of most language tutors featured in this book, which is on pronunciation rather than on discourse. Gómez et al.'s chapter also explains why invoking the visual modality may help to teach second-language auditory distinctions, thus setting the stage for visualization techniques offered in later chapters. Both Gómez et al. and Clifford and Granoien emphasize that language learning cannot occur just by exposure, just by listening and repeating.

Clarifying the Limitations of ASR in Interactionist Language Teaching

Clifford and Granoien provide a cautionary voice for technology in language learning. The desiderata they set forth for CALL derive from contemporary trends in educational theory that see all learning as socially mediated and interactively constructed (e.g., Collins, Brown, & Newman, 1989; Lave & Wenger, 1991). Social constructivist theory has been applied to education in schools, revealing how classroom discourse serves to scaffold learning (Cazden, 1988; Newman, Griffin, & Cole, 1989). First developed around core school subjects such as mathematics (Schoenfeld, 1987) and reading (Langer, 1985), social interactionist explanations have more recently found solid and detailed substantiation in patterns of second language acquisition, both natural and instructed (e.g., Doughty, 2003, 1999; Gass, 2004; Gass, Mackey, & Pica, 1998; Meskill, 2005; Swain, 2000).

Examining interactionist desiderata, Clifford and Granoien conclude that automated speech recognition (ASR) and related technologies are not sufficiently mature to equip CALL to meet these desiderata, in particular, to support authentic communicative dialogues. They propose that speech technologies take a limited, well-defined position in CALL where they can excel, such as shaping pronunciation. This proposal is tacit in each of the ensuing chapters. Absent from this volume, for example, are the "systems for having conversation" that appeared in the 1999 CALICO special issue (Holland, 1999). Their absence reflects the limited progress in speech-interactive CALL beyond the initial realization of dialogue practice as reading from the screen. Instead, focus has moved toward pronunciation diagnosis and the integration of speech visualization into learning systems. Speech recognition has far to go, contend Clifford and Granoien, to provide useful discourse interaction for language learners.

Experimental work that may lead to conversational CALL is not entirely dismissed. Clifford and Granoien acknowledge the efforts of the Spoken Language Systems Group at the Massachusetts Institute of Technology, for example, which leverage multilingual research in fundamental speech recognition algorithms to fashion prototype conversational tutors (Seneff, Wang, Peabody, & Zue, 2004). Another research program that should be noted is the Tactical Language Trainer by the Center for Advanced Research in Technology for Education (CARTE) at the University of Southern California, Information Sciences Institute (Johnson et al., 2004). This program draws on agent-based frameworks from computer science (Bradshaw, 2002;

Klusch, 1999), and the extension of those frameworks to intelligent pedagogical agents (White, Shimoda, & Frederiksen, 2000), which can teach in
virtual worlds (Landauer & Bellman, 1998). Pedagogical agents attempt not
only to model the learner for error diagnosis and feedback, as in traditional
intelligent tutoring systems (Anderson, Boyle, Corbett, & Lewis, 1990), but
also to interact with the learner as socially intelligent characters, modeling
relationships in society and culture (Maatman, Gratch, & Marsella, 2005;
Rickel et al., 2002) and in the dynamics of conversation (Traum, Swartout,
Marsella, & Gratch, 2005). In this way, the goals of pedagogical agent technology respond to the desiderata of social constructionist theory in general and second language interactionist theory in particular. Johnson et al.'s
Tactical Language Trainer is designed to use agent technologies to prompt
second-language utterances in believable scenarios, respond in scenario-
appropriate ways, and evaluate learner input on several levels for feedback
and assistance. Thus, the long-term design of the system acknowledges and
addresses the multiple difficulties not only of recognizing and categorizing
learner speech, but also of responding realistically and flexibly.

Research efforts such as these are evolving gradually, beginning with demonstrations of pronunciation diagnosis for fixed utterances, such as Chinese
in the Spoken Language Systems Group (Peabody, Seneff, & Wang, 2004)
and Modern Standard Arabic in the Tactical Language Trainer (Mote, Sethy,
Silva, Narayanan, & Johnson, 2004). Because errors in free-form utterances
can derive from many levels and sources, say a mispronunciation versus a
lexical mix-up, their automatic classification remains a challenge. The direction for current speech-interactive CALL indicated by Clifford and Granoien is to find and refine that niche where the technology is reliable and
useful.

The Challenge of Learning the Sounds of a Second Language

Taking us into that niche is the work cited by Gómez et al. Their chapter
begins with a theory of language learning at an entirely different level—the
theory of feedback loops connecting speech perception and speech production—a short-term, local loop whose constraints are established by perceptual physiology and neurology. Research at this level is relevant to learning
and teaching of pronunciation in second languages and lays the foundation
for how speech technologies might best be employed for this purpose. Here,
ear training and tongue training may be legitimately rote and decontextualized, to be recombined with the higher levels of language learning and use
assumed in Clifford and Granoien's interactionist framework. Gómez et al.
show that perception of the sounds of a first language is based deeply in neural organization, from the auditory nerve to the brain. That is why, after a
certain level of maturity, adult learners are so resistant to producing native-
like sounds and have difficulty hearing and saying the distinctions that are
natural to native speakers.

Exploiting Spectrograms to Teach Speech: The Semantic Gap

The biological basis of speech perception offers a compelling justification for the use of visualization methods to facilitate teaching and learning: These methods provide an alternative to an auditory channel already exhausted by first-language discriminations that are neurologically wired from early childhood. Gómez et al. recognize, nevertheless, that turning spectrograms into useful visual aids is by no means guaranteed. By defining the "semantic gap" between what spectrograms show and what learners need to know, Gomez et al. set up a thoroughgoing critique of visualization techniques in CALL. The issue, they say, is "how the information provided by speech visualization technology is to be supplied to the user. Just showing spectrograms is arguably ineffective as a tool for learning." How to manipulate and transform the spectral display so that it communicates to learners is a question ripe for research. Gómez et al. offer some display possibilities as seeds for a visualization tutor at the end of their chapter.

The issues voiced by Gómez et al. concerning the comprehensibility and validity of speech visualization are replayed in the chapter by Dalby and Kewley-Port, who use visual game metaphors deemed familiar to students to show students how far they are from an articulatory target, and in the chapter by Molholt and Hwu, who trust the communicative value of pitch contours and pitch-energy displays, and to some extent spectrograms, assuming that the link between acoustic features and articulatory gestures will be apparent to language teachers as well as advanced students.

As a background chapter, Gómez et al. provide for the interested reader an abundance of technical detail on speech perception and its physiology as well as on speech acoustics and how its physics are expressed in spectrograms. These sections of their chapter are marked for those who want to read closely.

REFERENCES

Anderson, J. R., Boyle, C. F., Corbett, A., & Lewis, M. (1990). Cognitive modeling and intelligent tutoring. *Artificial Intelligence, 42,* 7–49.
Bradshaw, J. (Ed.). (2002). *Handbook of agent technology.* Cambridge: AAAI/MIT Press.
Cazden, C. (1988). *Classroom discourse: The language of teaching and learning.* Portsmouth, NH: Heineman.
Collins, A., Brown, J. S., & Newman, S. (1989). Cognitive apprenticeship: Teaching the crafts of reading, writing, and mathematics. In L. Resnick (Ed.), *Knowing, learning, and instruction: Essays in honor of Robert Glaser.* Hillsdale, NJ: Lawrence Erlbaum Associates.
Doughty, C. (1999). Cognitive underpinnings of focus on form. *University of Hawaii Working Papers in English as a Second Language, 18*(1), 1–69.
Doughty, C. (2003). Instructed SLA: Constraints, compensation, and enhancement. In C. Doughty & M. H. Long (Eds.), *The handbook of second language acquisition.* Malden, MA: Blackwell.

Gass, S. (2004). Conversation analysis and input-interaction. *The Modern Language Journal, 88,* 597–602.

Gass, S., Mackey, A., & Pica, T. (1998). The role of input and interaction in second language acquisition. *Modern Language Journal, 82*(3), 299–307.

Holland, V. M. (Ed.) (1999). Tutors that listen: Speech recognition for language learning. *CALICO Journal, 16*(3), 243–468. Special issue.

Johnson, W. L., Marsella, S., Mote, N., Si, M., Vilhjalmsson, H., & Wu, S. (2004). Balanced perception and action in the tactical language training system. *Proceedings of the International Workshop on Autonomous Agents and Multi-Agent Systems (AAMAS WS 2004),* New York.

Klusch, M. (Ed.). (1999). *Intelligent information agents.* Berlin: Springer–Verlag.

Landauer, C., & Bellman, K. (Eds.). (1998). *Proceedings of the Virtual Worlds and Simulation Conference (VWSIM '98),* San Diego, CA: The Society for Computer Simulation International.

Langer, J. (1985). A sociocognitive view of literacy learning. *Journal of the Teaching of English, 19,* 235–237.

Lave, J., & Wenger, E. (1991). *Situated learning: Legitimate peripheral participation.* Cambridge, UK: Cambridge University Press.

Maatman, R., Gratch, J., & Marsella, S. (2005). *Natural behavior of a listening agent.* Proceedings of 5th International Conference on Interactive Virtual Agents, Kos, Greece.

Meskill, C. (2005). Triadic scaffolds: Tools for teaching English language learners with computers. *Language Learning & Technology, 9*(1), 46–59. [Retrieved on November 21, 2006, from http://llt.msu.edu/vol9num1/meskill]

Mote, N., Sethy, A., Silva, J., Narayanan, S., & Johnson, W. L. (2004, May). Detection and modeling of learner speech errors: The case of Arabic tactical language training for American English speakers. *Proceedings of InSTIL/ICALL Symposium: NLP and Speech Technologies in Advanced Language Learning Systems,* Venice, Italy.

Newman, D., Griffin, P., & Cole, M. (1989). *The construction zone: Working for cognitive change in school.* Cambridge, UK: Cambridge University Press.

Peabody, M., Seneff, S., & Wang, C. (2004, May). Mandarin tone acquisition through typed interactions. *Proceedings of InSTIL/ICALL Symposium: NLP and Speech Technologies in Advanced Language Learning Systems,* Venice, Italy.

Rickel, J., Marsella, S., Gratch, J., Hill, R., Traum, D., & Swartout, W. (2002). Toward a new generation of virtual humans for interactive experiences. *IEEE Intelligent Systems, 17,* 32–38. (Special issue on AI in Interactive Entertainment).

Schoenfeld, A. H. (Ed.). (1987). *Cognitive science and mathematics education.* Hillsdale, NJ: Lawrence Erlbaum Associates.

Seneff, S., Wang, C., Peabody, M., & Zue, V. (2004, October). Second language acquisition through human computer dialogue. *Proceedings of 8th International Conf. on Spoken Language Processing (ICSLP 04),* Jeju, Korea.

Swain, M. (2000). The output hypothesis and beyond: Mediating acquisition through collaborative dialogue. In J. Lantolf (Ed.), *Sociocultural theory and second language learning.* Oxford, UK: Oxford University Press.

Traum, D., Swartout, W., Marsella, S., & Gratch, J. (2005). Fight, flight, or negotiate: Believable strategies for conversing under crisis. *Proceedings of 5th International Conference on Interactive Virtual Agents,* Kos, Greece.

White, B. Y., Shimoda, T., & Frederiksen, J. R. (2000). Facilitating students' inquiry learning and metacognitive development through modifiable software advisors. In S. Lajoie (Ed.), Computer as cognitive tools, Volume 2: No more walls. Mahwah, NJ: Lawrence Erlbaum Associates.

2 Applications of Technology to Language Acquisition Processes
What Can Work and Why

Ray Clifford and Neil Granoien

THE PROMISE OF SPEECH TECHNOLOGY FOR LANGUAGE LEARNING

Recent developments in speech technology have enabled a human–computer interaction in which the user can converse directly with a machine for the purpose of transferring information. For example, one can make airline reservations and check on weather and traffic conditions. With a leap of the imagination, one can picture an intelligent tutor that can work with a student in a learning situation, overcoming issues of distance as well as affording tantalizing economies of scale. Such a system might seem ideal for language learning, given its ability to recognize and parse the user's speech. Indeed, the chapters in this volume illustrate the variety of systems, from reading coaches to second language tutors, that have adapted speech technology for language learning. These chapters assume that speech technology to automate selected teaching processes is desirable, and some chapters (e.g., Aist & Mostow; Mostow et al.) put forth evaluation results that suggest the effectiveness of this automation. However, to address comprehensively the implications of speech technology for computer-assisted language learning (CALL), it is useful first to examine the minimum requirements for learning in a computer-assisted context, then to look at what remains to be done to make such a capability an instructional reality. We begin by observing common pedagogical limitations of CALL, then introduce a framework for CALL that reflects contemporary theories of second language acquisition, and finally examine how speech-interactive CALL systems, in particular the ones in this volume, relate to this framework.

COMMON LIMITATIONS OF CALL

In recent years, we have seen increasing attention paid to learning outcomes and educational standards. In the field of foreign language education, this revolution has meant a shift from the past, when for decades the professional debates were about competing teaching methods, to a more refined discussion of the methods or techniques best suited to accomplishing specific proficiency objectives. However, the transition from process to outcomes has not yet occurred in CALL.

Continued Focus on Method

In general, the tendency in CALL has been for the charm of the technology itself to outweigh considerations of learning. Software functionality and system structure have had a tendency to influence learning design (Plass, 1998). Even the best-planned activity has had to be abstracted and bent to fit system requirements. Historically, the key consideration has been how the computer system processes and stores information, rather than how the human user acquires language skills. As a result, most programs are based on "bottom-up" assumptions of the learning process, where the material to be learned is reduced to its minutest logical constituents and presented according to a predetermined sequence. The Programmed Logic for Automatic Teaching Operations (PLATO) authoring system, which saw wide acceptance in the earlier days of mainframes, was used in this manner to generate CALL activities. A typical PLATO lesson would begin by displaying a list of native language–target language vocabulary, then move to a reading passage contrived to display semantic and syntactic features, followed by a multiple choice check of comprehension (Dawson & Provenzano, 1981). The actual process of acquisition was left to the learner.

Most common CALL approaches in use today still appear to be related to assumptions of teaching that are two decades and more old. The outdated teaching method that focuses on semantic and syntactic comparisons between L1 and L2, for example, finds a common reflection in the automated phrase book format, or in links of words and phrases to graphic illustrations. What the learner is expected to do may not be spelled out, but surely implicit is the directive to memorize everything by rote. Single sentences, narratives, or dialogues repeated in audio files belong to the same practice. Also mimicking some older classroom practices are numerous examples of multiple choice activities that focus on definitions, morphological manipulations, sentence structure, or the content of texts. These are written by designers who assume that there is a connection between testing and learning.

Primacy of Interface

What many see as advantageous about CALL activities is often limited to superficial characteristics, particularly to the presentation and the interface. A good multimedia presentation can impress (Kaiser, 1998), as can the function of recognizing speech, but presentation leaves many questions about the learning process unanswered. Production values in a software program can be first rate, with all learner needs ostensibly covered by linked supplementary resources such as word definitions and grammar rules. But attractive graphic design, good programming, and, more recently, novel input modalities can mask pedagogical shortcomings. In contrast to classroom instruction, the prevalent trend in CALL appears to be that learning is by and large an informational construct. In other words, learning something is the natural result of repeated exposure, and higher order cognitive skills such as analysis and synthesis happen automatically.

Hence, one can know vocabulary or know grammar rules, and it is hoped that when a situation requiring communication arises, the capability to perform will somehow emerge without prior instruction or practice in this higher order activity. We have learned, however, that such is not the case. Repetition and memorization of a set corpus of material, whether presented by a teacher or a software program, do not lead to communicative capability on the part of the student. This holds not only for reading or hearing words (conventional CALL) but also for saying them (speech-interactive CALL).

It is not the computer itself that is good or bad for learning, but rather the use we put it to (Ortega, 1997). The authors recall a demonstration some years ago given by a programmer and a theoretical linguist, who proudly announced that they had faithfully replicated in their computer program the classroom practices of a particular teacher. What they had failed to question in the first place was whether the practices were effective. It should be obvious that, if a program is indeed intended to emulate teaching, then the teaching model should be a good one. For this reason, the director of the German Bundessprachenamt has admonished his faculty, "If you can be replaced by a computer, you ought to be."

Speech recognition technology has had a particular allure for CALL, and developers have increasingly sought to incorporate it as the technology becomes widely available and accessible. Speech recognition is featured in many commercial packages, where, in general, the method continues to outweigh considerations of learning. Some of the weaknesses in commercial packages that promise authentic dialogue experiences and professional pronunciation scoring have been documented (Hincks, 2003; Wachowicz & Scott, 1999). Here, however, we intend to distinguish the commercial realm from the research realm and address those systems, such as the ones presented in this volume, that stem from a well articulated research base and that make their inner workings and design principles explicit.

CONTEMPORARY VIEWS OF SECOND LANGUAGE ACQUISITION (SLA)

Acquisition Through Social Interaction

Over the last decade or so, a consensus has emerged in the field of second language acquisition that learning occurs in the course of language use

(Doughty & Long, 2003; Ellis, 1998; Gass, Mackey, & Pica, 1998; Polio & Gass, 1998; Swain, 2000). At once a communicative and a cognitive activity, language use is seen to stimulate learning through social interaction (Gass & Varonis, 1994) and collaborative construction (McDonough, 2001). Interacting with native speakers provides learners with the most favorable opportunities for acquisition. In this interaction learners purposefully engage in modifying their communication by negotiating comprehension, and in due course, they adjust their interlanguage, or internal representation of syntax and morphology (Gass et al., 1998). An underlying assumption of the interactivist viewpoint is that communication and negotiation of meaning help the learner develop language competence. In responding to a native speaker, learners construct hypotheses about structures and meanings in the target language and use their output, spoken or written, to test these hypotheses. In doing so, they encounter difficulties in encoding and decoding messages. Hypothesis testing can be cued by interlocutors through recasts, expansion, or reformulation of a learner's utterances, which can shift the focus from the meaning of a message to its form. Through this process of "noticing" errors, a kind of cognitive dissonance is created, which can lead learners to make the adjustments needed to improve their language competence. The dialogic interaction between nonnative speaker and native speaker also helps to develop a metalinguistic function in learners, giving them the capability for systematically monitoring their own errors and for making and internalizing corrections (Polio & Gass, 1998).

The view of language learning as arising from the interaction of native and nonnative speaker in negotiating meaning and form has roots in a more general theory of learning described in the early twentieth century by Lev Vygotsky, whose works were later compiled and published (Vygotsky, 1978). Vygotsky found a range of mental functions developing in collaborative activity rather than in independent, isolated activities (Moll, 1990). His construct of the Zone of Proximal Development (ZPD) has the learner working with material and tasks that are partly familiar and partly beyond his or her current capability, a situation roughly equivalent to the notion of comprehensible input that stretches the language learner's capabilities, or i + 1 (Krashen, 1982). Beyond simply providing input, however, Vygotsky's teacher must actively mediate by scaffolding the lesson's activities between the learner's existing ability and the outcome to be achieved. Refining this concept of scaffolding for the second language classroom, SLA researchers such as Doughty (1999). Gibbons (2002), and Gifford and Mullaney (1999) regard learning as a joint problem-solving enterprise, with teacher and learner functioning in a kind of master–apprentice relationship.

From Input Hypothesis to Interactionist Hypothesis

The assumption that input alone can lead to acquisition (Krashen, 1982), which was called into question over two decades ago (Higgs, 1985), is the foundation of a majority of language learning software. If the premise that input, along with the lowering of affective barriers to learning, were adequate, then the practice afforded by any computer-learning program should suffice.

Contemporary interactionist and constructivist frameworks, however, view acquisition as resulting from performance, from the learner's working with output and not merely comprehension of input. In this manner, the learner is obliged to move from mere semantic decoding to syntactic processing, which facilitates grammatical competence. Interaction becomes the basis for the development of syntax, as language learners modify and restructure their interactions with native speakers in order to achieve message comprehensibility (Swain & Lapkin, 1998). Gass and Varonis (1994) posit this development as arising from conversation, which is the common classroom form of interaction.

We can hypothesize that written interaction may have the same result, and indeed, be even more effective for the reflective, analytical learner. A growing body of research yields positive evidence for the use of computer-mediated communication, or CMC (Cziko & Park, 2003; Ortega, 1997; Smith, 2003; Warschauer, 1997; Wible, Kuo, Chien, Liu, & Tsao, 2001). In this mode, learners communicate with each other, following a defined communicative task, and their messages are displayed on a scrollable screen in posting sequence. The benefits of CMC are that learners communicate in a social context, work at their own pace (which accommodates the need to reflect), and are under less stress to respond immediately than would be the case with face-to-face communication. The major drawback is that learners are communicating mostly with each other, without the modeling and formative feedback that the expert teacher provides.

In current pedagogical theory, therefore, learners can be brought to noticing and correcting their shortcomings only through stretching their linguistic resources while constructing meanings for communication with a native speaker. Chapelle (1998) illustrates the process with the schematic shown in Figure 2.1.

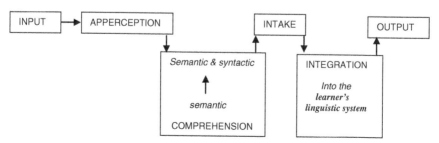

Figure 2.1 Basic components in the SLA process in interactionist research (adapted from Chapelle, 1998).

According to Figure 2.1, the process of language acquisition begins as the learner is exposed to the target language (input), which may be modified by means of simplification, elaboration, or redundancy. The learner next becomes aware of specific features (apperception), which then have the potential to be acquired. Only when the learner understands the message content of the input (comprehension) is the result the intake of linguistic features. These features may then be used in producing output as they are integrated into the learner's linguistic system. The teacher responds to the learner's output with a recast or restatement of the output, either confirming or disconfirming accuracy, and the process begins anew.

Another way of illustrating the acquisition process, with the role of the teacher made more patent, may be seen in Figure 2.2.

Input and Apperception

As shown in Figure 2.2, the first opportunity for language acquisition begins when the learner encounters the second language (L2). This opportunity, however, may not result in learning. Before this language "input" can be received by the student, it must first pass through his or her personal sensory filters—filters that have been tuned through the acquisition of the first language (L1) to classify non-L1 features as "noise" and reject them. Thus, this stage requires more than perceiving; it requires the conscious relating of newly observed features to past experience filters (or apperception).

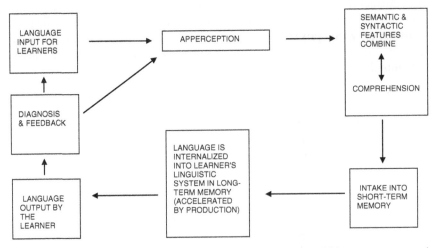

Figure 2.2 Language acquisition process recognizing the role of learner output and diagnosis.

Comprehension and Short-Term Memory

If the L2 input passes through these personal perception filters, then the input moves into sensory memory and the mind can begin attempts to make sense of the acoustic or graphic symbols of the language input. Only if the learner is immediately able to make sense of the semantic and syntactic features now in sensory memory can the input be organized into meaning elements and entered into short-term memory.

Transfer to Long-Term Memory

Focused attention and repeated rehearsals can then move the language chunks from short term to long-term memory. Research indicates that this process is accelerated through L2 production activities.

Output, Diagnosis, and Feedback

The first external indication that the language acquisition process has begun is the learner's "output." This output is usually in the second language, but there may also be evidence of comprehension in the learner's L1 or inter-language production. In addition to accelerating the internalization of the L2 system, the learner's output provides the "data" needed by the teacher to diagnose the effectiveness of the learner's apperception of the original input. The teacher tailors feedback to the learner either through direct correction or through adjusted L2 input, and the process is repeated. Exactly how explicit this feedback should be is part of a continuing discussion in the field of second language acquisition (Doughty, 2003; Long, 1998; Norris & Ortega, 2000).

APPLYING CONTEMPORARY FRAMEWORKS TO CALL

Implementing the Interactionist Approach in CALL

The implications of interactionst principles for language learning software have been articulated by Chapelle (2001, 1998), Laurillard (2002), and McDonough (2001), among others. Most basically, the software must be able to work with a learner's output to set the stage for acquisition. Even the simplest output processing, that is, single-sentence parsing and feedback, has been shown to be superior to presentation alone for retention (Nagata, 1998). Tools such as Delmonte describes in this volume exploit techniques from the field of intelligent tutoring to process learners' output. These techniques include a linguistic knowledge database and reasoning algorithms that, like Nagata's parser, work on learners' constructed responses.

More specifically, the way in which the acquisition process is actualized in a computer program crucially affects the design of the learning interface.

Chapelle (2001, 1998) provides some key considerations for CALL design that follow the models of second language acquisition discussed here (Figures 2.1 and 2.2).

First, to facilitate *apperception,* the linguistic characteristics that learners are to pay attention to should be made salient. This can be accomplished by mechanical means such as highlighting on the screen or by linking with graphics or supporting text. It can also be done by having the learner perform communicative subtasks, such as formulating questions to elicit information or making multiple responses to posted questions. These tasks should be framed in a logical context, in order to provide the meaning focus found in authentic communication as well as to provide the cognitive connections needed for retention.

Second, to facilitate *comprehension,* learners should receive help in decoding semantic and syntactic aspects of linguistic input. Simplification, elaboration, and redundancy are techniques for aiding the learner with semantic and syntactic comprehension. Activities that use scaffolded layers of inferencing can also help in this regard by leading incrementally to the minimal level of comprehension needed to attack a reading or listening text.

Next, there must be opportunities for the learner to produce comprehensible *output.* It is only through this output that the learner's degree of acquisition can be determined and miscues can be analyzed to provide the learner with feedback and with the adjusted input necessary for improvement and advancement.

How do these considerations relate to speech-interactive CALL? Earlier work in this area sought to build dialogue simulations that would permit learners to converse in a second language with a computer character. These systems aimed to implement aspects of the interactionist approach, that is, to simulate communicative interactions with native speakers a shared, meaningful context. However, as evidenced in this book, speech-interactive CALL has more recently focused on lower-level skills: speech pronunciation and oral reading (word identification). By limiting their goals to these more tractable subskills, which are, in fact, building blocks of communicative interactions, the systems in this book respect current limitations of the technology. None can be said to implement the interactionist approach as we have defined it, where learners construct meanings to communicate with a native speaker. Eventually, however, the interactionist model we have sketched may be brought to bear on a more comprehensive suite of CALL, in which pronunciation training is embedded as one process, a possibility we will consider in more detail toward the end of this chapter.

Incorporating Learning Outcomes into CALL

So far, we have been discussing the process of acquisition and the ways in which a computer-based learning program should accommodate that process. The other side of the discussion concerns learning outcomes. The CALL programs currently available tend toward lower level cognitive objectives. Applying Bloom's taxonomy (Bloom, et al., 1956), one can see that most would fall under the rubrics of knowledge, comprehension, and application, or what are usually referred to as lower-order skills. Falling into this category are the "able-tos" of a matching activity, fill-in-the-blank, sentence completion, or paraphrasing, which can be scored using "right–wrong" answer-judging routines. Higher-order cognitive skills, coming under the rubrics of analysis, synthesis, and evaluation, result in open-ended responses which, given current technologies, are difficult to judge without human intervention. These include activities that have learners following inductive or deductive threads of reasoning, discriminating factual information from values statements, drawing conclusions, forming hypotheses, judging the correctness and reliability of an argument, establishing standards of usefulness or validity, and so forth.

In the field of foreign language learning, the most widely accepted scales for measuring L2 language development are the American Council on the Teaching of Foreign Languages (ACTFL) and Inter-agency Language Roundtable (ILR) proficiency guidelines (ILR, 2005). Since the ACTFL scale was derived from the ILR scale, and the scales retain their comparability at the base levels, a review of the ILR scale will suffice to demonstrate the need to add a developmental dimension to Chapelle's (Figure 2.1) and the authors' (Figure 2.2) acquisition cycles. The ILR scales rate, in behavioral terms, what an individual can do in listening, reading, speaking, and writing based on what is called a *functional trisection*. The functional trisection consists of (a) *language function*, or what is done with the language, (b) *context*, or the topical domain in which the task is performed, and (c) *accuracy*, or the quality of performance. A simplified summary of the scale for speaking skill, or oral proficiency, is shown in Table 2.1. [Place table 2.1 here.]

Defining Outcomes Practically for CALL

We recognize that the theoretical discussion above needs to be framed more practically if the L2 acquisition principles presented here are to be applied to the design and assessment of CALL or of web-assisted language learning programs. Practical definitions are difficult because the acquisition process is by its very nature complex and multidimensional. The authors' proposed solution to dealing with this multidimensionality of process is to start with desired outcomes for the process and then devise the learning activities assumed to lead to those outcomes. Important factors in activity design are language functions, structure, and vocabulary—each of which should be appropriate to the communicative tasks and to the contexts in which communication takes place. Additionally, tasks can be chained into extended activities that incorporate more than one language skill, for example, listening and speaking, or reading, writing, and speaking. Sample tasks are shown in Figure 2.3. Note that, despite overt similarity among them, the three tasks

Table 2.1 Oral Proficiency Scale Summary (With 5 as High End-Point)

Oral Proficiency Level	Function (Tasks accomplished, attitudes expressed, tone conveyed)	Context (Topics, subjects, areas, activities, and jobs addressed)	Accuracy (Acceptability, quality and accuracy of the message conveyed)
5	Functions equivalent to an educated native speaker (ENS).	All subjects.	Performance equivalent to an ENS.
4	Fluent and accurate; able to tailor language to fit audience; can counsel, persuade, negotiate, represent a point of view and interpret ofr dignitaries.	All topics normally pertinent to professional needs as well as in unfamiliar fields.	Nearly equivalent to an ENS. Speech is extensive, precise, appropriate to every occasion, with only occasional errors, e.g., in register or pronunciation.
3	Can converse in formal and informal situations, resolve problem situations, deal with unfamiliar topics, provide explanations, describe in detail, offer supported opinions and hypothesize; able to use irony and sarcasm.	Practical social, professional, and abstract topics, particular interests, and special fields of correspondence.	Errors virtually never interfere with understanding and rarely disturb the native speaker; control of cohesive devices, but not of idioms or cultural references.

Level	Functions	Topics	Accuracy
2	Able to participate in casual conversations, express facts, give instructions, describe, report, and narrate current, past, and future activities.	Concrete topics such as personal interests, family, work, travel, and current events.	Grammar not completely controlled; frequent errors, minimal cohesive structures; uses appropriate high-frequency vocabulary, but otherwise limited range. Intelligible to a native speaker not used to dealing with foreigners.
1	Can create with the language, ask and answer simple questions, participate in short conversations.	Everyday survival topics and courtesy requirements.	Severely limited control of grammar; narrow range of vocabulary, frequently misused. Intelligible to native speakers used to dealing with foreigners.
0+*	Can enumerate, can repeat learned words and phrases.	Memorized material, e.g., numbers, weather expressions, time, foods, names of family members, occupations.	Frequent errors in stress, intonation, tone; little or no control of grammar. Often unintelligible to native speakers.
0	No functional ability. Able to reproduce isolated words.	Insufficient to match or establish a context.	Generally unintelligible, even at the word level.

*"Plus" levels also exist for levels 1-4, but are not represented here for the sake of brevity.

a. Using the chart you have been given, list the number and location of accidents that occurred between 2 and 4 a.m. (Writing, level 0+)

b. Scan a series of accident reports, tabulate data regarding type, frequency, and severity and prepare a report in chart form for government officials. (Writing, level 2)

c. Collate and interpret accident data from the past twelve months, then prepare a decision paper for city administrators, discussing at least three options for improving highway safety, identifying the pros and cons for each, and justifying your proposed course of action. (Writing, level 4)

Figure 2.3 Writing tasks at various proficiency levels (cf. Table 2.1 for oral proficiency levels).

differ markedly in difficulty due to the implicit variation in cognitive and linguistic complexity among them. Partly as a result, activity (a) can be computer-scored, but activities (b) and (c) cannot.

The first step in designing (or evaluating) a CALL program should be defining the desired learning outcomes. For example, is a given CALL program to lead to the memorization of vocabulary or phrases (an achievement outcome associated with Novice or 0 + level skills)? Or is it to lead to a real-world performance outcome requiring the comprehension and production of extended narratives and the organization of factual events into appropriate logical sequences (which is related to level 2 activities)? Or is it to lead to the writing of an editorial on a controversial topic that is intended to persuade opposing factions to reach consensus (related to level 4)? Making such distinctions in outcome will enable the CALL field to move from its current state of automated worksheets and sentence-level activities to higher order learning objectives and to the kinds of communicative interactions that will bring learners to meaningful levels of language proficiency.

The speech-interactive CALL systems described in this volume find a niche in pronunciation or reading aloud rather than seeking to address other outcomes of SLA. Pronunciation flaws tend to span the proficiency scale in Table 2.1 and can be considered a relevant goal for all but the highest skill levels.

Given this discussion of the language acquisition process, one can see that many complex interactions must be considered in designing computer-based learning activities. It should be apparent that using a computer for presentation alone is inadequate for learning. If the computer is used only to present information, the learner is then obliged to fill in all the spaces, to make sense of new material, to figure out how it connects to what he or she already knows, to determine how to modify what is already known to fit with new information, and, perhaps most importantly, to assimilate everything into a usable whole that can be retrieved when needed.

Defining Interactivity In CALL

Many CALL programs purport to go beyond presentation and are billed as *interactive*. But the interactions are usually limited. The very term *interactive* may even be misleading. The computer demonstration mentioned previously, which purported to replicate the practices of a particular teacher but which we deemed an example of questionable teaching, boasted a touch screen that connected displayed words and phrases to audio files. But does that qualify as interactivity? One can interact with objects on the screen, eliciting responses from a program. One can interact with the structure of a program, navigating from screen to screen, from object to object. One can also interact with accessible help, in order to navigate or perform functions correctly. Apart from these mechanical functions, however, there is no true communicative interaction between human and computer. The only link in such programs, and it is a tenuous one, is between the learner and the absent designer.

In order to define effective communication in a computer-based medium, Laurillard (2002) uses interactivity as one of the constructs for her "conversational framework." Analogous to a real-time tutorial interaction, her framework is based on four notions:

1. Teacher–student communication must be discursive. That is, the teacher's and learner's conceptions must by mutually accessible, so that the learner can negotiate with the teacher to clarify and understand the content as well as the task.
2. Teaching must be adaptive. The teacher needs to be able to alter the mode or the content of the presentation, so that the learner can maintain focus and understanding.
3. The teacher/learner relationship must be interactive. The learner should perform a task that will give the teacher an indication of the level of competence attained. The teacher can then make a diagnostic assessment and provide the learner with meaningful feedback.
4. The learning process must be reflective. The teacher should provide an opportunity for the learner to return to the original task and make corrections. In comparing the corrections to his or her original performance, the learner reflects on the differences, and learning takes place. Thus, the essence of true interaction is enabling the learner to comprehend where adjustments need to be made.

Applying Laurillard's framework to a computer program, we can ask four questions to evaluate its instructional efficacy:

1. Is it discursive? (Does the program have sufficient capability to sustain a dialogue with the learner, to describe a concept or an action and receive the learner's recasting of the concept or action?)
2. Is it adaptive? (Does the program collect and interpret learner input and adapt the dialogue to meet the learner's individual needs for recasting or corrected task performance?)
3. Is it interactive? (Does the program provide for both analysis of learner task input and meaningful specific feedback on performance?)
4. Is it reflective? (Does the program provide the opportunity for the learner to return to the task and modify the original input?)

IMPLICATIONS FOR SPEECH TECHNOLOGY IN CALL

Speech Recognition for Support of Dialogue

We have suggested that a CALL program, in order to support language acquisition and proficiency, must be capable of interacting with the learner, of recording, analyzing, and interpreting learner output, and of providing feedback for correction, all in a context of meaningful tasks with authentic input. We have further suggested that speech technology is not currently capable of providing this range of interaction. The questions that remain are how speech technology might fit into the cycle of learning, and what kind of interface it is capable of providing.

Two dimensions of functionality of automatic speech recognition can be posited as necessary for language learning. First is the degree of accuracy with which the program can *recognize* the individual learner's speech characteristics. Second is how comprehensively the program can *analyze* the learner's output to provide corrective strategies.

In terms of accuracy of recognition, a number of variables come into play, such as acoustic quality, differences among speakers, and variations in linguistic and phonetic shape (Mariani, 1999). Speech recognition is domain specific; that is, a computer can recognize only what it is programmed to recognize (Ehzani & Knodt, 1998). It follows, then, that the narrower the linguistic domain in which the natural language functions, the more successful the program. One can have a very high degree of accuracy within a very small domain, or lower accuracy within an expansive domain. The adult native speaker can operate in a broad range of linguistic competence, as suggested in Table 2.1. The computer, on the other hand, performs best in narrow subdomains. The function of information access, for example, such as making an airline reservation or requesting a weather forecast, is usually predicated on a small set of possible utterances. Moreover, such an exchange can be system initiated, further limiting the range of responses expected of the human user and enabling speech recognition to perform robustly. Thus, experimental speech interfaces for small-domain information access were not only effective but also realistically conversational (Zue & Glass, 2000;

Zue et al., 2000), and these have been followed by commercial use of speech recognition for interface applications ranging from credit card billing inquiries to flight information requests.

In the meantime, investigations are proceeding in mixed-initiative spoken dialogue systems (Chung, Seneff, Wang, & Hetherington, 2004; Glass & Seneff, 2003), and in the extension of these systems to language learning (e.g., Seneff, Wang, Peabody, & Zue, 2004). Yet the support of unconstrained, spontaneous dialogue remains outside the realm of possibility for CALL at present for several reasons. First, the topical domain in spontaneous conversation can shift unpredictably. Moreover, informal speech is replete with disfluencies, such as hesitations, mispronunciations, false starts, interruptions, and ellipses. Add to disfluencies the variability in the population of speaker-learners, and speech recognition difficulties are compounded. Nevertheless, modeling authentic conversation was the ultimate goal of early research-based CALL systems, as it is the advertised promise of many commercial packages today. The early research-based systems (reviewed in Holland, 1999) were careful to place limits: they showed learners what to say, offering them a choice of three or so utterances on the screen, and branching the scenario according to which response the learner uttered. When the production values are superb, as in the dramatic characters built into the interactive video lessons of Harless, Zier, and Duncan (1999), the effect of talking to a person can appear startlingly real. The jury is still out on whether and how much these read-from-the-screen versions of interaction help to advance the second language learner. Perhaps because of the difficulty of enabling freer expression, some developers have put aside the broad goal of communication and negotiation of meaning for a focus on speech subskills.

Speech Recognition for Support of Word Pronunciation

If the goal of employing speech technology for learning on a limited scale is within reach, what is its value? Pronunciation significantly contributes to the perception of nonnativeness in a language learner, as pointed out by Precoda and Bratt (this volume); it is therefore worth isolating as a subskill for practice and shaping. Indeed, the majority of work reported in this volume deals with applying speech technology to the diagnosis and correction of pronunciation (words, phrases) or with applying the tools of pronunciation diagnosis to oral reading (Mostow et al., Aist & Mostow) or proficiency testing (Bernstein).

According to Laurillard's desiderata, none of these prototypes is discursive, because none purports to carry on conversations. Yet, all prototypes or designs provide for adaptive, interactive, and reflective participation by the learner in the realm of pronunciation. In addition to the projects described in this book, it is important to mention the work of the Spoken Language Systems Group at the Massachusetts Institute of Technology (MIT), which is developing a pronunciation tutor for Chinese. This work builds on research by the MIT group to extend dialogue-based information access systems from English to new languages, such as Mandarin Chinese (Wang et al., 2000). The goal of the pronunciation tutor is to enable a learner to correct errors in vowel quality, in consonant formation, and in tones. Development of the tutor is based in part on models of native speech and learner speech built from a corpus of utterances provided by native Mandarin-speaking teachers and English-native students at the Defense Language Institute Foreign Language Center. The tutor for Mandarin tone uses varying teaching approaches and attempts to assess tone quality automatically, contrasting pitch contours extracted from a learner's utterance with contour models of the native speaker. The learner is provided with auditory and visual cues for self correction. This tutor has developed sufficiently to support laboratory trials with users (e.g., Peabody et al., 2004), and experiments are ongoing with methods of teaching and correcting tones. A key principle of exercise design is to designate vocabulary for pronunciation by means of conversational prompts calling for specific responses. This design embeds the exercise in a realistic context while at the same time defining the targets narrowly enough for speech recognition to be successful.

Much more complex is the process of analyzing a learner's utterances beyond the phoneme level. For each level of language proficiency, the perplexity of grammar and the range of vocabulary grows significantly, reaching, if we take Chomsky at his word (1959), an astronomical number of permutations in educated native speech. At the lowest levels of proficiency an advantage can be had, in that the words and phrases used by learners are usually limited to a narrow range of language tasks (Ehzani & Knodt, 1998). Thus, training a system to handle the disfluencies of early learners is possible. One needs to bear in mind, however, that the training process must be repeated for each content domain. Taking into consideration the language learning cycle depicted in Figure 2.2, the system will have to capture the output, analyze the errors, and provide diagnostic feedback in detail sufficient to enable the learner to correct the error. It will also have to organize adjusted or modified language samples that will serve as input in the succeeding cycle of learning.

Computers acting in place of a human instructor may be adequate for certain lower level cognitive and psychomotor processes, such as phoneme reproduction, the rudimentary association of sound and symbol, or routine dialogue responses. These processes can be computer-scored, although doing so reliably and validly and embedding them in appropriate learning contexts, takes years of research, as the chapters in this book bear witness. However, eliciting higher level cognitive processes from the learner within the complexities of a language-learning situation is farther down the road.

The model proposed in the next chapter, by Gómez et al., provides a subskills view of SLA, focused on hearing and producing speech sounds in a second language. Gómez et al.'s schema of feedback loops reflects what we have called apperception: where the student must notice phonological distinctions that depart from his or her personal sensory filters—filters that have been tuned to the phonemes of the first language. Indeed, it is this problem of acquiring phonology that concerns most of the chapters in this volume. In this way, Gómez et al.'s model closely anticipates the succeeding chapters.

REFERENCES

Bloom, B. S., Englehart, M. D., Furst, E. J., Hill, W. H., & Krathwohl, D. R. (1956). *Taxonomy of educational objectives: Handbook I, cognitive domain.* New York: David McKay.

Chapelle, C. (1998). Multimedia CALL: Lessons to be learned from research on instructed SLA. *Language Learning and Technology,* 2(1), 22–34. [Retrieved on August 16, 2003, from http://llt.msu.edu/vol2num1/article1/index.html]

Chapelle, C. (2001). *Computer applications in second language acquisition: Foundations for teaching, testing and research.* Cambridge, UK: Cambridge University Press.

Chomsky, N. (1959). A review of B. F. Skinner's "Verbal Behavior." *Language, 35,* 26–58.

Chung, G., Seneff, S., Wang, C., & Hetherington, L. (2004). A dynamic vocabulary spoken dialogue interface. *Proceedings of Interspeech 2004,* Lisbon.

Cziko, G., & Park, S. (2003). Internet audio communication for second language learning: A comparative review of six programs. *Language Learning and Technology,* 7(1), 15–27. [Retrieved on August 12, 2003, from http://llt.msu.edu/vol7num1/review1/default.html]

Dawson, C., & Provenzano, N. (1981). PLATO sitcom dialogs for Russian. *Studies in Language Learning, 3*(1), 92–97.

Doughty, C. (1999). Cognitive underpinnings of focus on form. *University of Hawaii Working Papers in English as a Second Language, 18*(1), 1–69.

Doughty, C. (2003). Instructed SLA: Constraints, compensation, and enhancement. In C. Doughty & M. H. Long (Eds.) The handbook of second language acquisition. Malden, MA: Blackwell.

Doughty, C., & Long, M. (Eds.). (2003). *The handbook of second language acquisition.* Malden, MA: Blackwell.

Ehzani, F., & Knodt, E. (1998). Speech technology in computer-aided language learning: Strengths and limitations of a new CALL paradigm. *Language Learning and Technology,* 2(1), 45–60. [Retrieved on August 18, 2003, from http://llt.msu.edu/vol2num1/article3/index.html]

Ellis, R. (1998). *SLA research and language teaching.* Oxford, England: Oxford University Press.

Gass, S., Mackey, A., & Pica, T. (1998). The role of input and interaction in second language acquisition. *Modern Language Journal, 82,* 299–307.

Gass, S., & Varonis, E. (1994). Input, interaction, and second language production. *Studies in Second Language Acquisition, 16*(3), 283–302.

Gibbons, P. (2002). *Scaffolding language, scaffolding learning: teaching second language learners in the mainstream classroom.* Portsmouth, NH: Henemann.

Gifford, C., & Mullaney, J. (1999). From rhetoric to reality: Applying the communication standards to the classroom. *NECTFL Review, 46,* 12–18.

Glass, J., & Seneff, S. (2003). *Flexible and personalizable mixed-initiative dialogue systems.* Paper presented at HLT–NAACL 2003 Workshop on Research Directions in Dialogue Processing, Edmonton, Canada

Harless, W., Zier, M., & Duncan, R. (1999). Virtual dialogues with native speakers: The evaluation of an interactive multimedia method. *CALICO Journal, 16,* 313–339.

Higgs, T. (1985). The input hypothesis: An inside look. *Foreign Language Annals, 18,* 197–203.

Hincks, R. (2003). Supplementing pronunciation tutoring with speech recognition: An empirical evaluation of the effectiveness of a leading CALL program. *ReCALL, 15*(1) (Selected papers from EUROCALL 2002, Jyväskylä, Finland).

Holland, M. (Ed.). (1999). Tutors that listen: Speech recognition for language learning. Special issue, *CALICO Journal, 16.*

ILR (2005). Interagency Language Roundtable Website: ILR Language Skill Level Descriptions. [Retrieved on February 27, 2006, from http://www.govtilr.org]

Kaiser, M. (1998). Twelve Chairs Interactive: A multimedia Russian language course. [Retrieved on September 15, 2003, from the University of California, Berkeley College Writing Programs website: http://www-writing.berkeley.edu/chorus/call/reviews/12chairs/index.html]

Krashen, S. (1982). *Principles and practice in second language acquisition.* New York: Pergamon.

Laurillard, D. (2002). *Rethinking university teaching: A framework for the effective use of educational technology.* London: Routledge.

Long, M. (1998). Focus on form in task-based language teaching. *University of Hawaii Working Papers in English as a Second Language, 16,* 35–49.

Norris, J., & Ortega, L. (2000). Effectiveness of L2 instruction: A research synthesis and quantitative meta-analysis. *Language Learning, 50,* 417–528.

Mariani, J. (Ed.). (1999). Multilingual speech processing (recognition and synthesis). In E. Hovy, N. Ide, R. Frederking, & J. Mariani (Eds.), *Multilingual information management: Current levels and future abilities.* [Retrieved on July 22, 2003 from Carnegie Mellon University, School of Computer Science: http://www.cs.cmu.edu/People/ref/mlim]

McDonough, S. K. (2001). Way beyond drill and practice: Foreign language lab activities in support of constructivist learning. *International Journal of Instructional Media, 28,* 75–80.

Moll, L. (1990). Introduction. In L. Moll (Ed.), *Vygotsky and education: Instructional implications and applications of sociohistorical psychology* (pp. 1–27). Cambridge, UK: Cambridge University Press.

Nagata, N. (1998). Input vs. output practice in educational software for second language acquisition. *Language Learning and Technology, 1,* 23–40. [Retrieved on January 18, 2003, from http://llt.msu.edu/vol1num2/article1/default.html]

Ortega, L. (1997). Processes and outcomes in networked classroom interaction: Defining the research agenda for L2 computer-assisted classroom discussion. *Language Learning & Technology, 1,* 82–93. [Retrieved on January 28, 2003, from http://llt.msu.edu/vol1num1/ortega/default.html]

Peabody, M., Seneff, S., & Wang, C. (2004). Mandarin tone acquisition through typed interactions. *Proceedings of InSTIL/ICALL Symposium: NLP and Speech Technologies in Advanced Language Learning Systems,* Venice.

Plass, J. (1998). Design and evaluation of the user interface of foreign language multimedia software: a cognitive approach. *Language Learning and Technology, 2,* 35–45. [Retrieved on August 16, 2003, from http://llt.msu.edu/vol2num1/article2/index.html]

Polio, C., & Gass, S. (1998). The role of interaction in native speaker comprehension of nonnative speaker speech. *Modern Language Journal, 82,* 308–319.

Seneff, S., Wang, C., Peabody, M., & Zue, V. (2004), Second language acquisition through human computer dialogue. *Proceedings of 8th International Conf. on Spoken Language Processing (ICSLP 04),* Jeju, Korea.

Smith, B. (2003). Computer-mediated negotiated interaction: An expanded model. *Modern Language Journal, 87,* 38–57.

Swain, M. (2000). The output hypothesis and beyond: Mediating acquisition through collaborative dialogue. In J. Lantolf (Ed.), *Sociocultural theory and second language learning.* Oxford, England: Oxford University Press.

Swain, M., & Lapkin, S. (1998). Interaction and second language learning: Two adolescent French immersion students working together. *Modern Language Journal, 82,* 320–337.

Vygotsky, L. (1978). *Mind in society: The development of higher psychological processes.* Cambridge, MA: Harvard University Press.

Wachowicz, C., & Scott, B. (1999). Software that listens: It's not a question of *whether,* it's a question of *how. CALICO Journal, 16*(3), 263–278.

Wang, C., Cyphers, S., Mou, X., Polifroni, J., Seneff, S., Yi, J., et al. (2000). Muxing: A telephone-access Mandarin conversational system. *Proceedings of 4th International Conf. on Spoken Language Processing (ICSLP 00),* 715–718(II), Beijing.

Warschauer, M. (1997). Computer-mediated collaborative learning: Theory and practice. *Modern Language Journal, 81*(4), 470–481.

Wible, D., Kuo, C.-H., Chien, F.-Y., Liu, A., & Tsao, N.-L. (2001). A web-based EFL writing environment: Intelligent information for learners, teachers, and researchers. *Computers & Education, 37,* 297–315.

Zue, V., & Glass, J. (2000). Conversational interfaces: Advances and challenges. *Proceedings of IEEE, Special Issue on Spoken Language Processing, 88,* 1166–1180.

Zue, V., Seneff, S., Glass, J., Polifroni, J., Pao, C., Hazen, T., & Hetherington, I (2000). Jupiter: A telephone-based conversational interface for weather information. *IEEE Trans. on Speech and Audio Processing, 8,* 100–112.

3 Applications of Formant Detection in Language Learning

Pedro Gómez, Agustín Álvarez, Rafael Martínez, Jesús Bobadilla, Jesús Bernal, Victoria Rodellar, and Víctor Nieto

INTRODUCTION

Speech technologies constitute an area of growing interest for computer-assisted language learning (CALL) as new speech processing tools become available with potential to serve learners. As schematized in Figure 3.1, language learning (or acquisition) is based on successive approximations, which can be called feedback loops. The primary loop is based on speech perception and speech production. The secondary loop is based on reading and writing (see Gómez, Martinez, Nieto, & Rodellar, 1994). Departing from the interactionist model put forth in the previous chapter by Clifford and Granoien, which widely frames the communicative processes of language acquisition, the feedback loop model closely frames the physiology of learning—in particular, hearing and articulating speech sounds and how these two processes work together.

In this chapter we explore the primary loop of speech perception and production, describe problems arising in the normal learning processes characterized by this loop, and look at possible solutions based on speech technologies, in particular, technologies that permit aspects of speech sounds to be visualized for learners.

PHYSIOLOGICAL MECHANISMS OF SPEECH PERCEPTION AND PRODUCTION

In a typical dialogue interaction, the primary loop begins with a listener's perception of speech through the auditory periphery and the speech centers of the brain. Having perceived a spoken utterance, the listener assigns it meaning (speech understanding) and, finally, utters a meaningful spoken response (speech production). Let us consider each process in turn.

Speech Perception

Like music, speech is a set of sounds with specific meaning for humans. Speech sounds may be seen as a sequence of ordered units related contextually and

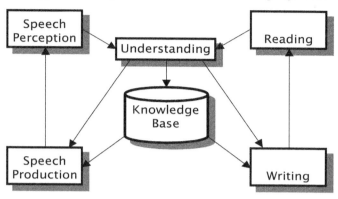

Figure 3.1 Feedback loops in language learning.

hierarchically. The smaller units are *phones* (also called *phonemes*): segments of sound to which a meaning may be attributed in the sense that distinctions between larger units (morphemes, words) depend on phone distinctions (e.g., the English phones /p/ and /b/ distinguish the words *pin* and *bin*). Phones are associated to form words, or individual units of meaning that are not acoustically separated in a sentence. Sentences are complete physical entities in that they present a clear acoustical beginning and end. They contain specific realizations of words concatenated according to grammatical rules. Speech perception consists in assigning specific symbols from a preestablished set to the segments of speech at lower levels, that is, phones and words.

Speech Understanding

Understanding is at a higher level than perception. It involves detecting the grammatical roles of words in a sentence to establish its syntactic and semantic structure.

Interaction of Processes

Speech perception and speech understanding are not independent. Perception does not rely exclusively on detection of the acoustic-physical qualities of speech but depends also on the listener's ability to assign meaning to an already received message and to predict the incoming message at different levels of meaning. This interaction of bottom-up and top-down processes is an essential finding in research on speech perception (Allen, 1994). The physiological processes of the primary (aural–oral) feedback loop may be roughly conceived as follows (see Figure 3.2).

- *Perceiving sound.* Incoming sound waves are transformed by the auditory nerve into a neural *speech trace* and relayed to the brain's speech processing centers.

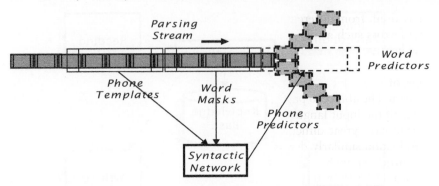

Figure 3.2 Parsing process in speech perception and understanding.

- *Detecting phones and syllables.* The speech processing centers detect the basic structure of the trace depending on its time-frequency distribution (changes in pitch over time). *Phonetic* qualities such as voicing, onsets, decays, glides, and frictions are determined, and depending on their distribution, distinct *phones* are hypothesized. A primordial symbolic stream is produced, schematized in Figure 3.2.
- *Parsing the symbolic stream.* The symbolic stream appears to be parsed by different automata working in parallel in different speech areas of the brain. As shown in Figure 3.2, aspects of a listener's prior knowledge of the language are applied: phone templates, words, and grammar in the form of a syntactic network. Thus, three levels of parsing can be defined: (a) in *phone matching and prediction* a sequence of variable length phones is preparsed and phone templates are labeled; (b) in *word matching and prediction* the chain of phones is parsed, and word hypotheses are produced and tested; (c) in *applying syntactic constraints*, a kind of mental syntactic network assigns values such as part of speech to the words detected and generates new word hypotheses.
- *Generating the sentence template.* The first stage in speech production can be viewed as invoking a database of sentence templates.
- *Establishing word sequences.* Next, word sequences are completed through what might be seen as a template filling process.
- *Defining the sequence of articulatory positions.* Each word in the planned sentence is associated with a sequence of articulatory positions (placement of lips and tongue) best suited to producing speech.

SOURCES OF PROBLEMS IN SPEECH PERCEPTION AND PRODUCTION

What are the most common problems found in these processes? At the level of auditory perception, a loss of part or most of the encoded speech trace may result from different degrees of deafness or from the influence of external factors such as noise. The process of phone and syllable detection may fail because of damage in auditory structures called the lateral olivary nuclei (Ferrandez, 1998). But for listeners with normal physiological functioning, one of the most common problems is improper parsing of the symbolic stream. The ability to parse depends highly on the listener's linguistic knowledge of the input language, and adults with little experience in a given language have great difficulty parsing it into phone and word units. Speech production similarly depends on linguistic knowledge, especially for defining articulatory positions. Production problems can also arise from physiological distortions that result from illness or malformations. An explanation for how linguistic experience comes to guide acoustic parsing can be found in the particular physiology of speech perception, viewed in terms of neural structures and their functions (Suga et al., 2003).

Neural Structures Involved in Speech Perception

Speech is perceived through a hierarchy of nerve structures, sketched in Figure 3.3. In the peripheral auditory system, the outer ear receives speech sound waves, which are passed as vibrations to the inner ear, or cochlea, where they stimulate the fibers of the auditory nerve. The auditory nerve transmits neural impulse in a kind of time-frequency representation of the sound. The stream of time-frequency information is carried to a nerve mass called the cochlear nucleus (CN), where a detection process begins. Other important nerve structures in the auditory transmission path include the superior olivary nucleus (SON), with sets of neurons tuned to different acoustic frequencies; the inferior colliculus (IC), with additional neurons;

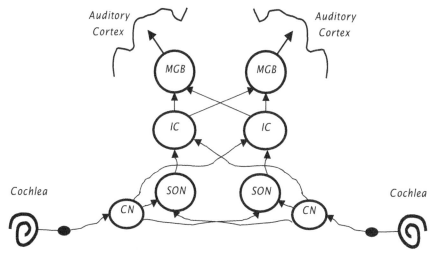

Figure 3.3 Auditory perception hierarchy from cochlea to brain.

the medial geniculate body (MGB), which seems to act as a prefiltering structure; and the brain's auditory cortex (called Wernicke's area), where the ultimate identification, classification, and recognition of speech take place.

Neural Functions Involved in Speech Perception

The auditory neural hierarchy has well established functions in speech perception. The distinctions we hear cannot be explained just by the sound wave but derive from processing imposed by the brain and intervening neural structures. Specific sets of neurons in the auditory path are specialized to detect phenomena in the acoustic trace significant for speech, such as energy bursts and peaks, frequency bands, and moving frequencies. These phenomena, called acoustic markers or spectral cues, map to the phonetic features that define phones. The parameters of these features can vary between languages, and the human auditory system becomes tuned to the settings of its particular linguistic environment. This tuning of auditory physiology develops as children are exposed to their mother tongue: neural organizations emerge, following the hierarchy in Figure 3.3, that reflect the phone classes of the surrounding language. With extended exposure, neurons come to fire in specialized groups, which precondition the speech sounds a listener can discriminate. Thus, listeners may not perceive the acoustic distinctions of a new language when those distinctions require different neuronal groupings from what the listener has acquired.

In summary, perception of the phones of a language is based deeply in neural organization, from the auditory nerve to the brain. That is why, after a certain level of brain maturity, language learners are resistant to hearing as well as producing some of the distinctions characteristic of native speakers.

WHY USE SPEECH VISUALIZATION TECHNOLOGIES TO AID SPEECH PERCEPTION AND PRODUCTION?

Reestablishing the Feedback Loop

Problems in speech perception and production cannot be overcome just by listening and repeating. Most of the time, as the above account suggests, the perception of phonetic features and their proper reproduction are impaired, if not by physiological defects, then by a lack of knowledge and exposure to the target language.

An alternative way to learn phonetic distinctions is through a modality independent of auditory perception. When the speech perception-production feedback loop is broken, we propose that it be reestablished through the visual channel. Toward this aim, visual representations can be extracted from the images of sound waves generated by instruments for analyzing sound: oscilloscopes and spectrographs. Oscilloscopes display the waveform as level of energy—amplitude or loudness (vertical axis)—plotted against time (horizontal axis), as seen in the narrow top window of Figure 3.4. Spectrographs analyze the waveform into a spectrum of frequency components (a spectrogram), as in the bottom window of Figure 3.4. A typical spectrogram plots frequency on the vertical axis against time on the horizontal. It also reflects amplitude in the darkness with which areas of frequency are presented. While the amplitude of an utterance can vary widely over people and situations, its frequency patterns, especially how energy is distributed across frequency, constitute invariants that are the main source of phonetic information for humans. Thus, spectrograms are our preferred basis for visualization techniques for learning phones.

Research suggests that spectrographic depictions of phone sequences can be designed with enough semantic content to depict usefully the differences between correct and incorrect perception and production (Germain & Martin, 2000; Gómez et al., 1996; Hunt, Howard, & Worsdall, 2000; Martin, 2003; Povel & Arends, 1991; Rossiter, 1995).

As framed by Clifford and Granoien in their interactionist model, visual representations of speech support apperception: the process by which language input must first pass through the student's "personal sensory filters—filters that have been tuned through the acquisition of the first language (p. 30)," thus requiring the conscious relating of newly observed features to past experience filters. Visual representations fulfill Clifford and Granoien's

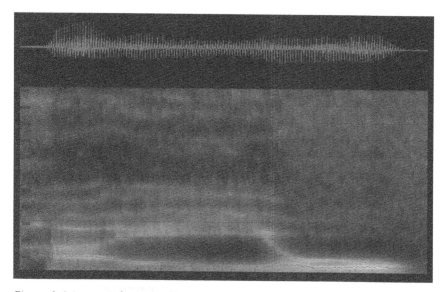

Figure 3.4 (top window) Oscilloscope display of waveform for utterance /aeiou/ with amplitude plotted over time; (bottom window) LPC spectrogram for same utterance highlighting bands of frequencies (formants) over time. (Note: /aeiou/ is the five cardinal vowels in Spanish produced continuously, without stops).

admonition that "the linguistic characteristics that learners are to pay attention to should be made salient . . . by mechanical means such as high-lighting on the screen or by linking with graphics . . ." (p. 32).

A Process for Creating Visual Representations

We examine the use of visual representations to depict the learner's own speech compared with a native standard. The visual record of the learner's speech can be adapted to this purpose by a logical process shown in Figure 3.5. This process assumes that the input speech, the content of a learner's utterance, is given. It assumes, then, an earlier stage of pedagogical decision: what to teach—here, which speech sounds to focus on. That stage is seen in the analysis by Precoda and Bratt (this volume) to determine those phones that learners of a given language most need to acquire or improve. We are concerned here with the subsequent series of decisions:

- *Time and frequency processing.* The first block in Figure 3.5 uses techniques from signal processing to extract basic characteristics of the speech signal, such as a spectrogram. The output template constitutes a raw representation of the frequency content of the signal and its variation over time.
- *Feature mapping.* Next, the time-frequency characteristics of the speech template are mapped to phonetic distinctions (for instance, voicing–unvoicing to distinguish English /p/ and /b/). The output of this block serves to describe the phonetic features of the input.
- *Semantic User Interface.* Finally, the phonetic features of the input are compared with those of a target (native) utterance and the comparison transformed into meaningful visual information for the learner. This end representation can reveal significant differences and suggest corrective actions.

The *semantic user interface* is the most critical block in this chain as it is the least well established. The issues posed by this interface for a developer of speech instruction occupy the rest of this chapter. One issue concerns which phonetic features to highlight in the visual interface to clue discrimination of phones. This question is treated in the section titled What Should be

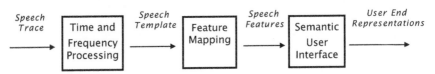

Figure 3.5 A process for creating visual representations of speech (*semantic* means understandable to learners).

Visualized? A second issue is how to show those features to learners, treated in the section titled How Should Formants be Visualized? Just presenting spectrograms is arguably ineffective for promoting learning.

WHAT SHOULD BE VISUALIZED? FORMANT-BASED VISUAL AIDS IN LANGUAGE LEARNING

Regardless of which phones are the focus of instruction, one of the most useful sets of features to show visually is the pattern of speech formants. When a speaker produces a sound wave, some frequencies in the wave will be relatively more intense (have more energy) than others. These energy concentrations, or resonances, of a sound are called *formants*. They reflect the regular opening and closing of the vocal cords, reinforcing the speech signal. The pattern of formants determines the phone class of a speech sound, most directly for vowels. When a single moment of speech has energy concentrations at different frequency levels, they look like horizontal energy bands (Figure 3.4). The band at the lowest frequency range is called the first formant (F_1), then the second (F_2), and so forth. While phone class depends on the first two to three formants, the higher formants are thought to contribute to perception of a speaker's voice quality. Frequency is typically represented on the vertical axis of a spectrogram (Figure 3.4, bottom, and Figure 3.6), measured in Hertz (Hz), from 0 Hz at the bottom of the axis up to 8000 Hz, since most phonetic information occurs in this span. Formant patterns can be seen in the distribution of energy bands by frequency and in how the distribution changes over time.

Formants are instructionally useful for several reasons. First, formants or formant-like structures are found in most speech sounds and form spectrographic patterns that characterize classes of speech sounds. Second, human speech perception across languages is physiologically based on formant positions and their dynamic changes. Indeed, formant values and patterns also correspond to the gestures of speech production: the configuration of the speaker's tongue and lips in producing particular vowels and other sounds. Third, formants give a clear time-frequency representation that is tractable by phoneticians and expert linguists who must adapt visualization technology for learners. These ideas are developed in the sections that follow.

Note that Molholt and Hwu (this volume) also treat the visualization of formants as a means to aid language learners and teachers. Their chapter illustrates how pictures of formants can highlight differences between native speakers' and learners' pronunciations in a range of languages. Here we are concerned not with particular languages but with methods to transform native-learner differences into visual metaphors that are familiar to learners.

Formants Characterize Classes of Speech Sounds

Speech sounds can be placed into two main groups, static sounds and dynamic sounds. These groups accord with the physiology of speech perception, since each group involves different neural mechanisms in their perception. Formants are central to both groups and form patterns in the spectrogram that reliably distinguish phone classes within each group as, illustrated in highly schematic form in Figure 3.6 (a–h).

- *Static sounds* have formants whose frequency distribution is relatively stable over time: approximately five speech frames (assuming a 10-ms frame, with formant position changing no more than 5% over frames). In this group are midsyllable, stable vowels, liquids, nasals, and fricatives (voiced and unvoiced). The two first formants establish the phonological quality of the vowel and vowel-like sounds. Figure 3.6 depicts these properties in abstract spectrograms: Figure 3.6a shows the structure of the first two formants of a stable vowel (e.g., /i/ as in *beat*, /u/ as in *toot*, /a/ as in *not*); Figure 3.6b–3.6c, the structure of liquids (/l/) and nasals (/n/); Figure 3.6d, the structure of an unvoiced fricative (e.g., /f/), in which formants widen and become noise-like, with energy bands above 2000 Hz. Voiced fricatives (/v/) combine both kinds of spectra. (In Castilian Spanish, the pronunciation of the initial consonant in *seis*, etc. classifies it as an alveolar fricative.)
- *Dynamic sounds* tend to be unstable over their duration. Formants move swiftly within several frames of speech, showing slopes up to tenths of Hz/msec (Allen, 1994; Haykin, 1996). If formant changes are smooth and prolonged, the sensation is that of glides (Figure 3.6e), as in /ωa/ of *water* and *away*, and approximants (Figure 3.6f), as in Spanish /β/. If the change is more abrupt, the sensation corresponds to voiced plosives (Figure 3.6g), such as /b/ in *bat*, or unvoiced plosives (Figure 3.6h), such as /p/ in *pat*. In the last case the change is very abrupt and accompanied by a burst of noise lasting very few (three to five) frames. In general, the unstable (dynamic) part of the spectrogram is associated with the perception of a consonant and the stable part, with a vowel, resulting in a first definition of the consonant-vowel-consonant structure of the syllable.

Speech Perception Is Physiologically Based on Formant Detection

We have seen that human speech perception depends on neural organization, which includes specialized auditory neurons sensitive to particular aspects of the speech trace. It is known that frequency bands are an organizing principle for neural specialization. For example, specific sets of neurons in the auditory path are tuned to detect the presence of certain bands of frequencies and not others, and a given neuron in the set will fire when the target

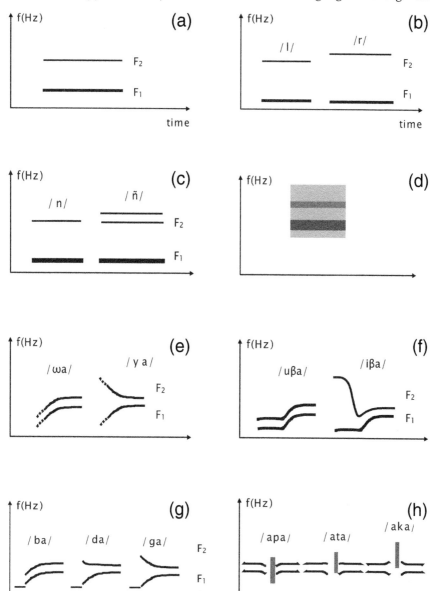

Figure 3.6 (a) Formant structure of vowels, (b) formant structure of liquids, (c) formant structure of nasals, (d) formant structure of unvoiced fricatives, (e) formant structure of glides, (f) formant structure of approximants, (g) structure of voiced plosives, (h) structure of unvoiced plosives.

frequency occurs in incoming speech. Sets of neurons are arranged according to the frequencies to which they are tuned (Suga et al., 2003). Neural tuning to frequency patterns establishes a primary role for formants in the automatic discrimination, or classification, of speech sounds by listeners.

How Listeners Use Formants in Classifying Speech Sounds

The essential factors in a listener's classifying a speech frame as a particular speech sound are as follows:

1. *Formants:* Individual energy bands.
2. *Moving formants:* Changes in the position of formants with time (slopes). Fast changes are associated with consonants (plosives), Figure 3.6g–3.6h; smooth changes, with glides (as /ωa/) and approximants (/β/), Figure 3.6e–3.6f.
3. *Voicing/unvoicing:* Bandwidth of formants. Narrow bands are associated with voicing, broad bands with unvoicing.
4. *Association of formants:* The relationship of the first two formants in vowel-like sounds determines the quality of the vowel.
5. *Stimulus duration:* Long formant duration (Figure 3.6a–3.6f) is associated with vowels or vowel-like consonants; short duration (Figure 3.6g–3.6h), with consonants (plosives or affricates).

Thus, discrimination of phones is based on the listener's ability to detect formants, their stability, bandwidth, association, and duration. The auditory system uses a complex combination of these clues from the acoustic trace for automatic and rapid classification of sounds. In more detail, vowel detection depends on the presence of frequency displacements in a tone, energy concentrated at particular frequencies, moving frequencies, and multiple peak stimuli. For plosive consonants (e.g., /p/, /t/, /k/), a small difference in formant duration determines the perception of the sound as voiced or voiceless. This feature, commonly viewed as voice onset time (VOT) of the vowel following the plosive, distinguishes minimal pair syllables such as /pa/ and /ba/ and constitutes a first level of differentiating meaning by opposition. The VOT threshold for binary classification of a given minimal pair differs for speakers of different languages and can be seen as neurally wired.

A Generalization of the Concept of Formant

The assumption that speech perception is driven by formant detection may seem extreme in the case of unvoiced consonantal sounds such as fricatives (e.g., /f/) and affricates (/č/ as in *chin*). The speaker's vocal cords are not exercised in the production of these sounds, which are not usually considered to have formants. However, we can reconceive the formant as a band of frequencies present as a local peak, or maximum, in the energy envelope of the speech spectrum. These *maxima* are associated with energy reinforcements produced in that part of the vocal tract closest to the place of articulation (e.g., the place or articulation for /f/ as in English *fin* is labiodental, formed by lip and teeth, while for /θ/ as in *thin*, it is interdental, formed between the teeth). Discrimination of fricatives is based on the presence in the spectrum of energy peaks differentiated by place or articulation. The extension and coloring of these peaks activate wide groups of auditory neurons and mark the quality of the fricative. Formants, then, reflect a property of the speech apparatus rather than the acoustic signal. They can occur whether excited by glottal pulses (voicing) or by turbulence generated at lips, teeth, palate, or glottis (unvoicing). This definition explains why listeners can detect the quality of vowels in unvoiced speech, such as whispering. It also explains why listeners can discriminate features of whispered consonants even though the voicing–unvoicing opposition disappears (e.g., whispered /p/ is distinguishable from whispered /t/ due to place of articulation but is indistinguishable from whispered /b/). The idea of a generalized formant will help in interpreting and creating meaningful visual representations of speech from a typical spectrogram (shown in Figure 3.7).

Formants Give Tractable Time-Frequency Representations for Instructional Manipulation and Marking

The conversion of speech waves into digital images permits manipulation and marking of phonetically significant constituents. Thus, a third rationale for focusing on formants is that, in general, they provide clear visual representations that can be enhanced and highlighted for experts en route to developing interfaces for learners. However, technical issues remain in detecting and extracting formants and in marking formant-based phonetic features, as discussed below.

Methods and Technical Challenges for Detecting Formants in the Spectrogram

While many methods are available to produce reliable representations of formants from the speech signal, no method is without complications. We call attention to two main groups of formant detection techniques, FFT-based and LPC-based, and comment on the accuracy and reliability of each.

Evaluation of the Fast Fourier Transform (FFT) spectrogram is one basis for formant extraction. The core idea is to detect the maxima or peaks in the spectrum of each frame and to spot (or mark) them from frame to frame. This technique has difficulties because strong peaks may hide weaker peaks; moreover, the harmonics of pitch may be confused with formants, especially in male voices. Various ways to overcome the difficulties, each with its own costs, are available (e.g., Bernal, 2000).

Another basis for formant extraction is *Linear Predictive Coding (LPC)*. The signal frame corresponding to each time window can be processed to obtain its LPC model. An LPC spectrogram appears in Figure 3.4 (bottom window). The parameters of the LPC model are used to estimate the envelope of the FFT spectrum. A process of peak detection helps to find the presence of formants in the spectrum of speech. One problem in this technique is that strong energy formants hide weaker formants if these are close enough. Another problem involves a degree of instability, or tilting, in formant peaks, which must be carefully traced and interpolated from frame to frame. A third problem is that certain sounds, like nasals, do not adhere well to the model. Several techniques have been published to overcome the first problem and to track efficiently the presence of formants between frames (Alvarez, Martinez, Nieto, Rodellar, & Gómez, 1997; Alvarez, Martinez, Gomez, & Dominguez, 1998; Bobadilla, 1998). The third problem may be partially treated by increasing the complexity of the model, which introduces larger computational costs.

Due to the intrinsic nature of the FFT, the structure of the voice harmonics characterizing an individual speaker are clearly marked on the spectrogram, appearing as horizontal lines especially visible in the lower frequencies of the spectrum. It may be inferred that producing algorithms to isolate formants from voice harmonics in FFT spectrograms is less straightforward than in LPC spectrograms. On the other hand, LPC spectrograms are less reliable than FFT, especially for nasal-like sounds.

Issues in Marking Formant-Based Features in Visual Representations

We have seen that listeners' classification of speech sounds depends on a complex combination of formants and formant-based features and relationships (see above section, How Listeners Use Formants in Classifying Speech Sounds). Visual representations of speech can be tailored to illuminate the five factors we have described as essential in this classification:

1. *Formants.* Highlighting formants in the visual record requires that they be measured frame by frame. First, frames must be short enough to ensure that formants within them are stable, leaving measurement of formant movements to a comparison between neighboring frames. On the other hand, the frame must be long enough to measure frequency with precision. A compromise established empirically in speech science is a time frame of around 10 ms. To prevent detection of false movements in formants, partially overlapping frames may be used. Another challenge in detection is that formants may appear, disappear, or overlap. Several techniques have been proposed to solve these problems.

2. *Moving formants.* A method to show displacement of formants must be devised, indicating the start and end positions and the speed of

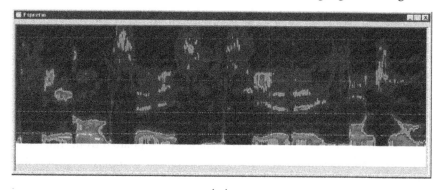

(a)

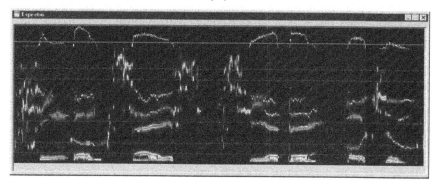

(b)

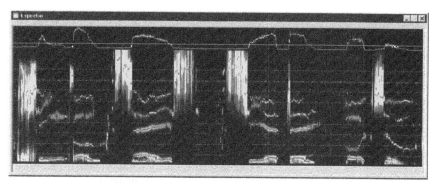

(c)

Figure 3.7 Presence of formants in voiced and unvoiced sounds in *cinco, seis, siete, ocho* (/θiŋko/, /seys/, /syete/, /očo/): (a) common spectrogram, (b) formants detected, (c) presence of fricatives (/θ/, /s/) and affricates (/č/) enhanced.

displacement. This feature is difficult to reflect in a meaningful way for nonexpert users.

3. *Voicing/unvoicing.* This feature may be established from the time-domain analysis of the speech trace. Algorithms may be applied to track pitch.

4. *Association of formants.* Essential for distinguishing vowels, associated pairs of formants may be mapped on a vowel triangle for the expert. A more sophisticated technique to communicate formant pairs to learners is to employ formant relationships to drive game-like interfaces (illustrated below in the section titled Examples of Visual Interfaces for Language Learners).

5. *Stimulus duration.* Essential for distinguishing vowels (long and short) and consonants, duration may be measured based on the number of frames in which a given feature is detected as stable.

Some aspects of these factors can be unambiguously identified for visual emphasis. Molholt and Hwu (this volume) tailor spectrographic displays to demonstrate the interplay of these factors in pronunciation differences between languages.

Using the Generalized Concept of Formant to Extend Visual Marking

The idea of a generalized formant was introduced above to explain how formants figure in the detection of unvoiced consonants (see section titled A Generalization of the Concept of Formant). Here we illustrate how this concept helps in illuminating voiceless as well as voiced segments in the spectrogram. Figure 3.7a shows the spectrum of four words in Castilian Spanish: the names of the numerals 5, 6, 7, and 8 (*cinco, seis, siete, ocho*). Figure 3.5b shows the extraction from the spectrogram of the frequency maxima (formants) for these words. Figure 3.5c shows the unvoiced segments enhanced for fricatives (/θ/ in /θiŋko/, /s/ in /seys/ and /syete/) and affricates (/č/ in /očo/), with their maxima spotted to give visual definition to distinguishing features.

Emphasizing Formants Through Vector Representations

Formants can be further emphasized in vector representations, which use the computer screen as an x–y map in which time is not explicitly plotted. These maps are especially useful to represent vowels and vowel-like sounds if the instantaneous values of the first two formants are normalized and plotted relative to the x and y axes (Gómez et al., 1997), as exemplified in Figure 3.8.

Figure 3.8 shows an x–y plot of the /aeiou/ utterance from Figure 3.4, with 5-ms templates used in analyzing the plot. The first formant (F_1) is plotted on the x axis and the second format (F_2) on the y axis. The normalization values are the lowest and highest values that these formants may

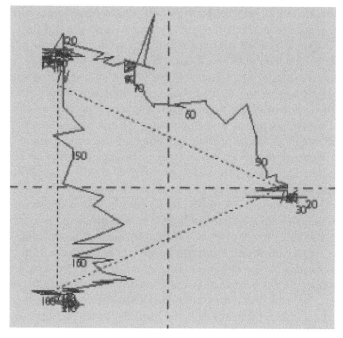

Figure 3.8 Vector representation for the utterance /aeiou/. Numerals shown in the graph give the ordinality of each 5-ms template in the plot. Vertices correspond to /u/ (bottom left), /i/ (top left), and /a/ (right).

take: the value of F_1 for the vowel /a/ is the rightmost point on the x axis; the leftmost point is the value of F_1 for /i-u/. The upper value on the y axis is given by the highest value of F_2 in /i/; the lowest value, by F_2 in /u/. In the emerging triangle in Figure 3.8, the trace starts on the rightmost part of the x axis (about 50 templates). From this point the trace follows a progression (dynamic glide) to the position of /e/ (templates 70–90), then /i/ (between templates 100–140). The transition through the position of /o/ is swift, and the utterance ends in /u/ (the last 30 templates). (See also the vowel triangles in Molholt & Hwu, this volume, which label the vowel locations.)

The possibilities of vector interfaces may be further exploited in three-dimensional (3-D) representations. A 3-D diagram can employ the first three formants to establish coordinates on the three main axes and then apply the successive template approach from Figure 3.8. However, standards for 3-D representations have not been fully established.

USER INTERFACES IN VISUAL REPRESENTATIONS

The remaining issue is how to help listeners who cannot detect or produce phonemic distinctions—whether these listeners have impairments in hearing and articulation (e.g., Dalby & Kewley-Port, this volume), or are learners of a language (e.g., Precoda & Bratt, this volume). It seems natural to use visualization of speech as a way to bypass listeners' difficulties at the physiological (speech perception) or psychological (phonological detection) levels.

The requirements of the visual interface for communicating speech features depend on who the user is. For users who are speech experts, we have sampled the variety of visualization formats available: oscillographic interfaces, spectrograms, and vector maps, for example. Phoneticians and acoustic engineers demand precise instrumental displays in which formant positions, segment duration, and vowel triangles are accurate. However, beginning language students, hearing-impaired children, and other non-expert users need engaging, meaningful, and simple interfaces. Depicting speech sounds for these users poses challenges not just at the technical level but at the cognitive comprehension level. The *semantic user interface* should present easily understood, discriminating information about when the pronunciation of a given sound is correct according to linguistic standards and about how to improve pronunciations that are deemed nonstandard.

The spectrographic interface is intended for the expert and will rigorously reflect the measurements obtained. The learner interface, by contrast, is intended to hide technicalities. This gap in knowledge and interpretation capabilities between expert and nonexpert users we term the semantic gap.

Bridging the Semantic Gap: A Videogame Interface With Microphone Joystick

The semantic gap poses a major obstacle for applying speech visualization techniques to language learning. The typical user of CALL systems lacks the background to interpret spectrographic data. One form of visual representation hypothesized to bridge the semantic gap is the videogame interface. Here we use the instantaneous values of the target speech features to define actions in a game, controlled by the user's microphone input instead of by the conventional joystick. The user is requested to produce a given speech sequence, which, following the chain proposed in Figure 3.5, is presented visually. A simple example of a videogame interface, where the user interacts through a microphone joystick, is presented in Figure 3.9.

The interface in Figure 3.9 has been integrated into a CALL lesson under the project ALAS (*Aprendizaje de Lenguas con Asistencia Sonora*, or Sound-Assisted Language Learning; originally, Povel & Arends, 1991). The lesson is designed to test the ability of Spanish-speaking students to reproduce English vowels. Short words containing opposing vowels such as *ball*, *bell*, and *bird* are used as pronunciation models. Through the classroom setting, a picture of the object associated with the word is presented to the student, and the standard pronunciation of a teacher can be heard. The student can obtain more repetitions by clicking on the loudspeakers in the picture. When

Figure 3.9 Videogame Interface in ALAS, a sound-assisted language learning demonstration.

the student wants to speak, he or she must click on the microphone in the picture and then speak.

Behind the scenes, a spectrographic analysis of the student's and the teacher's utterances enables the vector positions of each utterance to be evaluated and their duration and centroids to be compared. The separation between centroids is evaluated, and this distance is used to simulate the casting of a dart. A good spectral match means a high scoring dart. The implementation of this system is rather straightforward: a computer function is responsible for evaluating the templates and distances from both speech traces, and it supplies the x–y coordinates that direct the dart. A similar principle underlies the visual interface in one of the pronunciation training aids described by Dalby and Kewley-Port (this volume).

Many other possibilities may be devised. The interface in Figure 3.10, for example, is oriented to the pronunciation of dynamic sounds such as glides.

The scenario shown in Figure 3.10 is that of a car racing game. The car is directed based on evaluation of the instantaneous distances in the x–y plane between the teacher's and the student's sound trajectories. When the trajectories between student and teacher are close enough by some predefined metric, the car follows the center line of the curve. Otherwise, the car moves to right or left the center line.

Other designs have been studied for giving feedback on additional conceptual speech features, such as voicing/unvoicing, pitch, rhythm, prosody, and coarticulatory phenomena (Eskenazi, Ke, Albornoz, & Probst, 2000; Martin, 2003; Povel & Arends, 1991; Rossiter, 1995). A pending issue is

Figure 3.10 Videogame interface to teach phones of dynamic type (such as glides).

how to integrate all these tools into a general CALL system. Another issue is how to produce enough data to implement a complete system, combining these techniques with other kinds of exercises.

A Look at Emerging Visualization Techniques

Here we present examples of recently developed acoustic visualization methods with potential for application to CALL. The example given in Figure 3.11 shows the application of a FFT-based technique originated by Bernal (2000) for detecting formants.

The upper picture of Figure 3.11 shows the spectrum of the Spanish word *cosa* (/kosa/), containing an unvoiced plosive and fricative, and two different vowels. The lower picture shows the result of detecting formants in the general sense. The accuracy of this method is remarkable, and it brings to

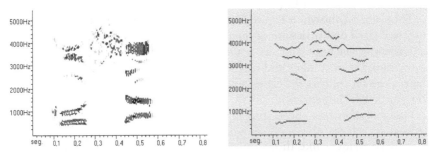

Figure 3.11 Example of an advanced formant detection technique (based on FFT).

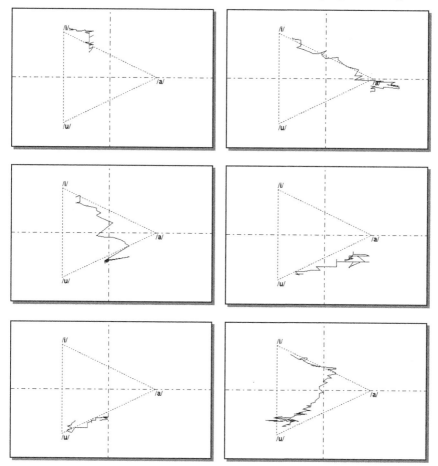

Figure 3.12 From left to right and top to bottom, plots for the English diphthongs /ey/, /ay/, /oy/, /aω/, /oω/ and /εω/.

light the coloring of the fricative /s/ (corresponding to places where energy peaks are present), which is indistinct in the upper picture. The examples in Figure 3.12 show a set of x–y plots for several English diphthongs. This method gives highly descriptive trajectories for most cases, the most notable being the lower right case, the /εω/ diphthong. The method works with both male and female voices if normalization is applied.

DISCUSSION

Before techniques like those just described can be tried with students, the main requirement is to validate the method in question using a wide set of speech traces from a specific speech database especially designed for this purpose. This same database can be used in production of exercises for a CALL system.

At this point in our research, we have reviewed a range of spectral analysis and display methods as well as techniques for manipulating displays to distill important features of pronunciation and to make them understandable to a learner. We are beginning the process of validating methods such as those depicted here and incorporating them into CALL pronunciation exercises that can be tried with learners. Then we can begin to evaluate the benefits to language learning of visualization in general and of specific alternatives.

ACKNOWLEDGMENTS

This research has being carried out under Grants ALAS (PASO No. 249), NATO CRG 960053, TIC97–1011, 07T–0001–2000 from the Plan Regional de Investigación de la Comunidad de Madrid and TIC99–0960 from the National Program for the Technologies of Information and Communications of Spain. The authors wish to express their recognition to the suggestions made by M. Holland on the improvement of the paper's manuscript.

REFERENCES

Allen, J. B. (1994). How do humans process and recognize speech? *IEEE Transactions on Speech and Audio Processing, 2–4*, 567–577.
Alvarez, A., Martínez, R., Gómez, P., & Domínguez, J. L. (1998). A signal processing technique for speech visualization. *Proceedings of STIL98 (Integrating Speech Technology in (Language) Learning)*, 33–36, Marholmen, Sweden.
Álvarez, A., Martínez, R., Nieto, V., Rodellar, V., & Gómez, P. (1997). Continuous formant-tracking applied to visual representations of speech and speech recognition. *EUROSPEECH'97*, 653–656, Rhodes, Greece.
Bernal, J. (2000). *Metodología para la visualización de los formantes, basada en la transformación de fourier, y su uso en el estudio espectral de la fonética acústica española*. Unpublished doctoral dissertation, Universidad Politécnica de Madrid, Facultad de Informática (in Spanish).
Bobadilla, J. (1998). *Desarrollo de algoritmos basados en filtrado adaptativo y su aplicación en el estudio de la fonética acústica española*. Universidad Politécnica de Madrid, Facultad de Informática, Ph.D. dissertation (in Spanish).
Eskénazi M., Ke, Y., Albornoz, J., & Probst, K. (2000). Update on the Fluency pronunciation trainer. *Proceedings of InSTIL 2000*, 73–76.
Ferrández, J. M. (1998). *Estudio y realización de una Arquitectura Jerárquica Bioinspirada para el Reconocimiento del Habla*. Unpublished doctoral disseration, Universidad Politécnica de Madrid, Facultad de Informática (in Spanish).
Germain, A., & Martin, P. (2000). Présentation d'un logiciel de visualisation pour l'apprentissage de l'oral en langue seconde. *Apprentissage des Langues et Systèmes d'Information et de Communication (ALSIC), 3*, 61–76. (Retrieved on

November 24, 2006, from http://alsic.ustrasbg.fr/Num5/germain/alsic_n05-rec7. htm).

Gómez, P., Martínez, D., Nieto, V., & Rodellar, V. (1994). MECALLSAT: A Multimedia environment for computer-aided language learning incorporating speech assessment techniques. In J. Colpaert, W., Decoo, & D. Markey, (Eds.), *Proceedings of the Second International Conference on Technologies & Language Learning* (pp. 99–108), Brussels: IBM Education Center.

Gómez, P., Pérez, M., Mayo, N., Rubio, F., Álvarez, A., Martínez, R., et al. (1997). Visual representations of the speech trace on a real time platform. *Proceedings of the IEEE Workshop on Signal Processing Systems: Design and Implementation*, 283–292, De Montfort University, Leicester, UK.

Haykin, S. (1996). *Adaptive filter theory* (3rd ed.). Englewood Cliffs, NJ: Prentice Hall.

Hunt, A. D., Howard, D. M., & Worsdall, J. (2000). Real-time interfaces for speech and singing. *Proceedings of the IEEE 26th Euromicro Conference*, II, 356–361. Maastricht.

Martin, P. (2003). *Some speech analysis techniques for language teaching*. Paper presented at the 11th ELSNET European Summer School on Language and Speech Communication, University of Lille, Villeneuve-d'Asq, France. (Retrieved on November 24, 2006, from http://www.elsnet.org/ess2003site.html)

Povel, D. J. L., & Arends, N. (1991). The visual speech apparatus: Theoretical and practical aspects. *Speech Communication, 10,* 59–80.

Rossiter, D. P. (1995). *Real-time visual displays for voice tuition*. Unpublished doctoral dissertation, University of York, UK.

Suga, N., Ma, X., Gao, E., Sakai, M., & Choudhury, S. (2003). Descending system and plasticity for auditory signal processing: Neuroethological data for speech scientists. *Speech Communication, 41,* 189–200.

Section II

Analyzing Needs

The Case of a Pronunciation Tutor

INTRODUCTION

An important but often overlooked stage along the path of CALL research is analyzing the needs of the intended learners so as to focus the technology efficiently. Systems built to showcase speech technology, such as many found in the commercial market, tend to base decisions about what to teach on conventional teaching wisdom. Although conventional wisdom may, indeed, lead to efficiently focused technology, it lacks validation against evidence. Viewing CALL as a branch of instructional science demands empirically based needs analysis as a guide for development. This section illustrates empirical methods for needs analysis in the chapter by Precoda and Bratt.

THE PROBLEM OF DECIDING WHAT SOUNDS TO TEACH

The question dealt with by Precoda and Bratt is what speech sounds to address in a pronunciation tutor. Other chapters in this book consider designs for teaching and shaping pronunciation once the instructional focus has been decided. Precoda and Bratt consider how to determine the set of mispronunciations most in need of remediation—a step that in their research precedes the expensive and demanding work of adapting automatic speech recognition (ASR) to detect mispronunciations. The criterion for importance, or salience, of pronunciation errors used by Precoda and Bratt is how foreign (*nonnative*) they make a language learner sound to native speakers. The measure of nonnativeness is ratings by native speakers listening to learners' utterances. When correlated with phonetically annotated transcriptions, these ratings serve not only to identify and prioritize phone-based errors but also, during subsequent stages of adapting recognition algorithms and developing a prototype, to benchmark the computer's scoring of learners' speech. Human listener benchmarking is, in fact, an established research practice in developing ASR for pronunciation assessment. Its use in the subsequent stage of developing pronunciation instruction is described by Franco et al. (2000) and by Dalby and Kewley-Port (this volume); its use in developing spoken language testing is described by Bernstein and Cheng (this volume).

The work of human listener benchmarking consists of collecting acoustic data from learners and establishing a listener baseline using native speakers and trained phoneticians. Precoda and Bratt describe a set of assumptions and a methodology for that work, of interest to developers of pronunciation training. Moreover, the rankings they reveal of errors in Spanish made by American English speakers should be useful to developers of Spanish pronunciation instruction.

A criterion for choosing pronunciation errors that is equally as compelling as their effect on perception of nonnativeness is, arguably, their effect on intelligibility, a variable brought up by Precoda and Bratt. Intelligibility is likely to correlate well with perception of nonnativeness, but applying the intelligibility criterion requires data collection from a more extensive set of human listeners with more time-consuming measures; in particular, intelligibility calls for performance measures such as the accuracy of listeners' repetitions or transcriptions of what they hear. Research on automatic detection of pronunciation errors significant for intelligibility can be found in Raux and Kawahara (2002) and in Dalby and Kewley-Port (Section IV, this volume). Dalby and Kewley-Port argue that nonnativeness (accentedness) can substantially reduce intelligibility. They provide supporting evidence from studies of listener performance that manipulate accent in input speech. They further adduce evidence that segmental errors in isolated words predict listener misunderstandings of sentences and longer units, lending to justification of the need for pronunciation tutors.

Another criterion relevant to needs analysis for language teaching is error frequency—which may be defined in terms of the most common errors made by a learner or set of learners, or as the frequency in the language of sounds, words, or constructions in which learners make errors. Applying this kind of criterion requires collecting a representative language corpus and examining the frequency in that corpus of entities of interest; and further, collecting a corpus of language learner errors and analyzing their relative frequency (see Bley-Vroman, 2002). Efficient teaching calls for addressing the most frequent entities and the most common errors first. Error frequency is the recent basis of computer-assisted pronunciation training developed by Truong, Neri, de Wet, Cucchiarini, and Strik (2005), whose research addresses not only training technology but also criteria for selecting what to train (Neri, de Wet, Cucchiarini, & Strik, 2004). Further inquiry into criteria for selecting pronunciation targets for CALL is taken up by Wang and Munro (2004).

To strengthen empirical analysis of needs, CALL programs that aim for substantial coverage are advised to link selection of content to linguistic theories of orderings and dependencies in the acquisition of phonology and other linguistic levels. Some relevant theoretical frameworks are discussed by Clifford and Granoien in Section I.

EXTENSIONS TO PRACTICE OF THE RESEARCH
ON PRONUNCIATION SCORING

While Precoda and Bratt concentrate their chapter on needs analysis methodology, we should note that a practical capability has emerged from the thorough benchmarking research in their lab at SRI: a software developer's toolkit called EduSpeak®, which performs both ASR and pronunciation grading in selected languages. It can now be found on the web (http://www.speechatsri.com/products/eduspeak.shtml) for use in developing speech-interactive educational software, including CALL. The kit supports native and nonnative versions of American and other varieties of English, other more commonly taught languages, and some less commonly taught languages, such as Egyptian Arabic, Japanese, and Tagalog. It also supports American English spoken by children. Examples of CALL that incorporates software from the kit include the multimedia lessons created by LaRocca, Morgan, and Bellinger (2002), which provide feedback on French pronunciation in the course of communicative exercises. A screen from one of those lessons appears in Figure II.1, depicting how the system informs a student about an utterance he or she has spoken in response to a multiple choice question.

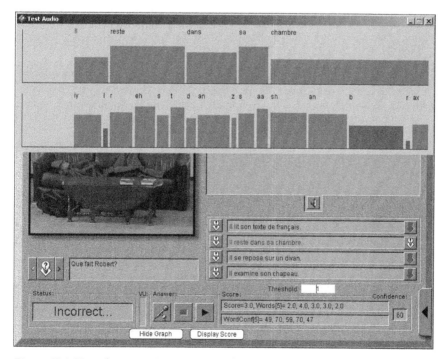

Figure II.1 Use of pronunciation scoring from EduSpeak® in multimedia French lessons at the United States Military Academy (from LaRocca et al., 2002).

The upper graph in Figure II.1 relates the height of the bar to overall quality (nativeness) of the utterance word by word (thus, *il* and *chambre* score low). The lower graph breaks down words by segment or phone, using bar height as well as color (with a tailorable threshold) to signal problems. Feedback in this example shows that the student has not only answered incorrectly the question "Que fait Robert?" but has also pronounced some words and phones below an instructor-set threshold of quality.

Besides EduSpeak®, other tools for automatic pronunciation scoring have emerged from research in speech recognition and human calibration. These include prototypes from Cambridge University (Witt & Young, 2000) and commercial products from Ordinate Corporation (Bernstin and Cheng, this volume) and Carnegie Speech Products (http://www.carnegiespeech. com/native_accent_ speech.html).

REFERENCES

Bley-Vroman, R. (2002). Frequency in production, comprehension, and acquisition. *Studies in Second Language Acquisition, 24*, 209–13.

Franco H., Abrash, V., Precoda, K., Bratt, H., Rao, R., & Butzberger, J. (2000). The SRI EduSpeak System: Recognition and pronunciation scoring for language learning. *Proceedings of INSTIL 2000*, 123–128, University of Abertay, Dundee, Scotland.

LaRocca, S., Morgan J., & Bellinger, S. (2002). Adaptation for successful recognition of student speech: Some first applications for Arabic learners. *Proceedings of EUROCALL 2002*, Jyväskylä, Finland.

Neri, A., de Wet, F., Cucchiarini, C., & Strik, H. (2004). Segmental errors in Dutch as a second language: How to establish priorities for CAPT. *Proceedings of the InSTIL/ICALL Symposium*, 13–16, Venice.

Raux, A., & Kawahara, T. (2002). Automatic intelligibility assessment and diagnosis of critical pronunciation errors for computer-assisted pronunciation learning. *Proceedings of International Conference on Spoken Language Processing (ICSLP) 2002*, 737–740, Denver. [http://www.cs.cmu.edu/~antoine/papers/icslp 2002a.pdf]

Truong, K., Neri, A., de Wet, F., Cucchiarini, C., & Strik, H. (2005). Automatic detection of frequent pronunciation errors made by L2 learners. *Proceedings of the European Conference on Speech Communication and Technology (EUROSPEECH 2005)*, 1345–1348, Lisbon. [http://lands.let.kun.nl/literature/ truong.2005.1.pdf]

Wang, X., & Munro, M. J. (2004). Computer-based training for learning English vowel contrasts. *System, 32*(4), 539–552.

Witt, S. M., & Young, S. J. (2000). Phone-level pronunciation scoring and assessment for interactive language learning. *Speech Communication, 30*, 95–108.

4 Perceptual Underpinnings of Automatic Pronunciation Assessment

Kristin Precoda and Harry Bratt

INTRODUCTION

One of the exciting promises of speech recognition technology in language learning is the ability to give automatic feedback on specific pronunciation problems and on the overall impression of nonnativeness produced by the learner's speech. There has been a substantial amount of work on the automatic detection of pronunciation problems (e.g., Brett, 2004; Eskenazi, 1996; Eskenazi, Ke, Albornoz, & Probst, 2000; Franco, Neumeyer, Ramos, & Bratt, 1999; Herron et al., 1999; Menzel et al., 2001; Neri, de Wet, Cucchiarini, & Strik, 2004; Tokuyama & Miwa, 2004; Witt & Young, 2000) and on automatically producing an overall assessment of nonnativeness (e.g., Cucchiarini, Strik, Binnenpoorte, & Boves, 2000; Cucchiarini, Strik, & Boves, 1998; Franco, Neumeyer, & Kim, 1997; Rypa & Price, 1999). There have also been preliminary efforts to incorporate this work into language tutors. For example, the Voice Interactive Training System (VILTS) developed by Rypa and Price (1999) provides overall assessments of nativeness. Using a communicative approach to elicit students' utterances, that system logs and stores student speech as a basis for delivering an overall pronunciation score. More recently, EduSpeak® (Franco et al., 2000), a software development toolkit, makes available to software developers speech recognition technology that can assess overall nativeness and estimate the nativeness of individual phones. EduSpeak® is described on the web (www.speechatsri.com/products/eduspeak.shtml) and has been applied in computer-based pronunciation tutors, for example, by LaRocca, Morgan, and Bellinger (2002) and by Vazulik, Aguirre, and Newman (2002).

At the same time as research on automatic pronunciation assessment advances, and equally importantly, we need to bear in mind and understand the behavior of humans listening to nonnative speech, since human listener reactions are the ultimate standard for what a computer-based pronunciation assessment system should produce. Human reactions to accented speech have been the subject of much research (see Markham, 1997), and perhaps one of the most obvious and important results is that listener judgments are strongly context-specific. As much earlier research has been concerned with more fundamental and wide-ranging problems, we are interested in beginning to bridge the gap to a near-term, implementable system that automatically assesses learners' speech pronunciation. To this end, this study will treat listeners as systems of inherent interest and will examine listener behavior within the particular context of a corpus of judgments collected to support work at SRI International on pronunciation assessment algorithms (e.g. Neumeyer, Franco, Digalakis, & Weintraub, 2000). These algorithms use information produced by a hidden Markov model-based speech recognition system to compare learner speech against native speech. This information consists primarily of phonetic segmentations and likelihoods of spectral vectors. The algorithms are evaluated by how well they can predict human ratings of pronunciation quality.

We will focus on two aspects of listener behavior. The first is the extent to which trained phoneticians who are also native speakers of the language being learned are able to label realizations of individual phones as native or nonnative, given their context. It would be highly desirable for an automatic system to be able to give very detailed feedback on the way in which a realization differs from nativeness, and a first, simpler task might be to detect whether a token is acceptable as native or not.

A second focus is the salience of different phone errors, that is, the amount to which errors in any given phone affect the overall impression of nonnativeness of the speaker. Clearly, understanding error salience could greatly contribute to designing a pronunciation assessment system by concentrating the system's and learner's efforts on the most significant errors.

A STUDY OF LISTENER BEHAVIOR

Data Collection

The acoustic data consisted of recordings of 206 native speakers of American English who spoke Latin American Spanish with varying and approximately balanced levels of pronunciation skill. Each speaker read between 75 and 150 sentences from newspapers, 79 sentences constructed to present potential phonetic problems, 10 strings of 10 digits, and 56 isolated words. Only the newspaper sentences are considered in this study.

Two kinds of listener judgments were collected. The first kind comprised ratings of overall nonnativeness, by one or more of a set of five native speakers of Spanish with no linguistic training. The ratings were on an ordinal scale from 1 to 5, where 1 was labeled "fuertamente extranjera/strongly foreign" and 5 "casi nativa/native quality." From this data, which included ratings of 14,062 utterances from news stories, we calculated a single nonnativeness index for each speaker by averaging all the ratings of her or his utterances (an average of about 68 ratings per speaker). If an utterance was rated by more than one listener, one listener's rating was randomly chosen to represent that utterance.

The second kind of listener judgment was in the form of phonetic transcriptions. Four native-Spanish-speaking phoneticians, who also spoke English, each transcribed 1,048 utterances. Among these utterances was a common set of 206 utterances transcribed by all the phoneticians, of which 10 were later discarded because of transcriber errors (e.g., typos). The 196 remaining utterances, which were taken from news stories, ranged from 5 to 12 words in length and contained a total of 8,267 phones in their canonical, mostly phonemic transcriptions. The phoneticians transcribed each segment as one of a limited set of likely phones, or as a nonnative realization of the intended or another phoneme, without further detail. For example, "lado" might be pronounced [lado] with a native-like [d], [laðo] with a native-like [ð], [lað*o] with an asterisk indicating a nonnative [ð], and so forth. For some of the following analyses, the transcriptions were further reduced to contain only labels of "native" or "nonnative" for each intended phone.

The set of phones and the number of occurrences of each phone in the set of 196 sentences are shown in Table 4.1. (A more detailed description of the data can be found in Bratt, Neumeyer, Shriberg, & Franco, 1998).

Results

Results will be discussed in two sections. First is the reliability with which native speakers perceive given speech phones as native or nonnative. Second is the degree to which particular phones contribute to the overall impression of a speaker as nonnative.

Native/Nonnative Phone Judgments

In general, there are likely to be several factors that influence whether a realization of a phone will be perceived as native-like or as nonnative. The quality of the realization itself is the most obvious: An American English retroflex approximant [r] is not a native-like sound when a Spanish trilled [rr] or tap [r] is required. There are instances where most or all listeners will identify a sound as nonnative, or as native; in our data, all four phoneticians agree on a sound's status as native or nonnative about 63% of the time.

A second factor influencing a listener's perception of a phone is that listener's overall tendency to label phones as native or nonnative in the particular task. This sensitivity corresponds to the response bias assumed in signal detection theory (e.g., Green & Swets, 1974), and will be called "response bias" or "threshold" here. It is useful in normalizing the responses of the individual phoneticians (P1–P4). The proportions of nonnative realizations of all phones are as follows: 24.1% (P1), 17.9% (P2), 30.8% (P3), and 27.0% (P4).

A listener's perception may also be partially determined by her or his internal targets or acceptable ranges for a given phoneme. One possible

Table 4.1 Set of Phones Used and Numbers of Occurrences in the 196 Sentences Transcribed by All Four Phoneticians

Phone Symbol	Example Word	Number of Occurrences
i	mi	418
e	mesa, papel	1117
a	la	1006
o	solo, menor	817
u	mucho	190
p	pasa	202
t	tasa	425
k	casa	310
b	tambien	40
d	donde	68
g	gracias, algun	29
β	cabo	177
ð	lado	278
γ	lago	46
m	cama	296
n	no	568
ñ	caña	10
ŋ	cinco	53
f	café	86
s	casa	781
x	caja	43
z	mismo, los dos	95
c	mucho	19
l	la	366
r	pero	452
rr	perro, sonrisa	62
y	estrella, bien	229
w	cuatro	84

source of differences in acceptable ranges might be dialect differences; there may be other causes as well.

In Figure 4.1 are shown the proportions of realizations of each phone labeled as nonnative by each phonetician over the 196 shared sentences, for those phones which occurred more than 50 times in the 196 sentences. One of the most striking features of these figures is how much these native-speaker phoneticians, who were listening to the same acoustic data, differed in the proportions of tokens they labeled as nonnative. We were interested in examining these differences with a view to whether they indicated differ-

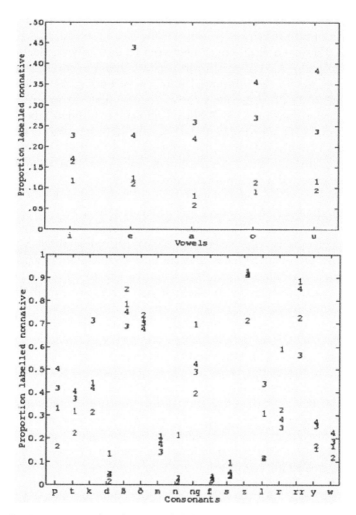

Figure 4.1 Proportion of realizations labeled nonnative for phones with more than 50 realizations ("ng" is [ŋ]). Numbers on figure indicate phonetician (P1, P2, P3, P4).

ences in response bias, that is, a type of sensitivity or threshold, or differences in acceptable ranges.

Consider the data for /a/ realizations labeled by P3 and P4. P3 and P4 have similar and fairly high rates of labeling /a/ realizations as somehow nonnative, 24.1% and 20.8% respectively, so any difference in overall response bias is small. If the differences between P3 and P4 were purely due to response bias and likelihood of labeling something as nonnative, we would expect to see some realizations which P3 labels as nonnative and P4 does not, since P3 labels a slightly higher proportion of /a/'s as nonnative. In the ideal case, the number of such realizations would be about 33, which is the difference between the nonnative /a/ rates for P3 and P4 times the total number of realizations. Cases that P3 labels as native and P4 as nonnative would be the result of error.

On the other hand, if differences between P3 and P4 were due to differences in acceptable ranges, possibly in addition to different response biases, we would expect to see substantial numbers of both cases in which one phonetician labels a realization as native and the other disagrees. Table 4.2 shows the actual data collected. While it is difficult to estimate labeling error rates, it seems high to attribute only to error the 101 utterances (>10%) falling into the P3-native/P4-nonnative category; and the 134 (13.4%) falling into P3-nonnative/P4-native is substantially more than the approximately 3.3% to be expected from a pure threshold difference.

We similarly considered ratings by all pairs of phoneticians for each phone. For the sake of a starting point, let us take a very crude model. Suppose an error rate of 3% is plausible: that is, a phonetician could make some kind of mistake and mislabel a token's nativeness about 3% of the time. If errors were equally likely to occur on any realization of a phone, the probability of one phonetician or the other making an error, but not both, is .059. (In fact, it is clearly not the case that errors are equally likely on any realization; presumably those that are extremely nonnative in quality have lower error rates.) 5.9% may thus serve as the threshold for the case in which the phonetician with the higher proportion of nonnative labels for a phone labels a token as native and the other phonetician labels it as nonnative. Out of 168 comparisons (28 phones, six pairs of phoneticians), 29 exceed this error threshold and appear to be likely candidates for differences in acceptable ranges. Phones that exceed the error threshold for at least two pairs of phoneticians are [p, t, k, g, l, r, rr, y, w]. There may also be cases in which a phone differs in acceptable range but the total number of tokens or proportion of nonnative realizations is so small that there are necessarily few tokens labeled in "error."

We were also interested in how many phones seemed to differ only in threshold or response bias and not in acceptable range. We arbitrarily defined a threshold difference as being those cases in which one phonetician's proportion of nonnative labels is at least 1.3 times another phonetician's proportion. This threshold seemed intuitively large enough to be more

Table 4.2 Realizations of the Phone /a/ (Vowel quality is considered but not vowel length. Total is slightly lower than in Table 4.1 because of dropping cases where one phonetician or the other labeled the phone as deleted.)

	P3: Native Quality	*P3: Nonnative*	*Total*
P4: native quality	654	134	788
P4: nonnative	101	106	207
Total	755	240	995

than just random fluctuation. Of the 139 comparisons that show less evidence of difference in acceptable ranges (139 = 168 − 29), there are 84 that exhibit a threshold difference by this definition. Phones showing a threshold difference for at least five of the six possible pairs of phoneticians are [i, a, o, u, k, d, g, n, f, s, c, l]; those showing a threshold difference for at least four of the six possible pairs are [e, p, ŋ, r, y, w].

Error Salience for Impression of Fonnativeness

In addition to their differences in threshold and acceptable range, phoneticians may differ in which of the segments they label as nonnative are the best predictors of ratings of overall nonnativeness.

For each phonetician, each speaker, and each phone, we calculated the proportion of nonnative realizations of the phone by that speaker, according to the given phonetician. This is the same data as is shown in Figure 4.1. A nonnativeness index was calculated as described in the Data Collection section above.

Exhaustive stepwise multiple regression was performed to determine which phones' nonnativeness proportions were the best predictors of the nonnativeness index. Table 4.3 shows those phones that contributed significantly ($p < .05$) to the proportion of variance accounted for by the multiple regression. It should be noted that phones that are rare are unlikely to be significant in a regression based on their rarity alone.

As indicated in Table 4.3, for every phonetician, /r/ is the single best predictor of nonnativeness of Spanish productions by native speakers of English. It can be seen that there is a fair degree of agreement between phoneticians on what phones most correlate with overall impression of nonnativeness; however, phoneticians differ in the details of relative importance and do have some more idiosyncratic perceptions. A question of consequence is whether speech recognition technology can extract the nonnativeness cues in /r/.

It is interesting to compare the best predictors for the individual phoneticians with the best predictors when all the judgments are treated as coming from a single, "average" phonetician, as seen in the last pair of

Table 4.3 Significant Phones in Order of Importance in Stepwise Regression, With Cumulative Multiple r2. (Regression is over all sentences transcribed by a phonetician, against speaker-level nonnativeness ratings averaged over all rated utterances)

P1		P2		P3		P4		Average	
Phone	Multiple r^2	Phone	Multiple r^2	Phone	Multiple r^2	Phone	Multiple r^2	Phone	Multiple r^2
r	.60	r	.51	r	.45	r	.43	r	.68
e	.68	e	.61	ð	.56	ð	.57	e	.77
o	.72	i	.67	e	.63	i	.63	β	.80
ð	.75	ð	.70	β	.65	β	.66	i	.82
a	.77	a	.71	ŋ	.67	ŋ	.69	n	.83
rr	.78	ŋ	.72	a	.68	l	.71	ð	.83
β	.78	u	.73	n	.69	y	.73	γ	.84
l	.79	k	.74	y	.70	u	.73	ŋ	.85
				o	.70			u	.85
								y	.86
all 28	.81		.76		.73		.75		.87

columns of Table 4.3. There remains fair agreement on the first few most salient phones, but beyond those it is more difficult to see convincing similarity. This could be due to any of a number of factors. One possible factor is that one phonetician's heightened sensitivity to some phone is cancelled out by another's lessened sensitivity. Another possibility is that a phone with only a weak correlation (perhaps due to a small number of occurrences) for each of the four individual phoneticians, appears to have a stronger correlation when the judgments are all considered together. Yet another possibility is that with so many observations, effects may appear to be of statistical significance without necessarily being of much practical significance.

From the last row of Table 4.3, it can be seen that for any individual phonetician, between 73% and 81% of the variance in the nonnativeness judgments is accounted for by purely segmental effects, so from 19% to 27% is not. Some of this unexplained variance is surely due to any number of causes not of present interest (e.g. listener inattention, individual differences between the listeners rating nonnativeness, typing errors, and many others). Some of the unaccounted-for variance may be correlated with prosodic or other linguistic effects. However, because segmental and prosodic performance may themselves well be correlated (e.g., as in Anderson-Hsieh, Johnson, & Koehler [1992] and to a lesser extent, in Munro & Derwing [1995]), without ratings of prosodic nonnativeness on these data, we are unable to distinguish between how much nonnativeness is uniquely predicted by segmental effects, how much uniquely by prosody, and how much by either variable.

As a final clarification, simple correlations for the six best single predictors of nonnativeness for each phonetician can be found in Table 4.4.

Table 4.4 Simple Correlations for the Six Best Single Predictors of Nonnativeness for Each Phonetician

P1		P2		P3		P4	
Phone	r^2	*Phone*	r^2	*Phone*	r^2	*Phone*	r^2
r	.60	r	.51	r	.45	r	.43
e	.37	e	.43	e	.29	ð	.37
ð	.32	ð	.36	ð	.29	e	.30
t	.31	o	.36	o	.25	β	.26
o	.30	t	.34	a	.25	o	.22
p	.24	i	.26	β	.24	l	.19

Discussion

Seeking Consistency in Listener Judgments

Although there is considerable agreement between phoneticians as to the phones that contribute to overall impression of nonnativeness, there is also evidence that, at least in some cases, listeners disagree on whether a particular sound is native-like or not, without any listener necessarily being wrong. The question then arises, should an automatic pronunciation assessment system try to mimic the judgments of a single listener, with her or his idiosyncrasies and level of self-consistency, or the judgments of a larger population of listeners, with their inconsistencies stemming from differences in threshold and acceptable range? We believe that the latter is appropriate, and that therefore a system's judgments must have reference to perceptual information from several listeners. We propose considering those realizations labeled nonnative by all available listeners to be the first set that the system should be trained to label nonnative; in our data, about 11% of the phone tokens were labeled by all four listeners as nonnative.

A slightly less conservative approach would be to consider the judgments of the listener with the lowest proportion of nonnative labels for each phone to be the "safest." Of the 1,322 tokens with these "safest" judgments in our corpus, 904, or 68.4%, are labeled nonnative by all four listeners, which can be compared with an agreement rate of 23.0% over all 3,927 tokens that are labeled nonnative by at least one phonetician.

An opposite approach would be to avoid giving feedback on phones that appear to show real differences in acceptable ranges. These phones will be the most difficult on which to give feedback, beyond the cases in which all or most listeners agree the realization is nonnative.

Impression of Nonnativeness Versus Intelligibility of Speech

Our results show error salience in the context of creating an impression of nonnativeness. This effect should be distinguished from intelligibility of a learner's utterance. The errors that contribute most to perception of nonnativeness of speech may or may not be those that are most salient for intelligibility of speech. Intelligibility is a human listener effect at least as important as perception of nonnativeness, and it is likely to be especially problematic for beginning learners of a language. Studies of the relative impact on intelligibility of a sample of segmental error types (e.g., vowel tenseness, consonant voicing) are referenced by Dalby and Kewley-Port (this volume).

Segmental Errors Versus Prosody in Impression of Nonnativeness

It is understood, as we have noted, that perception of speech as nonnative can be influenced by prosodic factors (Jilka, 2000), such as those illustrated in the chapter by Molholt and Hwu (this volume). The use of text-independent prosodic information has been shown to improve the correlation of automatic with human scores of the nativeness of student pronunciation (Teixeira, Franco, Shriberg, Precoda, & Sonmez, 2000). However, the relative importance of segmental and prosodic cues to nonnativeness and intelligibility is not well understood, and previous reports have been mixed. Anderson-Hsieh et al. (1992) found that ratings of prosodic nativeness were more highly correlated with ratings that combined intelligibility and acceptability, than were segmental error ratings. Their study was based on English read by 60 speakers of a variety of native-language backgrounds (the largest groups were 21 Chinese, 12 Koreans, and 13 speakers of languages from the Indian subcontinent). Similarly, Johansson (1978) found that in a very small amount of data from native Swedish speakers speaking English, prosodic cues appeared more important than segmental errors to native English speakers' judgments of accent, and for Swedish learners from several native-language backgrounds, Langlais, Öster, & Granström (1998) found that prosodic ratings were more highly correlated with overall accent ratings than were segmental ratings. However, Fayer & Krasinski (1987) reported that many more native English speakers considered "pronunciation" to be distracting than considered intonation to be distracting, when hearing spontaneous English speech produced by native speakers of Spanish.

In our data the multiple r^2 for predicting nonnativeness from segmental errors is quite high. (The most analogous, though not entirely comparable, result, in Anderson-Hsieh, Johnson, & Koehler, 1992, is $r^2 = .45$. Schairer, 1992, reported an r^2 of .81 between comprehensibility and a selected set of segmental errors, for nonnative Spanish. Langlais, Öster, & Granström, 1998, reported an r^2 of .49 between ratings of phonetic deviance and a "global" rating, for nonnative Swedish.) We have no ratings of prosodic nonnativeness on our data set of Americans speaking Spanish, but it would be surprising if prosodic nonnativeness were an even stronger predictor of overall nonnativeness for these data.

We suspect, together with Munro & Derwing (1995), that one reason for the variable results mentioned above may be that the importance of prosody to nonnativeness is directly related to the particular first and second languages under study and their prosodic characteristics, rather than that there is any universal relative importance of prosody and segmentals. For the language pair and the population addressed in our study, it appears that feedback on segmental effects alone may be sufficient.

IMPLICATIONS FOR FOCUSING SPEECH RECOGNITION IN SECOND LANGUAGE PRONUNCIATION TUTORS

The study we have described examines human perceptions of second language learners' pronunciation. It is understanding these perceptions, we argue, that should guide the use of speech recognition in a second language pronunciation tutor.

The preceding discussion suggests several considerations for the design of a pronunciation tutor. One of these considerations is the fact that whether or not a phonetic segment is perceived to be of native quality may depend on the listener as well as on the segment. For some realizations listeners show good agreement, and the decision that an automatic pronunciation tutor should make is clear. For many other realizations, "nativeness" is ill-defined and other factors will determine any feedback from the tutor.

Second, to be most effective, a speech-interactive pronunciation tutor should take into account the acceptability both of articulatory production and of durational and intonational aspects of the speech. The relative importance of these aspects is an open and challenging question.

Another consideration is that not all errors have equal impact on listeners' perception of a learner's speech. Much research remains to be done in this area, and it is likely that the salience of an error hinges in part on the language being learned. We have shown that for American English speakers learning Spanish, there is agreement across listeners as to the several phonetic segments whose errors best predict overall nonnativeness. A speech-interactive pronunciation tutor might profitably focus a learner's efforts on those segments first. For other languages, other segments may be most important.

Finally, it is important to distinguish between intelligibility and nonnativeness in defining the goals of a pronunciation tutor. The salience of particular errors for intelligibility, along with the relationship between nonnativeness and intelligibility, is an area for continued research.

REFERENCES

Anderson-Hsieh, J., Johnson, R., & Koehler, K. (1992). The relationship between native speaker judgments of nonnative pronunciation and deviance in segmentals, prosody, and syllable structure. *Language Learning, 42*(4), 529–555.

Bratt, H., Neumeyer, L., Shriberg, E., & Franco, H. (1998). Collection and detailed transcription of a speech database for development of language learning technologies. *Proceedings of the International Conference on Spoken Language Processing, 98,* 1539–1542.

Brett, D. (2004). Computer generated feedback on vowel production by learners of English as a second language. *RecALL, 16*(1). Selected Papers from EUROCALL 2003.

Cucchiarini, C., Strik, H., Binnenpoorte, D., & Boves, L. (2000). Pronunciation evaluation in read and spontaneous speech: A comparison between human ratings and automatic scores. *Proceedings of New Sounds 2000:Fourth International Symposium on the Acquisition of Second-Language Speech,* Amsterdam.

Cucchiarini, C., Strik, H., & Boves, L. (1998). Automatic pronunciation grading for Dutch. *Proceedings of the ESCA Workshop on Speech Technology in Language Learning* (STiLL 98), 95–98.

Eskénazi, M. (1996). Detection of foreign speakers' pronunciation errors for second language training: Preliminary results. *Proceedings of the International Conference on Spoken Language Processing, 96*, 1465–1468.

Eskénazi M., Ke, Y., Albornoz, J., & Probst, K. (2000). Update on the Fluency pronunciation trainer. *Proceedings of InSTIL 2000* (Integrating Speech Technology in (Language) Learning), 73–76.

Fayer, J. M., & Krasinski, E. (1987). Native and nonnative judgments of intelligibility and irritation. *Language Learning, 37*(3), 313–336.

Franco, H., Abrash, V., Precoda, K., Bratt, H., Rao, R., & Butzberger, J. (2000). The SRI EduSpeak system: Recognition and pronunciation scoring for language learning. *Proceedings of InSTIL 2000* (Integrating Speech Technology in (Language) Learning), 123–128.

Franco, H., Neumeyer, L., & Kim, Y. (1997). Automatic pronunciation scoring for language instruction. *Proceedings of the International Conference on Acoustics, Speech and Signal Processing*, 1471–1474.

Franco, H., Neumeyer, L., Ramos, M., & Bratt, H. (1999). Automatic detection of phone-level mispronunciation for language learning. *Proceedings of Eurospeech 99*, 851–854.

Green, D. M., & Swets, J. A. (1974). *Signal detection theory and psychophysics.* Huntington, NY: R. E. Kreiger.

Herron, D., Menzel, W., Atwell, E., Bisiani, R., Daneluzzi, F., Morton, R., et al. (1999). Automatic localization and diagnosis of pronunciation errors for second-language learners of English. *Proceedings of Eurospeech 99*, 855–858.

Jilka, M. (2000). *The contribution of intonation to the perception of foreign accent: Identifying intonational deviations by means of F0 generation and resynthesis.* Ph.D. Thesis, Institute of Natural Language Processing, University of Stuttgart. AIMS, Arbeiten des Instituts für Maschinelle Sprachverarbeitung 6, 3. (http://ifla.uni-stuttgart.de/~jilka/papers/diss.pdf)

Johansson, S. (1978). *Studies of error gravity: Native reactions to errors produced by Swedish learners of English* (Gothenburg studies in English 44). Göteborg: Acta Universitatis Gothoburgensis.

Langlais, P., Öster, A.-M., & Granström, B. (1998). Automatic detection of mispronunciation in non-native Swedish speech. *Proceedings of the ESCA Workshop on Speech Technology in Language Learning* (STiLL 98), 41–44.

LaRocca, S., Morgan, J., & Bellinger, S. (2002). Adaptation for successful recognition of student speech: some first applications for Arabic learners. *Proceedings of EUROCALL02*, August, Jyväskylä, Finland.

Markham, D. (1997). *Phonetic imitation, accent, and the learner* (Travaux de l'institut de linguistique de Lund 33). Lund: Lund University Press.

Menzel, W., Herron, D., Morton, R., Pezzotta, D., Bonaventura, P., & Howarth, P. (2001). Interactive Pronunciation Training. *ReCALL, 13*, 67–78.

Munro, M. J., & Derwing, T. M. (1995). Foreign accent, comprehensibility, and intelligibility in the speech of second language learners. *Language Learning, 45*(1), 73–97.

Neri, A., de Wet, F., Cucchiarini, C., & Strik, H. (2004). Segmental errors in Dutch as a second language: How to establish priorities for CAPT. *Proceedings of the InSTIL/ICALL Symposium*, 13–16, Venice.

Neumeyer, L., Franco, H., Digalakis, V., & Weintraub, M. (2000). Automatic scoring of pronunciation quality. *Speech Communication, 30*, 83–93.

Rypa, M., & Price, P. (1999). VILTS: A tale of two technologies. *CALICO Journal, 16*(3), 380–395.

Schairer, K.E. (1992). Native speaker reaction to non-native speech. *The Modern Language Journal, 76*(3), 309–319.

Teixeira, C., Franco, H. Shriberg, E. Precoda, K., & Sonmez, K. (2000). Prosodic features for automatic text-independent evaluation of degree of nativeness for language learners. *Proceedings of ICSLP 2000*, Beijing, China.

Tokuyama, K., & Miwa, J. (2004). A method of pronunciation assessment for word accent in consideration of Japanese intonation. *Report of the Speech Technical Committee, Institute of Electronics, Information and Communication Engineers (IEICE), SP2003-177*, 13–18.

Vazulik, J., Aguirre, J., & Newman, T. (2002). Speech-enabled multimedia lessons using several authoring systems: A comparison. *Proceedings of CALICO*, 26–30, University of California, Davis.

Witt, S. M., & Young, S. J. (2000). Phone-level pronunciation scoring and assessment for interactive language learning. *Speech Communication, 30*, 95–108.

Section III

Adapting Speech Technology

The Examples of Visualization and Synthesis

INTRODUCTION

From the analysis of learning needs, exemplified in Section II, we arrive at research to explore, adapt, and refine core speech technologies so that they work for identified needs. Representing research at this stage are two chapters. Molholt and Hwu address adaptation of speech visualization technologies for pronunciation instruction in second languages. Delmonte addresses adaptation of speech synthesis for a range of learning activities enabled by intelligent tutoring methods.

REFINING SPEECH VISUALIZATION AND SYNTHETIC SPEECH FOR LANGUAGE LEARNING

Molholt and Hwu's work on acoustic analysis of speech builds on the foundation laid by Gómez et al. in Section I, which explains why it is hard to hear and pronounce sounds in a new language and why visual displays of acoustic data might be hypothesized to help. Molholt and Hwu sample problematic distinctions for learners of a range of languages and show how spectrograms as well as pitch contours and pitch-energy displays can illuminate both the nature of those distinctions in native speech and departures from those distinctions in a learner's speech. Acoustic displays, they propose, can help not just the learner but also the instructor who seeks to diagnose pronunciation problems. It can, as well, inform the researcher in language education who needs concrete evidence about pronunciation patterns and their variation in languages to be taught.

Implicit in this proposal is an assumption that the acoustic picture plainly reflects articulatory gestures and that learners will be able to interpret and benefit from this picture. By comparison, Gómez et al. point to the "semantic gap" between image and interpretation, prompting questions about the value of acoustic displays for students and nonexpert teachers. Clearly needed are studies of instructional utility: Can a student understand and learn from these displays? Such studies would examine not just spectrograms in raw form but also visual transformations of spectrographic data designed to communicate to language learners. In addition, these studies would explore how teachers can effectively employ visualization in teaching pronunciation and how learners differ in their ability to use visual information to identify and correct pronunciation errors. While it is true that some commercial CALL software now offers voice visualization as an incentive for the buyer, research is incomplete on ways to adapt this technology and on its added value.

In addition to segmental or phone-based features, Molholt and Hwu show how suprasegmentals, or prosodic features, can be revealed by acoustic displays. For example, comparing pitch contours of the learner to those of a native speaker can highlight anomalies in the learner's intonation. The potential of visualization to help teach intonation patterns has long been recognized (Anderson-Hsieh, 1994; Chun, 1998; Hardison, 2004; James, 1979; Komissarchik & Komissarchik, 2000; Martin, 2005): here, the semantic gap is narrower than with phonemes, and acoustic displays can be refined to map the rise and fall of intonational pitch. Instructors' use of displays to show prosodic features should be distinguished from projects aimed at automatic identification of prosodic errors (e.g., Eskenazi, 1999)—an ongoing research endeavor that requires extensive data collection, normalization, and validation. Use of the acoustic display in Molholt and Hwu's examples assumes that the instructor already knows the learner's error when invoking the display to demonstrate that error.

Delmonte's chapter on text-to-speech synthesis defines the technology, compares it with speech recognition, and describes procedures for employing it in language lessons, such as marking up a text passage for computer voicing. With examples from the web-based environment SLIM (System for Interactive Multimedia Language Learning), developed to teach English to Italian speakers, Delmonte shows how speech synthesis can be applied to instruction in syntax, phonology, and listening and text comprehension. At the same time, his chapter points to a range of work in the United States and Europe on multilingual speech synthesis and its application to CALL, from student-manipulable synthesis labs (e.g., Martin, 2005) to the animated speech of conversational agents (e.g., Massaro, Ouni, Cohen, & Clark, 2005).

Speech synthesis can be used out of the kit, with no CALL-specific modification. The challenge, instead, involves exploring the appropriateness and maturity of the technology for language learning—appropriateness in terms of the intended learning activities and maturity in terms of the language to be learned. Indeed, use of synthetic voice for language learning recalls the questions of authenticity and fit introduced by Clifford and Granoien in Section I. Delmonte acknowledges that synthesis cannot replace the live or recorded human voice for teaching language, but he argues that synthetic output is necessary in a generative framework such as characterized by SLIM—one in which text, exercises, and feedback are computationally generated rather than preprogrammed. Generative frameworks build on earlier research in intelligent tutoring systems (Wenger, 1987; for language, Swarts & Yazdani, 1992, and Holland, Kaplan, & Sams, 1995) and in their more flexible successors, computer-based learning environments (e.g., Lajoie, 2003). These frameworks typically incorporate knowledge bases, learner modeling, and reasoning rules, and may, in the case of language tutors, use natural language processing and generation. These technologies enable the computer automatically to vary exercises, to diagnose a student's responses, and to adjust new content to identified errors, such as by populating text templates with words the student has previously confused. For content created dynamically in this way, synthesis is the only means to voice it, short of massively recording all possible word and text combinations from a lesson. Delmonte demonstrates the exploratory work of finding exercise forms for which text-to-speech synthesis is suited or demanded.

The second direction of exploration in adapting speech synthesis to CALL—identifying languages for which synthesis is available and mature—is clear-cut for SLIM. Its lessons target English, which has relatively advanced commercial synthesis, as do most European languages. Less commonly taught languages, or those spoken in less developed regions, usually lack ready-made synthesis. Efficient porting of synthesis to new languages is a current topic of research (e.g., Maskey, Black, & Tomokiyo, 2004).

Given the investigational status of speech synthesis in CALL, its benefits have yet to be established, although evaluation criteria have been proposed (Handley & Hamel, 2003, 2005). Evaluating speech synthesis for language learning requires going beyond technical performance tests of synthesizers. Technical performance measures include standardized rhyme tests to assess intelligibility of synthesized voice and native speaker judgments to assess acceptability and "naturalness" of the voice (Black & Tokuda, 2005). Given a speech synthesizer ranked as best-of-breed in technical performance, the question becomes whether its use in CALL can benefit learning and retention and what performance threshold it must meet in order to realize benefits (Handley & Hamel, 2005). Preliminary findings suggest that carefully chosen applications of synthesized voice can help language learners. Hincks (2002) found benefits of using synthetic utterances for teaching syllabic stress; Wang and Munro (2004) found that training with a combination of synthetic and natural voice improved second language learners' perception of vowel contrasts and that this improvement remained after several months. As speech science moves synthesis toward greater naturalness (e.g., Langner & Black, 2005), we might expect to see the fit to CALL more fully defined and demonstrated.

Adaptation of speech visualization and synthesis to the needs of language learning presupposes an understanding of what those needs are and which ones are worth pursuing with advanced technologies. The work presented in this section grounds that understanding in informed intuition rather than in empirical needs analysis such as conducted by Precoda and Bratt (Section

II). Delmonte, Molholt, and Hwu represent the perspectives of individual instructors seeking to enhance local programs of instruction—instructors who already know what content they want to teach. The adaptations they describe can be applied by other instructors to a range of content. Nevertheless, we would expect that CALL programs intended to put complex speech technology into wide and regular use would base decisions about content on systematic analysis of needs, considering evidence on the frequency and cost of learners' problems, together with analysis of orderings and dependencies from theories of second language acquisition.

REFINING SPEECH RECOGNITION FOR LANGUAGE LEARNING

Besides adaptations of visualization and synthesis methods, there have been significant efforts to adapt automated speech recognition (ASR) for language learning and testing. These efforts are documented in long-term research programs such as the Tactical Language Trainer at the University of Southern California Information Sciences Institute (Johnson et al., 2004; Sethy, Mote, Narayanan, & Johnson, 2005), Project Listen at Carnegie Mellon University (Mostow, 2004; in this volume, Aist & Mostow and Mostow et al.), the Cambridge University SCILL project (Spoken Conversational Interaction for Language Learning; Ye & Young, 2005), the work leading to EduSpeak® by SRI International (Precoda & Bratt, this volume) and to Versant testing by Ordinate Corporation (Bernstein & Cheng, this volume), and the work in multilingual dialogue systems by the Massachusetts Institute of Technology (MIT) Spoken Language Systems Group (Seneff, Wang, Peabody, & Zue, 2004).

These programs demonstrate two directions in refining ASR for CALL: recognizing the words learners say and assessing how well learners say them. Assessing speech quality calls for modifying ASR so that it can produce scores for pronunciation, fluency, or other dimensions of speaking skill (a function critically reviewed by Kim, 2006). Iterative experiments are performed to tune ASR features and to calibrate the algorithms against expert human scores. Human calibration experiments are referenced by Precoda and Bratt in Section II and in the chapters by Dalby and Kewley-Port and by Bernstein and Cheng in Section IV. In pronunciation scoring, learners or examinees are given a word or phrase to repeat or read, so the computer knows in advance what is being said.

On the other hand, adaptations to recognize the words uttered are based on an assumption of variability in what is said. The intent is to give learners a measure of expressive freedom, moving CALL interactions toward simulated conversation. Adaptations in this case are meant to enable recognition *despite* deficiencies in speaking skill, such as nonnative pronunciation and disfluencies. Experiments may involve developing and manipulating models of learner speech, creating error models, varying recognition confidence intervals, altering features used to classify errors, and adjusting the tradeoff between detecting errors and rejecting correct speech. Adaptations of this sort underlie the Tactical Language Trainer, which has focused on dialogue-based tutoring for Modern Standard Arabic. As discussed by Sethy et al. (2005), speech recognition is supplemented with a model of expected learner errors for particular utterances, from mispronunciations to wrong word choices to grammatical mistakes. By narrowing utterance choices and applying error models, Sethy et al. aim to recognize students' speech and classify their errors with some degree of certainty. More open conversational interfaces for language learning are sought by the MIT Spoken Language Systems Group (Seneff et al., 2004), whose continuing innovations in ASR have led to prototype tutors for Mandarin Chinese (discussed by Clifford & Granoien in Section I of this volume). Fundamental research at Cambridge University (Ye & Young, 2005) seeks to make continuous speech recognition more robust to nonnative articulation in explicit support of the long-term goal of conversational CALL.

The prospect of conversational CALL in turn challenges CALL design to limit what learners are likely to say in order to minimize misrecognition of their speech. Methods to constrain learners' utterances can be external, such as display of on-screen response choices, or internal, through the structure of the task or discourse (Raux & Eskenazi, 2004; Holland, 1999).

REFERENCES

Anderson-Hsieh, J. (1994). Interpreting visual feedback on suprasegmentals in computer assisted pronunciation instruction. *CALICO Journal, 11*, 5–22.

Black, A., & Tokuda, K., (2005). Blizzard challenge 2005. *Special session of INTERSPEECH 2005*, Lisbon. [http://www.festvox.org/blizzard/blizzard2005.html]

Chun, D. (1998). Signal analysis software for teaching discourse intonation. *Language Learning & Technology, 2*, 61–77. [http://llt.msu.edu/vol2num1/article4/index.html]

Eskenazi, M. (1999). Using automatic speech processing for foreign language pronunciation tutoring: Some issues and a prototype. *Language Learning & Technology, 2*, 62–76. (http://polyglot.cal.msu/llt/vol2num/_article3/_index.html)

Handley, Z., & Hamel M. (2003). Text-to-speech (TTS) synthesis in CALL: Developing an evaluation methodology to determine the suitability of TTS output for integration in CALL applications. *Recall, 15* (Selected papers from EUROCALL 2002, Jyväskylä, Finland).

Handley, Z., & Hamel M. (2005). Establishing a methodology for benchmarking speech synthesis for Computer-Assisted Language Learning (CALL). *Language Learning & Technology, 9*, 99–120. [http://llt.msu.edu/vol9num3/pdf/handley.pdf]

Hardison, D. (2004). Generalization of computer-assisted prosody training: quantitative and qualitative findings. *Language Learning & Technology, 8*, 34–52. [http://llt.msu.edu/vol8num1/hardison/default.html]

Hincks, R. (2002). Speech synthesis for teaching lexical stress. *TMH-QPSR (Sweden), 44*, 153–156. [http://www.speech.kth.se/~hincks/papers/fon02bh.pdf]

Holland, V. M. (Ed.) (1999). Tutors that listen: Speech recognition for language learning. *CALICO Journal, 16*(3). Special issue.

Holland, V. M., Kaplan, J., & Sams, M. (Eds.) (1995). *Intelligent language tutors.* Mahwah, NJ: Lawrence Erlbaum Associates.

James, E. (1979). Intonation through visualization. In H. Hollien & P. Hollien (Eds.), *Current issues in the phonetic sciences* (pp. 295–301). Amsterdam: John Benjamins.

Johnson, W. L., Marsella, S., Mote, N., Si, M., Vilhjalmsson, H., & Wu, S. (2004). Balanced perception and action in the tactical language training system. *Proceedings of the International Workshop on Autonomous Agents and Multi-Agent Systems (AAMAS WS 2004).* New York, NY.

Kim, I. (2006). Automatic speech recognition: Reliability and pedagogical implications for teaching pronunciation. *Educational Technology and Society, 9,* 322–334. [http://www.ifets.info/journals/9_1/26.pdf]

Komissarchik, E., & Komissarchik, J. (2000). BetterAccent tutor: Analysis and visualization of speech prosody. *Proceedings of INSTIL 2000,* Dundee, Scotland.

Lajoie, S. (2003). Transitions and trajectories for studies of expertise. *Educational Researcher, 32,* 21–25.

Langner, B., & Black, A. (2005). Improving the understandability of speech synthesis by modeling speech in noise. *Proceedings of ICASSP,* Philadelphia.

Martin, P. (2005). WinPitch LTL, un logiciel multimédia d'enseignement de la prosodie. *ALSIc: Apprentissage des Langues et Systèmes d'Information et de Communication, 8,* 95–108. [http://alsic.u-strasbg.fr/v08/martin/alsic_v08_13-rec7.pdf]

Maskey, S., Black, A., & Tomokiyo, L. (2004). Bootstrapping phonetic lexicons for new languages. *Proceedings of ICSLP 2004,* Jeju, South Korea.

Massaro, D. W., Ouni, S., Cohen, M., & Clark, R. (2005). A multilingual embodied conversational agent. In R. Sprague (Ed.), *Proceedings of 38th Annual Hawaii International Conference on System Sciences (HICCS'05),* Los Alimitos, CA: IEEE Computer Society Press.

Mostow, J. (2004). Advances in children's speech recognition within an interactive literacy tutor. In A. Hagen, B. Pellom, S. van Vuuren, & R. Cole (Eds.), *Proceedings of the Human Language Technology Conference 2004,* North American Chapter of Association for Computational Linguistics: Boston, MA.

Raux, A., & Eskenazi, M. (2004). Using task-oriented spoken dialogue systems for language learning: Potential, practical applications and challenges. *Proceedings of INSTIL 2004,* Venice. [http://sisley.cgm.unive.it/ICALL04/index.htm]

Seneff, S., Wang, C., Peabody, M., & Zue, V. (2004). Second language acquisition through human computer dialogue. *Proceedings of ICSLP 2004,* Jeju, South Korea.

Sethy, A., Mote, N., Narayanan, S., & Johnson, W. L. (2005). Modeling and automating detection of errors in Arabic language learner speech. *Proceedings of EUROSPEECH 2005,* Lisbon.

Swarts, M., & Yazdani, M. (1992). *Intelligent tutoring systems for foreign language learning: The bridge to international communication.* New York: Springer–Verlag.

Wang, X., & Munro, M. (2004). Computer-based training for learning English vowel contrasts. *System, 32,* 539–552.

Wenger, E. (1987). *Artificial intelligence and tutoring systems.* Los Altos, CA: Morgan Kaufman.

Ye, H., & Young, S. (2005). Improving speech recognition performance of beginners in spoken conversational interaction for language learning. *Proceedings of INTERSPEECH 2005.* Lisbon.

5   Visualization of Speech Patterns for Language Learning

Garry Molholt and Fenfang Hwu

INTRODUCTION

In the exhibit hall of a recent conference a linguist was trying out some of the new pronunciation software. An attractively arranged display caught his eye. When he clicked on the thumbnail drawing of a loaf of bread, it expanded to fill the screen, along with directions on how to speak and receive feedback. When he said the word "braid," the computer voice said, "Very good." When he said "Fred," again it was accepted. Upon saying "convention center," he got the response "try again." At a competitor's booth, the linguist started working on a screen flashing a white number on a black background. He said /paib/, and it was accepted. He said /flf/, and it was accepted also. As with the first package, when he said "convention center," it was rejected. A few weeks later this same linguist was reviewing CDs and web sites for pronunciation training. In the promotional material for one of the CDs was a statement comparing the regular beat of English to the beat of a rock and roll song. He wondered why rock and roll had become so popular if it was just the same old rhythm people used every day. At a web site he made some errors typing the dictated sentence, "Sinking fins are thought to be thin." A help routine popped up to inform him that the first word is a gerund and the fourth word a past tense verb, oblivious to the possibility that in this context they might be present and past participles.

Several questions arise from such experiences. As we journey through the transition from textbook-based language learning to computer-assisted language learning (CALL), to what extent are we merely bringing along old, untested ideas into a new format? To what extent are we losing quality control? To what extent are we actually making use of the power of computers to help us with the complex pattern recognition required to analyze speech and provide feedback? To what extent can we test some of the older hypotheses and revise, enhance, or replace them?

Speech visualization technologies, in particular, present new opportunities to assess and enhance hypotheses about patterns of speech sounds and to illuminate those patterns for teachers and learners. The technical foundations of acoustic analysis of speech and its visual results are presented by Gómez et al. in Section I. The current chapter focuses on two related questions: How can acoustic analysis be deployed to test hypotheses about the organization of speech patterns? How can acoustic displays be used to communicate these patterns to teachers and to students?

We address these questions through demonstration. In a section on English we show how common forms of visual display can be used to reveal defining aspects of speech sounds and patterns. We then invoke acoustic analysis to assess traditional hypotheses about syllable-timed versus stress-timed rhythm in Spanish and English. We illustrate the teaching potential of speech visualization with displays of suprasegmentals (prosody), vowels, and consonants in English and Spanish; tone variations in Mandarin Chinese; and consonants in Hindi that have proven difficult for learners. These examples provide a representative set that gives direction to ongoing work rather than offering exhaustive coverage.

Our intent is to inspire new ways of looking at computer-assisted analysis and teaching of speech patterns. We envision acoustic analysis as a research tool for studying pronunciation in different languages, as an information source to ground graduate programs for second language teachers, as a diagnostic tool for use by pronunciation teachers, and as a means for teachers to communicate with language students trying to master pronunciation and prosody. We are aware of the "semantic gap" described by Gómez et al. (this volume) between acoustic analysis and instructionally useful information, but we think the features made explicit in spectrograms and other displays provide a path to visualization of problematic distinctions that can eventually help students. Arguments and some evidence for the benefits of speech visualization can be found in the literature, for example, Hwu (1997), Levis and Pickering (2004), Molholt (1998), and projects referenced by Delmonte (this volume) such as WinPitch (http://www.winpitch.com/winpitch_ltl.htm).

All displays presented in this chapter were produced on a Kay Elemetrics (now KayPentax) Visi-Pitch 3300 with real-time pitch and energy displays, a real-time acoustic vowel chart, and real-time spectrograms. Text in the displays was added after the analyses were completed.

ENGLISH SUPRASEGMENTALS, VOWELS, AND CONSONANTS

Suprasegmentals and the Stress-Timed Hypothesis

Learning stress patterns in words and sentences is an area of concern for language learning. Through acoustic analysis we can test hypotheses about the relationships among the suprasegmental features of pitch, intensity, and duration in the creation of stressed syllables. Strong hypotheses state that increased pitch, greater intensity (energy or amplitude), and longer duration are all necessary to give stressed syllables prominence over unstressed syllables. For example, according to Van Riper and Smith (1992, p. 35), "syllable stress affects the pronunciation of a word, and you must sharpen your listening skills to hear the alternation of pitch, duration, and intensity that occurs on the accented syllable." Prator and Robinett (1985, p. 44) offer a milder version, stating that "often, but by no means always, a syllable with sentence stress is spoken on a higher musical note than the unstressed syllables. In such cases, intonation is one of the elements of stress, the others being loudness and length." This is similar to the statement in Edwards (1997, p. 335) that "syllables spoken with primary stress will typically be higher in pitch; they will also be slightly louder and slightly longer than syllables without primary stress." A weaker form of the hypothesis about the roles of pitch, intensity, and duration in the creation of stress is given by Celce Murcia, Brinton, and Goodwin (1996, p. 131), who state that "stressed syllables (or rather the vowels of stressed syllables) are often longer, louder, and higher in pitch, but in any given stressed syllable this entire combination of features may not be present."

We are also able to test a related hypothesis regarding what has been called the stress-timed nature of English rhythm. Again, the hypothesis takes strong and weak forms. According to Celce Murcia et al. (1996, p. 152), "just as in music, English moves in regular, rhythmic beats from stress to stress—no matter how many unstressed syllables fall in between. This stress-timed nature of English means that the length of an utterance depends not on the number of syllables (as it would in a syllable-timed language like Spanish or Japanese) but rather on the number of stresses." This strong form gives the impression that we speak in a regular meter similar to poetry or the lyrics of a song. Similarly, Kenworthy (1987, p. 19) noted that "there must be an alternation of stressed and unstressed syllables, with the stressed syllables occurring on a regular beat, and the unstressed syllables must have a less-than-full vowel." Again, Prator and Robinett (1985, p. 44) offer a milder statement that speakers should give "proper emphasis to stressed syllables, making them occur rather regularly, within a thought group."

These hypotheses are significant for teachers and CALL developers because these notions sometimes give rise to recommendations about how to teach pronunciation. Yet, significantly absent from the literature are studies that provide objective evidence from an acoustic perspective supporting either the strong form of the stress-timed hypothesis or the view that stress actually occurs on a regular beat. Also missing from the literature is proof that stress is made up of increased pitch, greater intensity, and longer duration for each syllable. Since acoustic analysis provides an objective means to observe patterns of pitch, intensity, and duration, it is an invaluable tool for the analysis and teaching of suprasegmental features. If we take a close look at the words in Kenworthy's statement above, the rhythm shifts several times throughout. There is no regular beat. We count 15 stresses, as follows: "There MUST be an alterNAtion of STRESSED and UNstressed SYLlables with the STRESSED SYLlables ocCURing on a REGular BEAT, and the UNstressed SYLlables must have a LESS-than-FULL VOWel."

It is difficult to imagine that we stretch the time it takes to make the two stresses in "STRESSED SYL . . .," or that we shrink the time it takes to say ". . . lables must have a" sufficiently to create equal beats for the stresses of "STRESSED SYLlables" and "SYLlables must have a LESS." In fact, in measuring one native speaker's utterance, we found the duration from the start of the first stressed vowel to the end of the following stressed vowel to be 0.377 seconds for "STRESSED SYLlables" but 1.23 seconds for "SYLlables must have a LESS" (or over three times as long). Ironically, even the rhythm within the definition of rhythm does not necessarily follow the intended formula. Attempts in language teaching to apply such formulas could unnecessarily detract from our understanding of the dynamic nature of communication by neutralizing interesting aspects of speech, whether such attempts are in textbook format, audio cassettes, video tapes, CDs, or web-based products.

It is well known that differences in pitch help us to understand word meanings, structural differences, and information about attitudes. For example, the top part of Figure 5.1 shows a pitch display for the noun *progress* and the verb *progress*. Note that the pitch is higher on the first syllable of the first word (noun) and on the second syllable of the second word (verb). In the bottom display of Figure 5.1, we have the word *president* on the left. It obviously has higher pitch on the first syllable, and we can distinguish three syllables. The right part of the bottom display shows a nonnative speaker's attempt, but it lacks the clear differentiation of pitch, and it omits the middle syllable altogether. This display makes explicit a common set of errors produced by nonnative speakers when they are first learning to produce multisyllabic words.

The upper part of Figure 5.2 shows a native speaker saying, "I need pens, pencils, and paper." The horizontal cursor is between the words *pens* and *pencils*. Notice that for the first two items in the series, the pitch rises, but for the final item of the series, the pitch falls. This type of "up-up-down" intonation is a signal that "there is more to come-there is more to come-the list is finished." The lower part of Figure 5.2 shows a nonnative speaker failing to produce the cues that indicate a series. Here the sentence sounds as if it is finished after the word pens. It is easy to imagine situations in which miscommunication could result from a nonnative speaker's either not hearing the cues given by a native speaker or not sending the signals to show that more information is coming. Such miscues could invite unwanted interruptions.

Utterances with quotations present a difficult structural problem for nonnative speakers. The top part of Figure 5.3 shows the pitch contour for "The boss said, 'John is in New York.'" The bottom part shows "'The boss,' said John, 'is in New York.'" Sentence pairs like these have been found to be difficult for nonnative speakers to differentiate. Who is in New York? Who said so? In the upper screen we can see that *John* has the highest pitch. For the lower screen it is *boss* that has the highest pitch. These are the cues we use to tell the difference between the utterances.

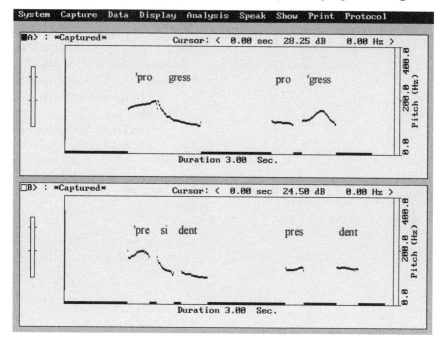

Figure 5.1 Word stress differences shown by pitch contours in an acoustic display. (Upper display contrasts progress as noun vs. verb; lower display contrasts native vs. nonnative pronunciation of *president*).

Finally, nonnative speakers of English are often unsure where to put stress, so they may "play it safe" by leaving out stress altogether. They do not realize that absence of stress may sound like absence of interest in the topic. While the upper part of Figure 5.4 is dynamic, the lower part is flat and ironic, given that the utterance is "I really want to get a job with this prestigious company."

English Vowels in Visual Displays: Spectrograms vs. Triangles

To discuss vowel patterns, we turn to a type of display called a spectrogram, distinct from the pitch and energy displays just discussed. We will start with an older type of display and show how it relates to the newer spectrogram display. Figure 5.5 has two parts. Both show the vowel sound /ae/ as in *cat*. The upper display is only 0.035 seconds in duration. We see five major cycles, each made up of four smaller cycles. If we looked further, we would find that the smaller cycles are each made up of three cycles. The number of cycles per second defines the frequency of a sound. Speech is complex because it contains several simultaneous cycles. Briefly, through a mathematical equation devised by Jean Baptiste Fourier, a French mathematician who accompanied

96   *Molholt and Hwu*

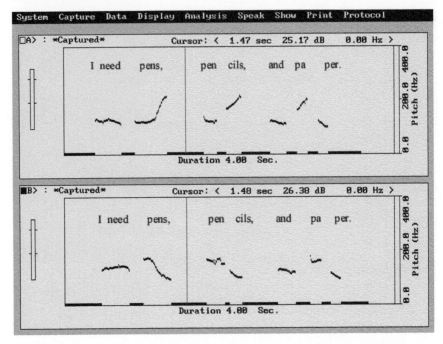

Figure 5.2 Pitch contours for words in a series ("pens, pencils, and paper").

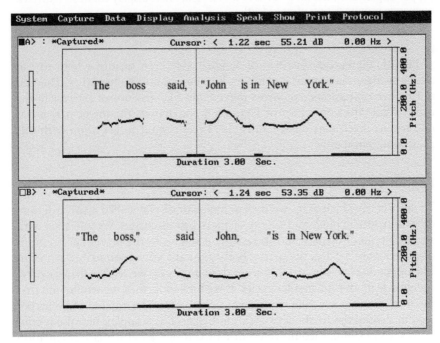

Figure 5.3 Pitch contours for utterances with quotations.

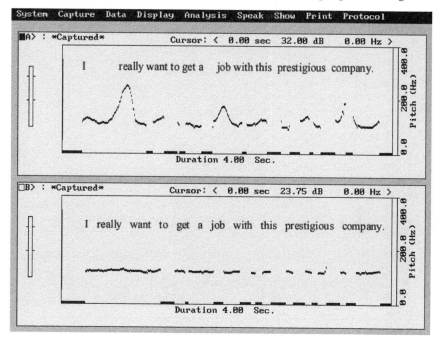

Figure 5.4 Contrasting attitude (serious vs. ironic) indicated by pitch contours.

Napoleon to Egypt in 1798, the components of a complex waveform can be separated and displayed as in the spectrogram in the lower part of Figure 5.5. Roughly speaking, five big cycles at 35 milliseconds (ms) equals a frequency of about 142.9 cycles per second for the vibration of the vocal cords (the pitch, or fundamental frequency, symbolized as F_0). Next, 20 medium cycles equals about 571.4 cycles per second for the first formant (F_1), which reflects the resonance frequency of the pharynx. Finally, 60 small cycles in 35 ms equals 1714.3 cycles per second for the second formant (F_2), which reflects the resonance frequency of the mouth. More information on how acoustic features reflect articulatory features, and on the central role of formants in speech perception and production, is presented in the chapter by Gómez et al. (this volume). According to physicists, the relationship between F_1 and F_2 frequencies gives our different vowel sounds.

Even if we do not understand fully the mathematics behind spectrograms, they can provide valuable information. Figure 5.6 gives spectrograms for the words *pat* (top) and *bat* (bottom). Here we can see important aspects of consonants. For example, the space between the explosion of the /p/ and the vowel /ae/ in *pat* is filled with turbulence (indicated by the unpatterned noise that contrasts with dark bands of frequency for the vowel). We call the duration of this space the voice onset time (VOT) since voicing does not start until the onset of the vowel. The lower display has a dark band at the

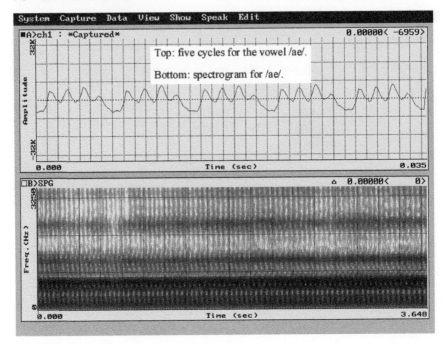

Figure 5.5 Acoustic displays for the vowel /ae/.

bottom before the start of the word *bat*. This is called prevoicing. Voicing itself is indicated by such a band at the bottom of a spectrogram. The gap before the final /t/ sound in both words results from closure of the air stream in anticipation of the stop. Were the words *pass* and *bass*, there would be no gap because the vowel moves smoothly into the turbulence of the following /s/. Voicing of consonants, especially at the ends of words, presents problems for nonnative speakers, as does initial aspiration of voiceless stops (/p/ in *pat*). Features on the spectrogram provide a potential path to visualization of problematic distinctions.

However, the raw spectrogram may be inadequate as a tool to communicate with teachers and students. It is relatively difficult, for example, to tell which vowel is displayed by looking at a spectrogram.

Fortunately, the F_1 frequency can be plotted against the F_2 frequency and set up to resemble a traditional articulatory vowel triangle (Figures 5.7–5.11). In Figure 5.7 what would normally be the high front tense vowel /i/ is in the upper left of the display; the high back tense /u/, in the upper right. We would argue that with appropriate editing and labeling, this type of real-time display, which shows movement across the vowel chart (in contrast to a static vowel triangle as in pronunciation textbooks), can help teachers and students understand the relationships among vowels. For example, instead of thinking that the high front lax vowel /I/, as in sit, is an

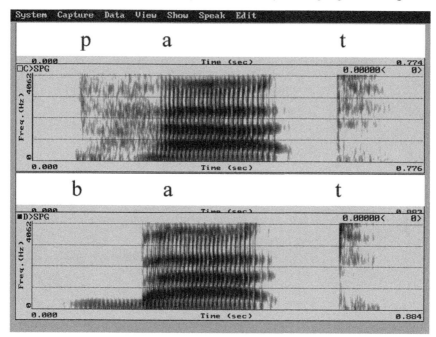

Figure 5.6 Voiceless (*pat*) and voiced (*bat*) initial stops.

isolated, difficult-to-find sound, students can see that it is related in important ways to sounds they already know how to say. Students already know how to say the tense vowel /i/. It is the most common vowel sound in the world, according to Maddieson (1984), occurring in 91.5% of languages. Those few students who do not have a schwa sound can be taught to relax and say uh. With those two sounds as anchors, if students say one of the sounds and move gradually to the other, they pass through the target area for /I/. Eventually, they can be taught to go slower and stop in the /I/ area. Then they know how to find /I/. It is no longer a sound floating somewhere out in space. They can control it.

The same technique can be used to find lax /U/ between schwa and tense /u/. These paths are clearly shown in Figure 5.7. Other examples of turning F_1, F_2 frequency plots into vowel triangles are found in the chapter by Gómez et al., this volume, using vector representations.

This approach may be extended to all vowels on the chart by working from known points of reference to find the locations for new sounds. Thus, Figure 5.8 shows the paths for locating the lax vowel between schwa and /e/ and the lax vowel between schwa and /o/. Figure 5.9 relates to dropping the jaw to reach the low vowels.

Figure 5.10 shows how to find /r/ and /l/ after vowel sounds by (a) starting at schwa and raising the tip of the tongue to move to the schwa-r position or

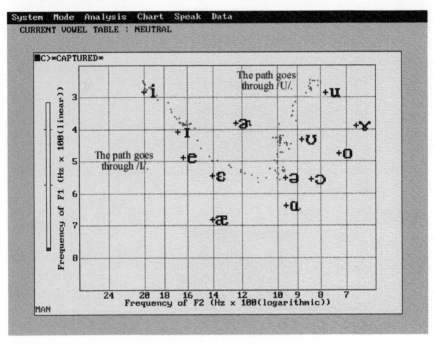

Figure 5.7 Finding lax high vowels /I/ and /U/ in a spectrographic vowel triangle using the tense vowels /i/ and /u/ as reference points.

(b) moving to the /o/ area, then moving the tongue to the back of the upper teeth for back-l position. Figure 5.11 displays the diphthongs /ai/ and /au/. Nonnative speakers of English often have difficulty with English lax vowels, diphthongs, back /r/, and back /l/. In addition, some speakers, especially Japanese, have difficulty with English /u/ because they frequently do not round their lips when trying to pronounce it.

English Consonants in Visual Displays

Spectrograms are quite useful for differentiating among consonantal features. Figure 5.12 shows the differences among stops, fricatives, and affricates in the words *tease, she's, cheese* (top) and *mat, mash, match* (bottom). Stops like /t/ have a characteristic vertical spike corresponding to the explosion of air. Fricatives like /sh/ (also represented as š) have a characteristic turbulence, and affricates like /ch/ (also represented as č) have both a spike and turbulence. As detectable in Figure 5.13, the turbulence of affricates tends to be lower in frequency and higher in amplitude (loudness) than the turbulence of fricatives, which feature aspiration.

Finally, Figure 5.14 shows *read* and *lead* (top) and *measure* and *major* (bottom). East Asian speakers, in particular, often omit the movement required

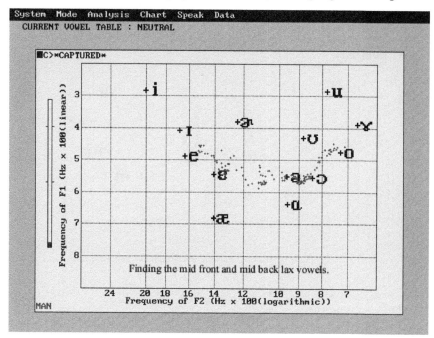

Figure 5.8 Finding lax mid vowels in the vowel triangle.

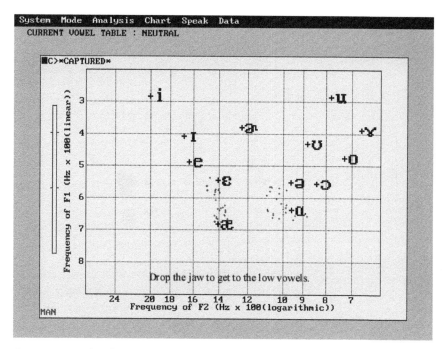

Figure 5.9 Finding low vowels in the vowel triangle.

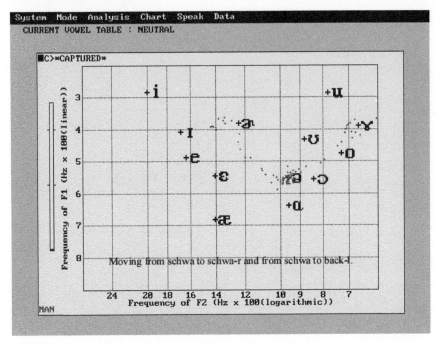

Figure 5.10 Finding /r/ and /l/ after vowels.

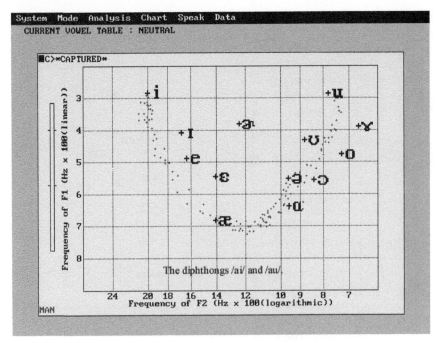

Figure 5.11 Finding two diphthongs in the vowel triangle.

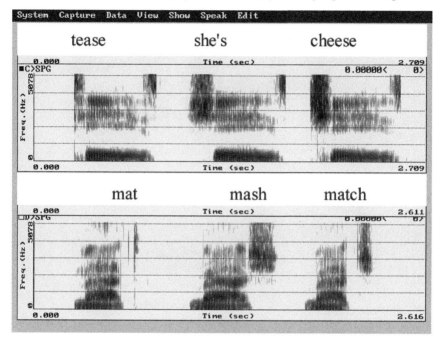

Figure 5.12 Spectrographic comparisons for stops, fricatives, and affricates.

for initial /r/ sounds in English, and they also fail to touch the tongue to the teeth and alveolar ridge to achieve stability in initial /l/ sounds. For the bottom displays, nonnative speakers often make their affricates too smooth or break up fricatives so they sound more like affricates. Thus, *major* could sound like *measure*. Again, the spectrogram could pave the way for learners to visualize these distinctions.

SPANISH SUPRASEGMENTALS, VOWELS, AND CONSONANTS

Suprasegmentals and the Syllable-Timed Hypothesis

According to conventional wisdom, Spanish is a syllable-timed language whereas English is a stress-timed language. In the strictest interpretation, this means that all Spanish syllables have the same length but that English syllables vary, with stressed syllables being longer and unstressed syllables shorter. Textbooks tend to omit discussions on the extent to which such concepts apply. They do not question whether these statements are true in all situations all the time. They do not ask if people deviate from such patterns in meaningful ways. For a more moderate view, Barrutia and Schwegler (1994) state that the durations of tonic (stressed) and atonic (unstressed)

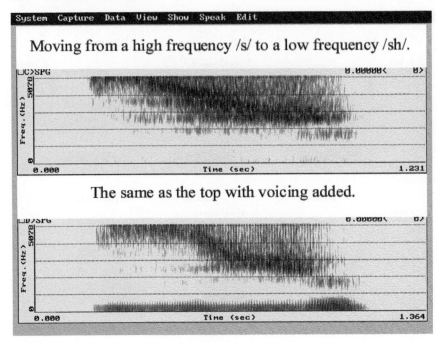

Figure 5.13 Changes in the amplitude–frequency relationship from fricative to affricate.

syllables are almost identical. So a word such as *consideración*, which has stress by way of increased intensity on the last syllable -*ción*, will have five syllables of relatively equal duration. English, on the other hand, lengthens the fourth syllable of consideration and reduces the others. Thus, Barrutia and Schwegler state, these factors may be sources of interference for English learners of Spanish.

According to Dalbor (1980, p. 258), when speakers of American English learn Spanish, "English stress-timed rhythm is transferred over to Spanish, which has a staccato syllable-timed rhythm. A concomitant feature is the incorrect substitution of a high central vowel, sometimes called a barred *i*, and schwa for unstressed vowels in Spanish since this usually happens in English in unstressed syllables." An alternative to viewing a second language learner's improper rhythmic pattern as interference by the first language, is viewing it as a product of the learner's interlanguage, that is, the current stage of the learner's emerging knowledge. As stated by Brown (1994, p. 203), "In recent years researchers have come more and more to understand that second language learning is a creative process of constructing a system in which learners are consciously testing hypotheses about the target language from a number of possible sources of knowledge. . . ."

Whichever perspective is taken, pronunciation problems can arguably be addressed by using visual displays of speech patterns to enhance

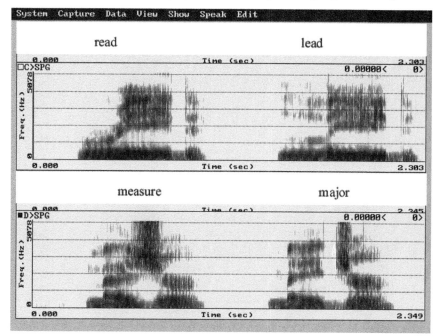

Figure 5.14 Initial /r/ and /l/ (top); voiced fricative and affricate (bottom).

communication between the instructor and the learner. Acoustic analysis equipment is neutral with respect to theories such as the notion that English is a stress-timed language while Spanish is syllable-timed. For this reason, acoustic analysis is ideal for testing the extent to which these notions actually apply and for determining if they apply more in some contexts than others. Acoustic analysis allows the focus of attention to go beyond general formulas so that language learners can better understand how language is used in particular situations. For example, it is easy to imagine an acting coach who can read any line from a play several different ways, each with a slightly different shade of meaning. The shades of meaning come from variations in pitch, intensity, and duration of syllables. Acoustic analysis allows us to go beyond general textbook definitions of language organization and to see those aspects that create interesting variations in communication. The following examples, therefore, are not intended to support any particular hypothesis. They are intended to show how the equipment may be used to acquire data about pronunciation.

Figure 5.15 displays the pitch contour of a native female Spanish speaker from Spain (top) and an American female studying Spanish (bottom), both saying the Spanish sentence, "La música clásica es bonita" (Classical music is beautiful). Even without detailed analysis, several points are clear in the display.

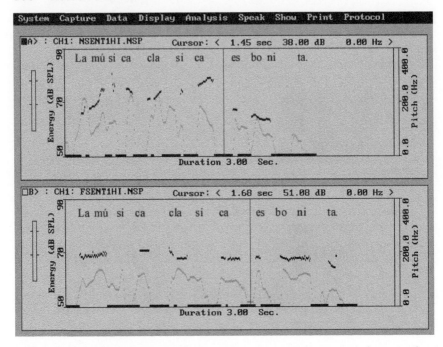

Figure 5.15 Native Spanish speaker's pitch contour (top) is more dynamic than Spanish learner's pitch contour (bottom).

First, Figure 5.15 indicates that pitch varies much more for the native speaker than for the learner. Also, loudness appears to vary more for the native speaker, based on the lighter gray lines that show amplitude. Thus, on two suprasegmental dimensions the native speaker's utterance appears more dynamic than the learner's. If the native speaker's utterance were actually produced in "staccato" style, as suggested in many textbooks, we would expect to see very short syllables separated by sizeable gaps. After all, in music the term *staccato* is relatively precise, meaning very brief notes separated by longer-than-usual spaces. Yet, looking at the utterance through the spectrographic displays in Figures 5.16 and 5.17, we do not immediately see a pattern of uniformly short syllables with large gaps between them. Since the notion of Spanish syllables as staccato comes from the syllable-timed hypothesis, a detailed analysis of the duration of the syllables may shed light on why this notion is not in evidence.

To compare the rhythm of the native speaker with that of the learner, we measured the duration of each syllable and of the total utterance in ms and calculated the percentage of total utterance duration contributed by each syllable. The results, shown in Table 5.1 (along with the average percentage and the standard deviation), indicate more variation in syllable duration for the learner than for the native speaker, with standard deviations of

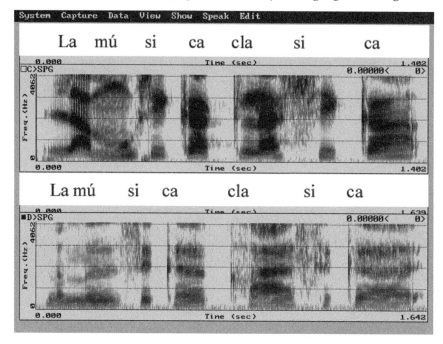

Figure 5.16 Spectrographic display of contrasting utterances from Figure 5.15.

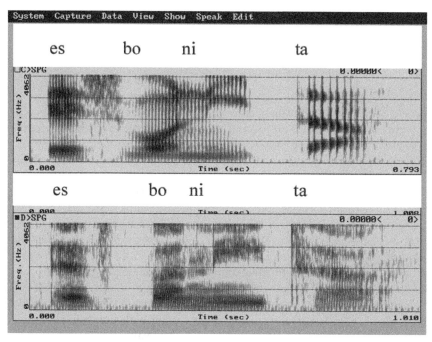

Figure 5.17 Spectrographic display of contrasting utterances (end) from Figure 5.15.

Table 5.1 Percentage of Total Utterance Duration
Accounted for by Each Syllable in Native's vs.
Learner's Utterance of Sentence From Figure 5.15

Syllable	Native %	Learner %
La	9.3	3.7
mu	8.6	11.0
si	7.4	6.3
ca	6.4	8.3
cla	10.2	14.3
si	12.3	7.6
ca	11.2	14.6
es	9.3	8.3
bo	7.3	4.8
ni	9.3	11.0
ta	8.7	10.1
TOTAL	100.0	100.0
Standard deviation	1.73	3.53

3.53 (student) versus 1.73 (native speaker). This finding, if replicated over a sample of speakers and utterances, might lend support to a hypothesis that syllable duration is more uniform in Spanish than in English. However, the data also show interesting variation within the Spanish native speaker: all syllables in the word *clásica* have longer duration than any other syllables in the utterance. Because this word also has the highest pitch and intensity, it appears to be the most prominent word of the utterance.

In addition, since the second and third syllables of *clásica* are the same sounds as the second and third syllables of *música*, and all of them are unstressed, there should be little difference in duration of the two *si* or the two *ca* syllables if the syllable-timed notion obtained. Moreover, if Spanish syllable durations were almost equal, then we might expect them all to contribute close to nine percent of total sentence duration. But this is not the case: the range of contributions in Table 5.1 is from 7.3% to 12.3%. At the same time, these data also challenge claims that Spanish is syllable-timed, with stressed syllables not being uniformly longer than unstressed, as well as claims that increased intensity is the most salient component of stress.

Spanish Vowels and Consonants in Visual Displays

Consider a comparison of the native Spanish speaker with the learner on more detailed phonetic features. The Spanish word *porque* "because" is usually spoken with stress on the first syllable, an unaspirated initial /p/, a tapped /r/, and little or no upward drift on the final vowel /e/. All these features become visible in the spectrogram.

In the upper part of Figure 5.18, a spectrogram of an utterance of *porque*, we see that the native speaker's first syllable lasts 96 ms and has higher pitch than the second syllable, which lasts only 75 ms. The VOT of the initial /p/ is only 12 ms, a sign that it is unaspirated. The gap before the /r/ signifies a tap. The bands of frequency at the end of the final vowel do not appear to slant upward. By contrast, for the learner (bottom part of Figure 5.18), the first syllable is shorter (168 ms) than the second syllable (314 ms), and has lower pitch, signifying that the second syllable is stressed. The VOT of the initial /p/ is 133 ms, signifying that it is highly aspirated. There is no gap before or during the /r/ sound, signifying that it is not tapped but has a smooth transition from the preceding vowel. The bands of frequency for the final vowel of the second syllable show obvious signs of upward drift. One word can provide a wealth of information.

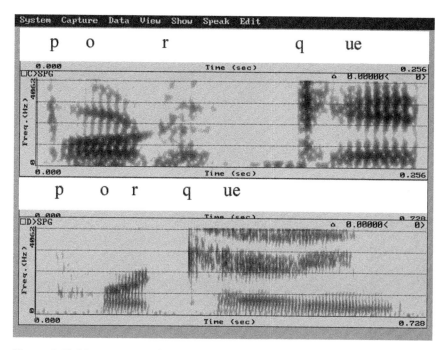

Figure 5.18 Nonnative speaker's pronunciation of Spanish *porque* (bottom) has many spectrographic deviations from native speaker (upper).

Integrating Spanish Suprasegmentals, Vowels, and Consonants

To integrate concepts of suprasegmentals, vowels, and consonants, consider the Spanish sentence, "A Roberto le gustan las ciencias" (Robert likes science). Figure 5.19 is a spectrogram of the first two words, *a Roberto*, and Figure 5.20, a pitch and energy display of the first four words of the utterance. The student, whose patterns appear in the lower part of the displays, is a male first-year Spanish student fulfilling a general language requirement.

While some points are clearer from the spectrogram, others are easier to see in the pitch-energy display. An overview of the spectrogram (Figure 5.19) reveals aspects of the phonetics of Spanish. From left to right, the native speaker starts the initial vowel sound /a/ with a slight glottal stop, indicated by the spike on the left. The gap between /a/ and the start of the syllable for *ro* reflects the speaker's tongue momentarily stopping the airflow for a tap or trill. The turbulence between the syllable *ro* and the syllable *ber* indicates that /b/ is less a stop with tight closure (typical of English) and more a fricative (like /v/) produced bilabially (point of articulation between the lips, typical of Spanish). The turbulence at the end of the syllable *ber* indicates a voiceless /r/. The final syllable, *to*, starts with a voiceless unaspirated /t/ with a VOT of only 6 ms. The /o/ lacks drift toward /u/.

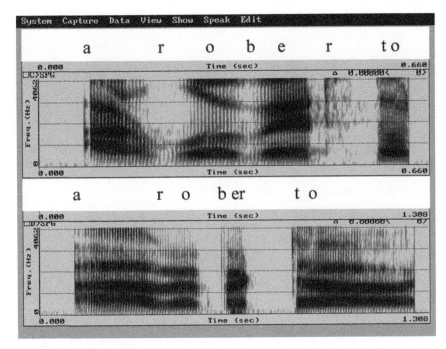

Figure 5.19 Spectrogram shows contrasts between a native (top) and nonnative (bottom) Spanish utterance.

Contrasting with these features is the learner's utterance of *a Roberto* (lower part of Figure 5.19). The learner's *a* does not start with a glottal stop, the smooth transition into the /r/ signifies no tap, and the short syllable *ber* ends with a smooth transition into /r/, lacking the turbulence of a voiceless /r/ or the gap of a tap. The very long final syllable includes drift, as indicated by the changes in relationships among the horizontal bands of frequency.

The pitch and energy display, Figure 5.20, makes it easier to see which syllables are stressed in "A Roberto le gustan." Again, it is clear that the native speaker's pitch varies much more than the student's. In the native speaker's utterance, the longer syllables with rising pitch, *ber* and *gus*, are perceived as stressed. The student has higher pitch on *ber*, but the duration of *to* is so long as to neutralize the concept of stress on *ber*. For *gustan* the second syllable is obviously stressed since it has higher pitch and energy and longer duration. As is the case with Table 5.1, Table 5.2 shows that the student's utterance varies more in syllable duration (standard deviation of 7.53) than does the native speaker's (5.95). As in Table 5.1, however, Table 5.2 shows that even the native speaker's syllables vary considerably as a percentage of total utterance duration (from 7.2 to 23.3 percent), counter to what the syllable-timed hypothesis might lead us to expect.

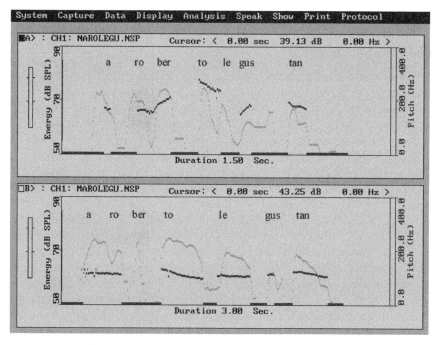

Figure 5.20 Pitch-energy display highlights Spanish native's dynamic pitch contour (top) with nonnative's static contour (bottom).

Table 5.2 Percentage of Total Utterance Duration
Accounted for by Each Syllable in Native's vs.
Learner's Utterance of Sentence From Figure 5.20

Syllable	Native %	Learner %
A	13.3	13.3
Ro	12.3	8.1
ber	19.5	4.4
to	7.7	21.7
le	7.2	23.6
gus	23.3	8.9
tan	16.7	20.0
TOTAL	100.0	100.0
Standard deviation	5.95	7.53

VARIATION IN MANDARIN CHINESE TONES

The Tone System and Its Complications

It is well understood that each lexical item of Mandarin Chinese has an associated tone. For example, *ma* spoken with different tones has different meanings. With the high flat first tone, it means "mother"; with the rising second tone, "hemp" ; with the low third tone that drops and then rises, "horse"; with the fourth tone dropping sharply, "to scold." When students of Mandarin Chinese produce words with the wrong tones, confusion often results. Thus, using the third tone instead of the fourth for the Mandarin word *wen* "to ask" transforms the question, "May I ask you something?" into "May I kiss you?" Elliot (1991) notes that, according to Shen (1989), the mispronunciation of Mandarin tones tends to lie in the register of pitch (which can be low, middle, or high) and not in the shape of pitch (which can be rising, falling, dipping, or level), since Mandarin has a significantly wider pitch range than English. Tones may be marked in transcribed Mandarin by cardinal numbers (1 for first tone, 2 for second, etc.). Research on teaching tone distinctions to learners of Mandarin through speech recognition and other innovative techniques is ongoing in MIT's Spoken Language Systems Group (Peabody, Seneff, & Wang, 2004; Wang & Seneff, 2004; see also Clifford & Granoien, this volume)

Tones in Mandarin Chinese also interact, and the problems these interactions pose for learners are less well understood. The first interaction has to do with what is sometimes called the "fifth tone." Although books and articles discuss Mandarin as a four-tone language, a fifth tone (sometimes termed the light tone, neutral tone, or no tone) is a falling tone that begins at a level related to that of the preceding syllable (Chao, 1968). In the second interaction, the tone of a word sometimes changes with the tone of the following word. For example, if two words each require the third tone, and they come together in a phrase, then the first word takes the second tone. A third interaction involves the dual role of tone. Tones can change as the speaker's attitude toward and relationship with the hearer changes. Thus, if a speaker utters a word with a tone other than the one expected, this indicates something about the speaker's stance. Not knowing that the tone is a cue for attitude, a nonnative speaker might perceive it as signifying a different word.

These interactions complicate the tone system and pose serious challenges for learners of Chinese. Pitch-energy displays offer concrete demonstrations of each of these interactions, as presented in the following sections (Figures 5.21–5.26), allowing us to examine how visual displays can help sort out complications.

Figure 5.21 depicts the basic Mandarin tones. The top part shows the word *hao* spoken with each the five tones. The first tone is relatively high and level; the second tone rises up to the high level; the third starts lower, drops, then goes up; the fourth starts high and drops sharply; and the fifth tone, which is much shorter, drops. The lower part of Figure 5.21 is a carefully spoken *hao* with the first tone.

Figure 5.22 shows the word *hao* with the second tone (top), then with the third tone carefully spoken (bottom). The speaker in this example distinguishes the third tone more by a gradual drop of pitch than by any upturn at the end of the drop. More casually spoken, *hao* with the third tone does not drop so far in pitch (Figure 5.23 top). Spoken with the fourth tone (Figure 5.23 bottom), the pitch drops sharply in relation to the gradual drop of the third tone.

Tone Changes With Following Tone

Figure 5.24 depicts two versions of *hao ma*. The word *hao* in each utterance means "good" so would be expected to have the same tone. In the upper screen, *hao* takes third tone and the tone for *ma* moves quickly up to the first level: *hao ma* would be heard as a question, such as "Is it good?" In the lower screen, since *ma* has the third tone, the first word cannot also have the third tone. It takes the second tone. Here, *hao ma* means "good horse."

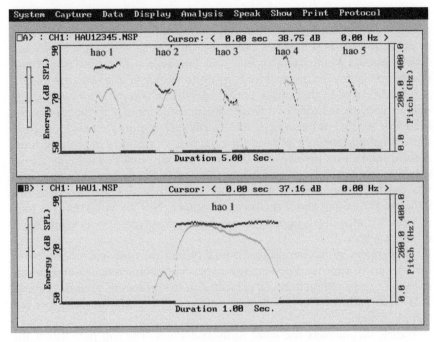

Figure 5.21 Five tones of Mandarin Chinese (top); first tone *hao* (bottom).

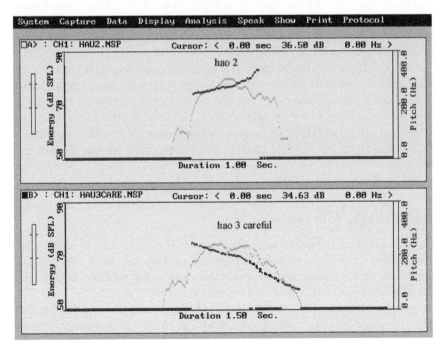

Figure 5.22 Second and third Mandarin tones for *hao*.

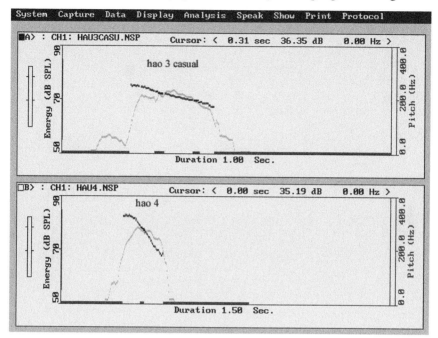

Figure 5.23 Third and fourth Mandarin tones for *hao*.

The Fifth Tone

The displays in Figure 5.25 demonstrate how the fifth tone consistently starts at the level of the preceding tone. At the top, "diao le" (It's lost) has fourth and fifth tones. At the bottom, "zou ba" (Let's go) has third and fifth tones.

Indications of Attitude Toward Hearer

Figure 5.26 shows two versions of "Ni zai gan shen me?" (What are you doing?). The ordinary pronunciation would use the tones: 3, 4, 4, 2, 5. To express strong curiosity in a friendly way to a child, the tones of the upper screen are appropriate: 1, higher 1, even higher 1, 3, 2. The same question asked of an adult in a demanding way is depicted in the lower screen: 1, higher 1, high 4, 3, 4.

HINDI CONSONANTS

Generalizations

Hindi is sometimes referred to as Hindi–Urdu since it has heavy influence from Islamic culture. Hindi, Urdu, and Hindi–Urdu are spoken throughout

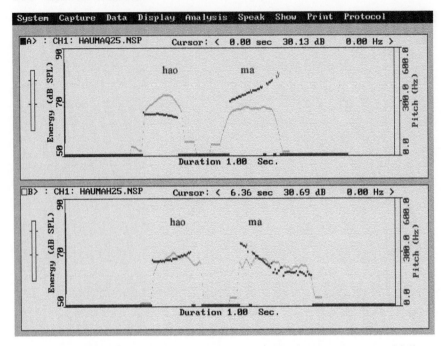

Figure 5.24 Third tone in *hao* (top) changes to second (bottom) because of following tone (meaning of *hao* does not change).

North India, and Urdu is a major language of Pakistan. English and Hindi
consonants have sufficient differences that many Hindi contrasts are subtle or indistinguishable to English ears (see Gómez et al., this volume, for
biological bases for this phenomenon). For example, the proper distinction
between initial English /p/ and /b/ (*pat* vs. *bat*) requires that /p/ be voiceless
and aspirated and /b/, voiced and unaspirated. Both features, voicing and
aspiration, must contrast. In Hindi one contrast is enough to distinguish consonant pairs. A voiceless unaspirated /p/ is classified as a different phoneme
than a voiceless aspirated /p/; both differ from voiced unaspirated /b/; all
differ from voiced aspirated (breathy) /b/ (Benguerel & Bhatia, 1980; Ohala,
1983). In his monumental study of phoneme inventories of 317 language
families, Maddieson (1984) noted that while 91.8% of language families
have a series of plain (unaspirated) voiceless stops, only 28.7% have a series
of aspirated voiceless stops. These statistics put the English initial voiceless aspirated stops /p, t, k/ in the minority compared to Hindi, Mandarin
Chinese, and Spanish, whose voiceless unaspirated stops may occur in syllable-initial position. Hindi also has a contrasting series of voiced aspirated
stops that, according to Maddieson, occur in only 2.2% of language families. Thus, Americans studying Hindi must learn both to speak and to hear
voiceless unaspirated stops as distinct from voiced unaspirated stops, and

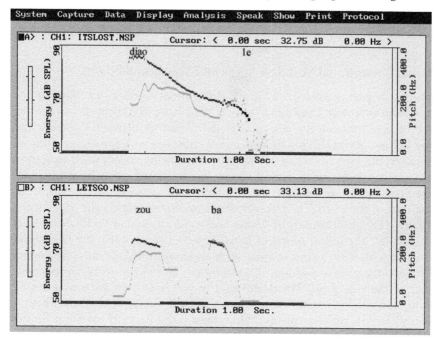

Figure 5.25 Fifth tone starts where previous tone ends.

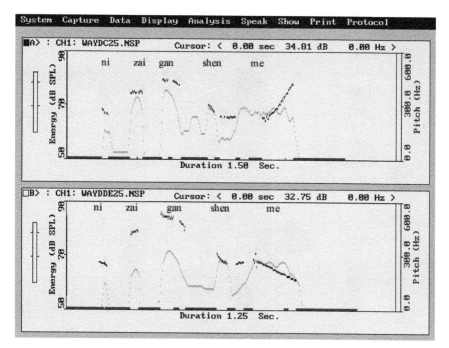

Figure 5.26 Tones reflect a change in relation and attitude toward hearer.

voiced aspirated stops as distinct from voiceless aspirated stops; and they must observe these distinctions in initial, medial, and final word positions.

Initial Unaspirated Voiceless Stops and Voiceless Sibilants

The upper part of Figure 5.27 displays the Hindi words *kana* "blind in one eye," *khana* "to eat," and *gana* "to sing." For *kana* (the leftmost word), note the vertical spike on the left and the short distance between the spike and the following vowel. This short distance contrasts with the longer distance between the start of /kh/ in *khana* and its following vowel, since aspiration fills the gap between spike and vowel. For the word *gana* the vocal cords are actually vibrating before the plosive part of /g/, so we see prevoicing at the start of the word. The plosive part of /g/ almost touches the onset of the vowel. The initial sounds of *khana* and *gana* are similar to English initial /k/ and /g/. The initial sound of *kana*, however, is more like the English /k/ occurring after /s/, as in *ski*, since both are unaspirated. Because the timing between the plosive portion of unaspirated /k/ and the vowel /a/ parallels that of the voiced /g/, Americans tend to perceive /k/ in *kana* as a voiced stop, and similarly with other initial voiceless unaspirated stops. Thus, if an Indian speaker were to say, "One could buy a new car for a time in my home village," an American might perceive the word *time* as *dime* and miss

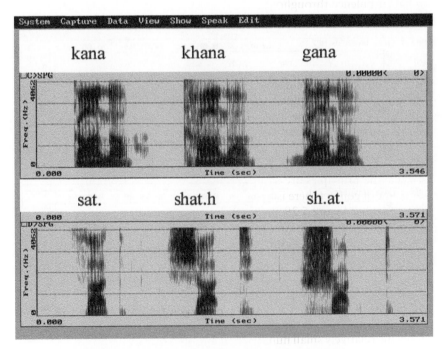

Figure 5.27 Hindi stops (top); Hindi sibilant frequencies (bottom).

the meaning of the sentence. Moreover, American speakers tend to use heavy aspiration in initial voiceless stops that Hindi speakers do not aspirate, which can lead to confusion when Americans pronounce Hindi words.

The lower part of Figure 5.27 displays words starting with three different voiceless sibilants (s-like sounds). The first two are similar to the English sounds /s/ and /sh/. The /s/ is a higher frequency sound made toward the front of the mouth, whereas /sh/ is farther back in the mouth so has a lower frequency. The third sound, retroflex /sh/, is even farther back so has an even lower frequency. Note that the initial portions of each word are progressively lower from one display to the next. The words are *sat.* "to stick", *shat.h* "dishonest", and *sh.at.* "six" (where a dot after a symbol represents a retroflex sound). The tendency of Hindi speakers to generalize native sibilant categories to English is illustrated in pronouncing *shave* as *save* or vice versa.

Voiced Aspirated Stops

As noted, voiced aspirated stops are very rare in world languages. To simplify pronunciation, Americans frequently drop the aspiration or add a vowel between the voiced stop and the aspiration. Either strategy has high potential for creating unintended meanings. The display in Figure 5.28 shows a Hindi speaker (top) and an American (bottom) saying the Hindi sentence, "Mujhe bhuk lagi" (I am hungry). Arrows mark the Hindi speaker's additional turbulence throughout the segments /jh/ and /bh/, a turbulence lacking in the American portion.

Hindi Flap

The retroflex flapped /r./ creates a display similar to tapped /r/ although the tongue is moving in a different direction. For tapped /r/, the tongue moves up quickly and taps the alveolar ridge. The contact is between the top of the tip of the tongue and the alveolar ridge as the tongue is moving up. For Hindi retroflex flap, the tongue is moving down from a raised position and hits the ridge with the underside of the tip on its way down. For both sounds, the principles are similar. The tongue moves and hits the ridge. At the point of contact there is a disturbance in the air stream, so a gap appears in the display. Figure 5.29 shows the Hindi word *lar.ki* "girl" along with an American attempt. The American's /r/ is not a flap so has no internal gap. The Hindi /r./ is a flap, so it has a gap indicating when the tongue hit the alveolar ridge.

CONCLUSION

From the relatively small number of examples discussed here, we have shown how to use speech technology to look for empirical evidence of prosodic and

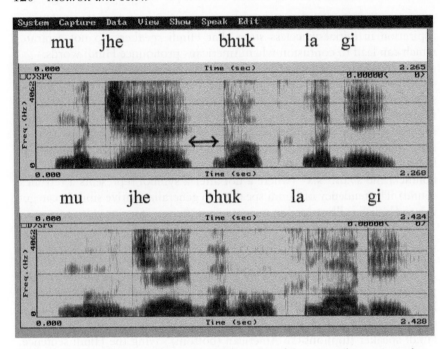

Figure 5.28 Voiced aspirated stops by Hindi (top) and American (bottom) speakers.

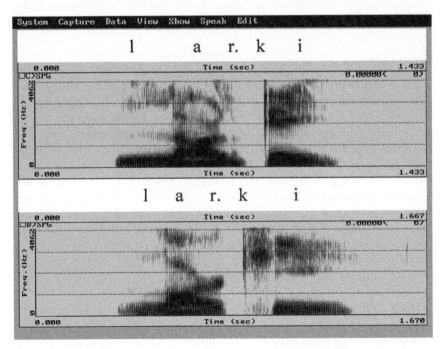

Figure 5.29 Retroflex flapped /r./ by Hindi (top) and American (bottom) speakers.

phonemic features addressed in second language courses. We have argued that it is better to focus pronunciation instruction on a true acoustic analysis of speech than on a set of partial, intuitive hypotheses formulated long before they could be adequately tested. For example, we did not find evidence of a regular beat (isochronism) in the rhythm of English, nor pervasive evidence of syllable-timing in Spanish, nor evidence of invariant tones in Mandarin. This points the way to further research since we can now verify hypotheses with hard evidence from speech analysis tools. This evidence has been lacking, in general, in graduate training programs for language teachers.

Furthermore, the displays presented here support a second argument: pronunciation features were evident in the pitch and energy displays, vowel charts, and spectrograms. Even critical features of Hindi consonants were made visible. These displays have the potential to become tools for communicating visually with teachers or students those pronunciation features that are difficult to hear. At present, utilization of high-quality acoustic analysis equipment for pronunciation training requires specially-trained instructors to help learners create and interpret displays and use them to modify their speech patterns. In the future, as research progresses in the instructional use of acoustic displays as well as in robust speech recognition, learners should be able to improve their speech via fully automated feedback.

Consider the questions that opened this chapter: To what extent is CALL using the power of computers for the complex pattern recognition needed in speech analysis and feedback? To test and revise hypotheses about language differences? We have presented the case that visual displays of speech can harness computer advances to convey phonemic and prosodic subtleties to language learners and to ground empirically the teaching of pronunciation.

REFERENCES

Barrutia, R., & Schwegler, A. (1994). *Fonética y fonología españolas: Teoría y práctica.* New York: John Wiley & Sons.

Benguerel, A., & Bhatia, T. (1980). Hindi stop consonants: An acoustic and fiberscopic study. *Phonetica, 37,* 134–148.

Brown, H. (1994). *Principles of language learning and teaching.* Englewood Cliffs, NJ: Prentice Hall Regents.

Celce Murcia, M., Brinton, D., & Goodwin, J. (1996). *Teaching pronunciation: A reference for teachers of English to speakers of other languages.* Cambridge, UK: Cambridge University Press.

Chao, Y. R. (1968). *A grammar of spoken Chinese.* Berkeley: University of California Press.

Dalbor, J. (1980). *Spanish pronunciation, theory and practice.* Orlando: Harcourt Brace Jovanovich.

Edwards, H. (1997). *Applied phonetics: The sound of American English.* San Diego: Singular Publishing Group, Inc.

Elliot, C. (1991). The relationship between the perception and production of Mandarin tones: An exploratory study. *University of Hawai'i Working Papers in ESL, 10*(2), 177–204.

Hwu, F. (1997). Providing effective and affective learning environments for Spanish phonetics with a hypermedia application. *CALICO Journal, 14,* 115–134.

Kenworthy, J. (1987). *Teaching English pronunciation.* New York: Longman.

Levis, J., & Pickering, L. (2004). Teaching intonation in discourse using speech visualization technology. *System, 32,* 505–524.

Maddieson, I. (1984). *Patterns of sounds.* Cambridge, UK: Cambridge University Press.

Molholt, G. (1998). *Accent reduction via acoustic analysis.* Lincoln Park, NJ: Kay Elemetrics Corporation.

Ohala, M. (1983). *Aspects of Hindi phonology.* Delhi: Motilal Banarsidass.

Peabody, M., Seneff, S., & Wang, C. (2004). Mandarin tone acquisition through typed dialogues. *Proceedings of InSTIL Symposium,* Venice, Italy.

Prator, C., & Robinett, B. (1985). *Manual of English pronunciation* (4th ed.). New York: Holt, Rinehart & Winston.

Shen, X. (1989). Toward a register approach in teaching Chinese: The problems with rising tone. *J. of the Chinese Language Association Teachers, 16,* 27–56.

Van Riper, C., & Smith, D. (1992). *An introduction to general American phonetics* (3rd ed.). Prospect Heights, IL: Waveland Press, Inc.

Wang, C., & Seneff, S. (2004). High-quality speech translation for language learning. *Proceedings of InSTIL Symposium,* Venice, Italy.

6 Speech Synthesis for Language Tutoring Systems

Rodolfo Delmonte

INTRODUCTION

The Case for Synthesized Speech

In this chapter we are concerned with the use of text-to-speech synthesis, or TTS, as a tool for second language learning. We present a number of language learning applications in which TTS plays a fundamental role. TTS can be used to foster awareness of the contrastive features of the phonology of the second language. It can be used to power a speaking tutor for any self-instructional system and to voice feedback on an exercise. It can be used as a reader for dictation exercises where the goal is to vary voice quality and speaking rate. TTS can also be used to give students hints about a listening comprehension task and other drills.

We shall illustrate these various roles for TTS in computer-assisted language learning (CALL). Of course, we do not assume that synthesized speech is the only way to cope with oral language practice. In general, a human tutor guarantees a much better result than TTS. The question is whether a human tutor may always be available when the student needs one. Because access to a human tutor is not always possible, TTS is worth pursuing. Moreover, there is at least one case in which a computer-based speaking tutor constitutes the only viable alternative to the human tutor: when mimicking the evolving levels of speaking proficiency in the second language (L2), also known as levels of interlanguage (Selinker, 1992), as will be explained further on. Finally, if feedback is generated on the fly—through automatic means such as filling template slots with words from an exercise—then use of synthesized voice is the only practical way to avoid having to predict and record all possible combinations of words in templates.

Most of these roles for TTS in CALL have been realized in the System for Interactive Multimedia Language Learning (SLIM), implemented at Università Ca' Foscari in Venice (Cosi et al., 2004; Delmonte, 2000, 1997; Delmonte et. al, 1996; Delmonte, 1995). SLIM is a prototype tutor for foreign language students at beginner to false-beginner level, which features the use of speech analysis and recognition as well as speech synthesis. In this chapter we use SLIM as a reference system to illustrate the TTS paradigm in language instruction. At the same time, we are aware that TTS has been prototyped in other systems (e.g., Bortolini, 2002; Mercier, Guyomard, & Siroux, 1999; Schröder & Trouvain, 2001).

We strongly believe that human–machine interaction should take place through speaking rather than reading. This tenet applies in particular to CALL, a field of interaction where speech is paramount.

Organization of the Chapter

The first section of this chapter is devoted an explanation of TTS and a discussion of naturalness in synthesized speech. The remaining sections present applications of TTS to CALL. We start from a web-based text-understanding application in which TTS gives voice to a computer tutor that reads text passages and gives feedback on comprehension. We next present common drills on written language, such as dictation, that take advantage of TTS to improve usability. We then move from written to spoken drills: Here, TTS serves as an interlanguage simulator and as a phonetics/phonology tutor that allows students to manipulate graphemes to explore the effects on pronunciation in the target language. Such a tutor can also serve children with language impairments. Implications of TTS for visualization of pronunciation patterns are discussed at this point, initiating a topic that is the focus of chapters by Gómez et al. and by Molholt and Hwu (this volume). To conclude, we point to a course on speech synthesis available on the web that addresses the use of TTS to produce CALL materials. We also provide an appendix with a sample of websites where TTS is freely available for most western and some eastern languages, or where tools are provided to implement TTS.

TTS: THE STATE OF PRACTICE AND THE STATE OF SCIENCE

TTS has been available since the end of 1960s. Yet, only in the last 15 years or so has it become a companion to many computer systems and applications. Thanks to the ease of use and implementation of TTS, it has been applied to virtual talking heads and intelligent agents, giving tutoring systems a more human-like appearance. Notable achievements in the progression of this technology include the following:

- There is increasing convergence on what synthesis approaches to use, leading to growth in the number and range of languages covered (e.g., Black & Lenzo, 2004; Chu, Peng, & Chang, 2001; Pfister & Romsdorfer, 2003; Ramakrishnan, Bali, Talukdar, & Krishna, 2004; http://tcts.fpms.ac.be/synthesis/mbrola.html).
- Several websites offer low-level, standardized, but full-fledged TTS for free, with accompanying tools to develop the modules needed

to improve naturalness and intelligibility; for example, the FestVox, MBROLA, and EULER Projects.

- Following books by Dutoit (1997) and by Sproat (1997), which O'Shaughnessy (1998) noted as among the few publications to that point to review TTS comprehensively, collections of advanced papers began to be published (e.g., ISCA, 2004, 2001; ICSLP, 2002; IEEE, 2002);

- Dialogue tutoring systems have introduced virtual talking heads equipped with standardized TTS of intelligible quality (e.g., the CSLU Toolkit using Festival speech synthesis), described in Cole et al. (2003) and Massaro (2004).

Nevertheless, as measured in terms of both intelligibility and naturalness, TTS has not reached a level of technological maturity comparable to that of automatic speech recognition (ASR), which achieved unprecedented heights with the advent of continuous speech recognition for large vocabularies in the 1990s. We predict that, following the path of ASR, improvements in TTS will result from a combination of advanced statistical procedures with phonetic and linguistic structural information.

The Question of Naturalness

Although the wide practical use of TTS in dialogue and tutoring systems is encouraging, we feel that it may dampen concern about the question of how to improve the quality, or naturalness, of synthesized speech. This tension between the call of practice and the requirements of research has been noted in van Santen, Sproat, Olive, and Hirschberg (1997) and Sproat (1997). To reach the goal of mimicking a human voice, these authors observe, requires ever more accurate models of the complex forms of coarticulation (where phonemes vary with context) found in human speech. It also requires deeper representations of knowledge of the world and of language to guide the placement of stress and intonation in speech.

We agree with this position and with the call for further research on TTS. The question of how to improve the quality of TTS will not be probed in detail here. We will, however, briefly sketch the foundations of TTS to help the reader better understand the rest of this chapter. More detailed coverage of the technology may be found, for example, in Bally, Benoit, and Sawallis (1992), Cole et al. (1997), Dutoit and Stylianou (2003), and van Santen (2004).

How TTS Is Achieved

Speech synthesis involves conversion of an input text (words, sentences, paragraphs) into speech waveforms. This conversion uses algorithms operating on real human speech data that has been previously stored and coded into small units. For synthesis of unrestricted text, the speech data are coded to the level of phonemes, the most basic speech sounds. If speech were generated *solely* from phoneme units, memory requirements for TTS would be small since most languages have only 30–40 phonemes. The spectral features of these short sounds (50–200 ms) must still be smoothed at their boundaries to avoid jumpy, discontinuous speech. If speech were, as printed text is, a succession of well-defined elementary symbols, the smoothing requirement would be simple and the problem of speech synthesis would have been solved long ago. However, pronunciation of a phoneme in a word or phrase changes with phonetic context (neighboring phonemes, intonation, speaking rate). For example, the initial /t/ in *tap* differs phonetically from initial /t/ in *top* and medial /t/ in *better*: none of these is an effective substitute for the other in a synthesized utterance. These coarticulation effects characterize all natural speech, merging phonemes into a complex acoustical continuum that carries as much information in its transitions as in its stationary parts. Examples of coarticulation across languages and its manifestation in spectrograms appear in chapters by Molholt and Hwu and by Gómez et al. (this volume). Because of the extraordinary difficulty of the problem, and despite well over thirty years of continuous effort, synthesis of text into fluent, intelligible, natural sounding speech remains an active research challenge.

Concatenative Synthesis versus Parametric Synthesis

Speech synthesizers can be characterized by the approach used to code, store, and generate voice. Two approaches have developed in parallel: concatenative and parametric/articulatory. Concatenative synthesis makes speech by stringing together acoustic units taken from a corpus of human speech. Parametric (rule-based) synthesis uses a set of segmental rules to model steady-state properties of phoneme realization and control how strings of phonemes are fused into connected speech.

Each approach has limitations. Parametric synthesis is limited by our incomplete understanding of coarticulation and thus our inability to build a full set of rules for how spectral parameters (features) of a phone are modified by its neighbor. Concatenative synthesis of phoneme-sized chunks has failed historically, as pointed out above, by failing to account for coarticulatory effects. More recent concatenative approaches have tried to circumvent this problem by storing diphones (two-phone syllables), which capture the articulatory transition from one phone to the next. This approach is effective to the extent that coarticulation influences only the immediately adjacent phones. However, in many cases coarticulation extends over several phones. Using only average diphones or those from a neutral context leads to lower-quality synthetic speech. Improved quality is possible using multiple diphones depending on context: effectively, this means storing triphones, which are longer units and substantially increase memory requirements. English, for example, requires calculation and storage of some 1,200 diphones to support speech synthesis. Thus, the main difficulty in concatenative approaches is the choice of an optimal set of units, with optimal depending on a negotiated tradeoff between parsimonious memory storage and natural sound quality. In the mid-1990s, researchers addressed this problem by turning to automatic, statistical optimization methods designed to find the best acoustic unit (e.g., Hunt & Black, 1996). In this way, starting from phonetically and phonologically annotated speech corpora, researchers devised greedy algorithms and other means to select optimal units ranging from phoneme to diphone and larger. The unit selection approach to concatenative synthesis was widely adopted. Advances in corpus-based synthesis techniques continue (Black & Tokuda, 2005).

Most rule-based TTS systems are structured on formal linguistic theory, which views synthesized voice as the outcome of three mappings in a pipeline: grapheme-to-phoneme mapping via orthography to phonology rules; phoneme-to-allophone via phonological or pronunciation rules; allophone to acoustic parameters via segmental rules. Each mapping uses an ordered sequence of symbolic context-sensitive rules.

TTS and ASR: Two Technologies in Comparison

Theoretically, the technologies of TTS and ASR can be regarded as integrating one another's internal architectures. To generate an appropriate feedback message for a user, a dialogue system with TTS needs a series of linguistic components that roughly parallel those required to analyze and understand a user's spoken utterance, as Table 6.1 illustrates.

This near parallelism between TTS and ASR cannot be regarded as strictly reversible, just as a computational system for text understanding cannot be regarded as reversible vis-à-vis a system for text generation. In particular, a TTS system can achieve good performance by selecting units derived from a single speech database produced by a single speaker; by contrast, an ASR system must adapt to an undefined number of speakers, and the performance may vary according to idiosyncratic traits of an individual speaker.

Current successful TTS systems choose the most appropriate speech unit by applying statistical measurements to a database of natural speech segments collected and annotated in advance for that purpose (Klatt, 1987; van Santen, 1997; van Santen, Shih, Mobius, Tzoukerman, & Tanenblatt, 1997; Segi & Takagi, 2004). That database must not only contain the legal inventory of phonetic segments of the language, with all relevant coarticulatory phenomena, but it should also reflect most prosodic features of the language and domain (*all* would be impossible due to the number of segments required to reach statistical significance).

This is another important difference between the two parallel domains: ASR can easily attain statistically good results, as measured by word error rates, even in a large-vocabulary domain. This is mainly because (a) the number of phonemes of a human language is very limited, and (b) their contextual

---

128 *Delmonte*

Table 6.1 Parallelisms Between TTS and ASR Technology Components

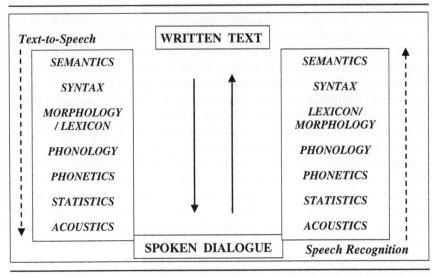

realization does not undergo dramatic changes beyond what can be reasonably encoded (Delmonte et. al, 1996). By contrast, as measured by ratings of naturalness of speech output, we would argue that TTS cannot now achieve statistical results comparable to the results of ASR because synthesis requires more information than realistically can be available to the system. This is a problem of sparseness: That is, an unmanageably large number of variables must be considered in order for TTS to produce a sensible mapping of all linguistically significant and perceptually relevant parameters. However, as we have indicated, corpus-based TTS systems can use statistical optimization methods to approximate the best possible selection of acoustic units as well as an optimal selection of text to serve as a reference corpus by the sampled speakers. This approach permits prosodic information to be preserved and reproduced to the best approximation. Still, the concatenative method, the choice of most current TTS, does not permit modification or adaptation of voice parameters so cannot in itself support varying modes of voice so as to render different emotions or to mark communicative function—say, declarative versus interrogative. These limitations notwithstanding, TTS is useful for CALL in ways that are discussed in the following sections.

APPLICATIONS OF TTS TO CALL

Pedagogical Assumptions

We agree with current approaches to language teaching, particularly in universities, that value learner autonomy and that emphasize learner-centered as well as self-directed learning (Littlemore, 2001). We agree that the Internet is among the primary new technologies that can support self-directed learning (Littlemore, 2001; Warschauer, Turbee, & Roberts, 1996). Therefore, many of the applications we describe have web-based implementations.

In addition, we consider self-assessment an important, although problematic, part of self-directed learning. Decisions about whether to go on to the next item, exercise, or unit, as well as decisions about the allocation of time to a specific skill or to remedial work, are all based on feedback from informal and formal assessment. We see self-assessment as an educational goal in its own right, and we assume that training learners in self-assessment is beneficial to learning. In fact, language learners regularly engage in self-assessment. They make exercises and check, by whatever means available, whether their responses are correct or not. In speech-interactive lessons, they check the computer's comprehension of their spoken language and adjust their speech when necessary.

To better support self-assessment, we assume that "intelligent" tools and natural language mechanisms are important. They can provide the diagnostic information by which students can assess themselves. Therefore, in many of these applications we have implemented rather complex underlying mechanisms to represent language knowledge and teaching knowledge, such as database structures, reasoning rules, and discourse models.

In terms of content, the applications that we illustrate concern learning English as a second language. One difficulty for learners of English is the phonotactics of the language, which is full of exceptions and requires much exercise to couple understanding and orthographic abilities. This complexity severely undermines students' ability to perform a complete phoneme-to-grapheme translation. Thus, a focus of many of these applications is exercises that test and provide practice in linking heard speech to its written representation.

Listening Comprehension Through Text Production: Using TTS to Read Passages and Voice Feedback

One goal of language learning is understanding spoken text: That is, listening comprehension for text passages. A system for CALL that is aimed at tutoring and testing students in understanding spoken text should ideally be equipped with a feedback module to provide explanation of a student's mistakes. However, most systems today replicate the traditional approach to feedback: An answer is either right or wrong and no explanation is made available. An additional limitation, drills for text understanding on the computer are usually of two types: multiple choice and true/false choice. Drills that permit students to answer questions by producing free text, even short segments, are rare because automatic analysis and feedback are hard to implement. Production tasks constitute a challenge in that the right feedback may be unavailable if the student makes an unanticipated mistake, one not included in a list of possible mistakes.

In this section, we present a first approach to teaching the understanding of spoken text through the twin objectives of permitting text production and providing explanatory feedback: the GETARUN system (Bianchi & Delmonte, 1999; Delmonte & Bianchi, 1998; Delmonte, Bianchi, & Pianta, 1992), recently implemented on the web. TTS is used in GETARUN both to read text passages aloud and to voice feedback on students' misunderstandings of a passage. Students may produce text in two ways: through answering questions about a passage by constructing response statements, and through constructing their own queries about a passage. GETARUN contains a knowledge base, called KL-One, and reasoning rules that permit it to answer students' queries and evaluate students' answers to questions. It can also generate feedback sentences.

Using GETARUN to Evaluate Students' Responses to Questions About Text Passages

In spoken text understanding, the student hears a passage read aloud either by the internal TTS module or by a previous recording. The passage is not available in written form. At the end of the listening activity, questions appear on the screen and the student is prompted to answer each one. The answers require aspects of text production, not simply recognition, as in multiple choice or true/false exercises.

Figure 6.1 shows the activity window for text understanding in an English lesson in web-based GETARUN. Here, a virtual dynamic face appears, whose lips and other features move to simulate a human speaking the selected passage. The student may choose between Practice and Test activities. In Practice activities, the student chooses a passage and may hear it as many times as desired. The student may also ask questions on its content to facilitate a full understanding. In Test activities, the system randomly chooses a passage and reads it twice to the student. After that, the student is asked questions on the passage content and must respond by building statements. The student builds these statements by activating menus on the lower part of the screen (e.g., Figure 6.2). These menus list all events, properties, and participants in the story along with a certain number of intruder words, which are phonetically close to the words used in the story.

As the language learner builds response statements, we can expect mistakes of three types:

- Case 1: The words chosen are not part of the text.
- Case 2: The words chosen are all part of the text; however, the statement built by the student is wrong and does not reflect the contents of the story.
- Case 3: The words chosen are all part of the text; the statement built by the student reflects the contents of the story; however, the statement has grammatical errors.

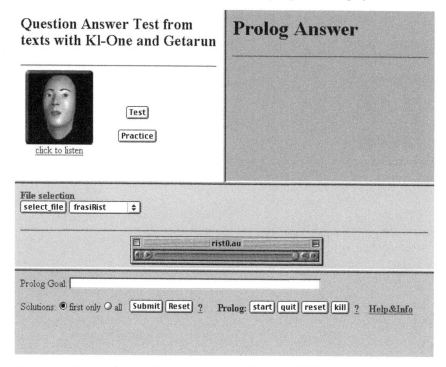

Figure 6.1 Text understanding activities in web-based GETARUN, where students answer questions about synthetically spoken text.

Feedback in Case 1 will indicate that the student has misunderstood or failed to process part of the text. Feedback in Case 2 is more complicated. The student has processed components of the text but has not fully integrated them into a representation of its content, or "discourse model." This misunderstanding is less serious than in Case 1. Depending on the type of error, the student may be assigned activities under Practice. In Case 3, the student has made a grammatical error. For feedback, students either are directed to a linguistic remedial activity or are shown a relevant grammar section. In all cases, students are informed about the kind of error they made and the possible reason they made it. Mechanisms supporting this kind of diagnosis and feedback are discussed below.

Using GETARUN to Answer Students' Queries About Text Passages

In a related activity for spoken text understanding, shown in Figure 6.2, the student assumes the role of questioner and builds queries about the text. This is done by activating menus at the lower part of the screen that contain question components. The same mechanisms support generation of answers

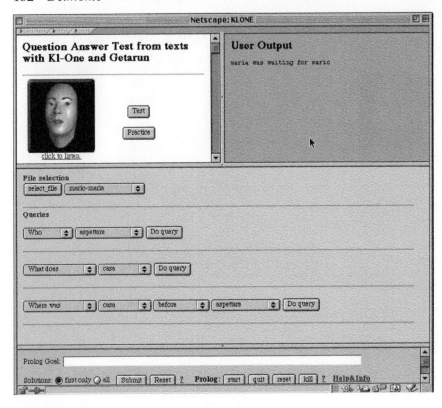

Figure 6.2 Text understanding activities in GETARUN, where students build queries (lower part of screen) about a synthetically spoken text.

to these queries as support diagnosis of response errors and are discussed in the next section.

Mechanisms by Which GETARUN Evaluates Students' Answers and Answers Students' Queries

For GETARUN to diagnose errors, formulate feedback, and answer questions, it must build a discourse model of the text offered to students for comprehension. Informally, a discourse model may be described as the set of entities "naturally evoked" (Webber, 1981) by a discourse, linked together by the relations they participate in. The discourse entities may be regarded as cognitive elements representing discourse referents. A discourse entity inhabits a speaker's discourse model and represents something the speaker has referred to. A speaker usually does not ascribe all at once the relevant properties of the referent of a discourse entity. Instead, the speaker may direct the listener's attention to that referent several times in succession. When the speaker wants to reaccess an entity already in the discourse model, he may do so with a definite anaphor (pronoun, as in it, or noun phrase, as in "the system"). In so doing, the speaker assumes that (a) a similar entity will be in the listener's evolving discourse model and (b) the listener will be able to reaccess that entity from the speaker's cues. The listener's problem, at least for definite anaphora, is identifying what discourse entities a text evokes.

To represent a discourse model in GETARUN involves these steps:

1. identifying the discourse entities a text evokes;
2. ascribing to them appropriate tags;
3. associating relations and properties to each tag.

Each text read to the student is kept in the form of a discourse model, with entities identified in the order they appear (id1, id2, id3, etc.). The entities, with tags and relations, are turned into a knowledge base structure, which allows reasoning to take place. The GETARUN feedback module uses the knowledge base and reasoning rules to build short feedback messages when a student's mistake is detected. We illustrate by commenting the system's behavior for the following short passage, "At the Restaurant" (Text 1).

Text 1.
"John went into a restaurant. There was a table in the corner. The waiter took the order. The atmosphere was warm and quiet. He began to read his book."

The following canned question can be posed to a student who has heard the passage:

"Where was John?"

This query is internally structured to match the KL-One knowledge representation:

?- where_was(id3)

The answer generated from the knowledge base is represented as follows:

After tes(f5_r01) was in id2

This answer might be worded as: "After entering, John was in the restaurant."

The student's menu-built answer is converted to KL-One structure and compared to the system's answer. Mismatches are detected and fed back to the student.

Alternatively, when the student queries the system and the system provides the answers, the system's internally generated answer is converted into a string of words, which is then voiced by TTS. For example, the student may ask the following questions and get the appropriate answer from the system:

"Where was the table?"

"Where was John after he entered?"

"Where was the waiter?"

"Who took the order?"

"Who ordered?"

"Who was reading the book?"

"What was in the restaurant?"

A valuable function of the discourse model is to allow recovery from failure in case the student's answer indicates a wrong inference. The inference error is diagnosed and appropriate feedback generated. For instance, if the answer to the question, "Who was reading the book?" is "the waiter," the feedback generated would be, "No, the waiter works in the restaurant: John is reading the book!"

Similar recovery strategies can be set up by back-retrieving information related to the wrong answer, then generating a message made up of two parts: an explanation of the error in a first sentence (the waiter works in the restaurant) and the right answer in the second sentence (John is reading the book). In all cases, the synthesized voice reads the feedback to the student.

Finally, to enable appropriate grammatical or orthographic feedback to be delivered, all words and utterances of the courseware are classified in a linguistic knowledge database in both orthographic and phonetic form, using a range of linguistic classifications. This database allows remediation to be targeted to the student's error.

A Pilot Test

A pedagogically useful extension of the Test activity is checking whether the student listening to the passage can recover the referential links between the pronouns in the last sentence and the antecedent, which is usually in the first sentence. Before the last sentence of the text is a decontextualizing sentence, which we call a "psychological atmosphere" sentence. To make the task more difficult, we allow the following variations from Text 1:

Text 2.
"John went into a restaurant. There was a man in the corner. The waiter took the order. The atmosphere was warm and quiet. He began to read his book."

Text 3.
"John went into a restaurant. There was a man in the corner. He waved at him. The waiter took the order. The atmosphere was warm and quiet. He began to read his book."

Text 4.
"John went into a restaurant. There was a man in the corner. The waiter took the order. John waved at him. The atmosphere was warm and quiet. He began to read his book."

Text 5.
"John went into a restaurant. There was a waiter in the corner. He waved at him. The waiter took the order. The atmosphere was warm and quiet. He began to read his book."

Text 6.
"John went into a restaurant. There was a man in the corner. The man waved at him. The waiter took the order. The atmosphere was warm and quiet. He began to read his book."

Text 7.
"A man went into a restaurant. John was sitting in the corner. The waiter took the order. The atmosphere was warm and quiet. He began to read his book."

Text 8.
"A man went into a restaurant. John was sitting in the corner. He waved at him. The waiter took the order. The atmosphere was warm and quiet. He began to read his book."

These texts were used in a pilot to elicit oral responses from students learning English, focusing on phenomena like anaphora resolution. We discovered that Texts 7 and 8 often caused confusion due to inherent ambiguity. We expect similar results from a web version of the exercise.

Expanding the System

GETARUN has been ported to SLIM, a self-instructional multimedia system for early language learners, with drills for both spoken and written language. GETARUN is intended to provide SLIM with a comprehensive feedback module to help the student working on these drills and to support self-assessment. Audiovisual materials are taken in part from commercially available courses. SLIM allows students to work either in an autonomous self-directed mode (Free Modality) or in a prestructured, programmed learning mode (Guided Modality).

Listening Comprehension via Automatic Dictation: Using TTS to Read, Vary Speed, and Change Style

Another method to address listening comprehension in language learning is dictation exercises. Dictation helps develop and test listening comprehension at the word-by-word level. They may be the simplest way to introduce TTS technology into CALL (Delmonte & Dolci, 1991). Because TTS can read any text, it is useful in cases where new texts must be introduced frequently, where having them continually recorded by a native speaker is not feasible. In addition, recording by humans can have unforeseen costs. First, reading must be done appropriately, as if the reader were addressing a student or a class. Also, the human's reading speed must sometimes be adjusted to make a portion of text more understandable. Moreover, the text must sometimes be read two or more times, to fit varying levels of student proficiency. These requirements can be efficiently satisfied by a TTS version of the dictation exercise. In addition, the use of TTS readily allows for different voices, both male and female, as well as for different accents or dialects.

We have implemented TTS-based dictation exercises in SLIM. Developing an exercise begins with a preediting phase in which the input text is chunked and coded, or marked up for intonation and pauses. The text is broken into fragments, each corresponding to a paragraph, and all punctuation is spelled out as a first approximation to pauses. Chunking can be done intuitively by a human, who goes through the text and marks with a slash those positions where a pause should be inserted by the synthetic voice. In addition, the nature of the pause needs to be indicated for the synthesizer. Some chunking can be done automatically by converting punctuation to spelled-out commands, for example, a period translates as "full stop". To illustrate a text marked up for TTS, we present a passage from Edgar Allan Poe's The Oval Portrait, with the empty list [] as the symbol for a pause:

> He occupied all his time—[dash] day and night—[dash] to complete this portrait of his love.[full stop] He almost never left his paints.[full stop] He wanted it perfect.[full stop] But he couldn't see that slowly she was getting weaker every day.[full stop] Her face was now white as snow. [full stop] He no longer was painting what was in front of him [ ] but was working on a picture he was in love with.[full stop]

When he finished his work in the middle of winter,[comma] he stood back and started to shake with happiness and fear.[full stop] All his color left his face.[full stop] He cried,[comma] "[open inverted commas] This woman is not made of paint![exclamation mark] She is alive".[close inverted commas & full stop] Then he turned to his wife that he loved so much,[comma] and saw she was now dead.[full stop]

Note that the mark-up cannot be fully automatic because the "inverted commas" command requires the human editor to search for the open/close pair manually. Also, the induced pause command [ ] is needed when the original text has no punctuation to indicate a pause.

When dictating a text, the human and the computerized tutor must observe a number of constraints to support students:

- chunking the text for semantic units;
- chunking the text for breath units corresponding to comprehensible and retainable portions of texts;
- allowing sufficient time for the student to transfer the text into orthographic form;
- providing a stretch of time, usually half an hour, for the exercise to be completed;
- reading every chunk twice;
- repeating as many times as required those chunks predesignated as hard to process;
- (only in the computer application) setting reading speed automatically to faster or slower by changing TTS speaking rate;
- (only by the human if students handwrite responses) producing a summary of the student's mistakes.

These tasks are done automatically and in real time by SLIM. Figure 6.3 shows the activity window for the complete dictation task (Detatto completo), which includes a written input section (lower screen). Students press the button (CONFERMA TESTO) on the low right-hand side after typing in and confirming what they heard from the synthetic voice. The system then checks for wrong or misspelled words in the student's response.

Options offered in the dictation task appear in the activity window shown in Figure 6.3. In the top part of the window are two menus: one (Voce) allows choice of voice type among a range of different synthetic voices; the other (Ritmo) lets the student change the speed with which the text is read. In the center are two scrolling spaces: the left one (Paragrafi) associated with paragraph numbering; the right (Schema/Testo) associated with chunks. The system gives each chunk a separate check when comparing a student's product with the original text. Words detected as misspelled are shown as crossed missing elements in that chunk.

Figure 6.3 Activity window for dictation exercise in SLIM courseware.

Other options shown in Figure 6.3 have also proved pedagogically useful in TTS-based dictation. Beneath the input section are buttons for exiting the activity either by returning to the main screen (first left button) or by going to the next activity (last right button). The four center buttons are organized as follows (from left to right): the clock tells how much time remains to write the dictation, the other buttons let the student hear the full paragraph, hear the current chunk, or move on to the next paragraph, respectively.

Listening and Reading Comprehension via True/False, Cloze, and Sentence Scrambling: Using TTS to Read Passages and Reorder Sentences

TTS can be profitably employed in three simpler exercises for written and spoken text comprehension. These exercises consist of true/false questions, the Cloze test, and sentence reordering. Key functions of each of these exercises will be described and illustrated with screen shots.

In the true/false exercise students listen to a text read aloud by the system and then validate statements about it. Beginners can also see the text displayed for a limited amount of time before responding. Figure 6.4 shows the true/false activity window for text listening comprehension (comprensione

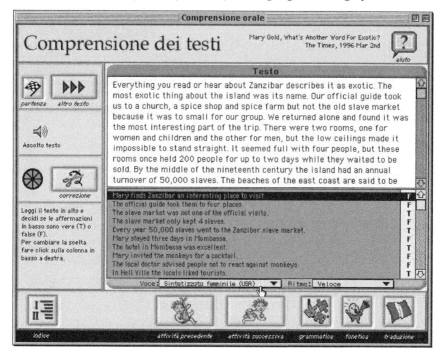

Figure 6.4 Activity window for true/false questions for listening text comprehension.

dei testi). The text scrolling part for beginners, under testo, appears after the text is spoken. Beneath that are listed true/false statements. At the left are buttons to start (partenza), choose-another-text (altro testo), speak (ascolto testo), and a clock and a correction button.

The Cloze test has students fill in slots where words have been deleted from a passage. Lower proficiency students can hear the text read with slots filled in. Figure 6.5 is a snapshot of the exercise with a list of word choices (parole) for the Cloze slots.

The reordering exercise displays a scrambled sentence (Figure 6.6). Lower level students can hear TTS read the sentence correctly. Students reorder the sentence manually, by positioning the words on screen, or (for advanced students) orally, using the ASR engine.

Lexicon Learning: Using TTS to Pronounce Words and Simulate Interlanguage

Besides spoken and written text comprehension and sound-grapheme correspondences, an important and related goal of second language learning is acquiring the lexicon. Indeed, lexical learning is the first challenge a second language student faces. A range of interesting problems might be helped by TTS:

Figure 6.5 Activity window for Cloze test.

- offering a first-level, linguistically appropriate exposure to the target language by presenting its sound system in context;
- allowing the student to couple meaning, sound, and sometimes image to words;
- providing an easy authoring facility that lets teachers increase the size of lexicon by adding new words to the database;
- allowing students to adapt to varying speaking rate, voice type, and voice quality (difficult to obtain with real life recording);
- exposing the learner to interlanguage and prompting comparison of word pronunciations by proficiency level.

Below we discuss how TTS might be applied to certain of these problems.

Presenting the Sound System of the Target Language in Context

The sounds of a language are organized in a phonological system, which children gradually induce upon exposure to their mother tongue. This gradual induction does not usually happen in second language learning. TTS in a CALL lexicon application may help because the sounds of the language are spoken in context of the lexicon of that language.

Figure 6.6 Activity window for sentence reordering.

Coupling Meaning, Sound, and Image to the Words to Be Learned

TTS in a CALL lexicon application may help simply because a rich, multi-sensory learning environment is more effective than a lean, one-dimensional one. Thus, we assume that it is more efficient and natural to learn words of a second language by associating sound to orthographic image than by orthographic image alone. Even better is to couple sound with a still image representing the concept behind the word, as usually happens with children.

Using TTS to Simulate Interlanguage: A Pilot Study

Lexical learning is, arguably, one of the most interesting applications of TTS because synthesis can simulate the stages of interlanguage (Selinker, 1992). Learners trying to read and pronounce written words in second language (L2) can be assumed first to apply their native (L1) phonological system. Interlanguage stages then proceed as follows: from *full beginner* level, where the learner pronounces L2 words (converts graphemes to phonemes) using no phonological rules of L2; to *false beginner*, where the learner knows some of the rules but has not mastered all L2 phonemes; to *intermediate*, where the learner has mastered the phonemes but not all prosodic (rhythm and intonation) rules; to *advanced*, or quasi-native speaker level, applying full phonetic and prosodic knowledge.

To study these phenomena, we experimented with modifying a TTS system for L2 by introducing phonetic and prosodic rules that mimic the interlanguage of an L2 learner who speaks a particular L1. Treating Italian as L2, we started with the Spoken Italian Word List (SIWL), a list of 30,000 Italian words with phonemic and prosodic transcriptions, lemmata, and morphosyntactic information (Delmonte & Stiffoni, 1995; Delmonte, 1998). To the SIWL we applied a TTS for American English. The idea was to use TTS to mimic the interlanguage stages of an American learning Italian. Similarly, to mimic a Spanish speaker learning English, we took the SLIM database of English and applied a TTS for Spanish American.

A TTS application may be fed a pure orthographic file or a phonetically transcribed version of the file. In the latter case, grapheme-to-phoneme rules and prosodic rules must be applied to generate an adequate format for synthesis. Table 6.2 shows the information flow for typical TTS, in which both phonetic and prosodic knowledge are required by the synthesizer. To this end, the Italian words in the SIWL were converted from graphemes to phonemes and the position of word-stress was marked in input strings, using long-established algorithms for synthesis of spoken Italian (e.g., Delmonte, Mian, & Tisato, 1984).

The procedure for mimicking levels of interlanguage is to manipulate the flow of information shown in Table 6.2. The interface for doing this appears in Figure 6.7, from the synthetic interlanguage application based on the SIWL. The FIND function at the upper right of the screen allows the user to type in a word and see it displayed with related linguistic information. Alternatively, the user may move to and from the current word by pressing on the arrows. As seen at the lower right side of the screen, each word may be synthetically pronounced at three levels of simulated proficiency:

Level 1: NO RULES
Level 2: NO PROSODIC RULES
Level 3: APPLY ALL RULES

The observations of listeners hearing the results of this procedure are as follows:

At *Level 1* the synthesized voice uses its own grapheme-to-phoneme rules and associated set of phonemes to produce a reading of input word(s). The impression one gets on hearing the TTS is of a native speaker of American English with no training on problematic words. The level of interlanguage competence in Italian is comparable to that of a false beginner. In particular, all L2 phonemes that coincide with L1 phonemes are pronounced correctly. But whenever a phoneme or a phonological rule is lacking in the L1 inventory, the grapheme-to-phoneme rules convert the word into an incorrect phonetic equivalent. The resulting utterance is often incomprehensible because of the distance between the Italian and English phonological sys-

Table 6.2 TTS Interaction With L2 Linguistic Rules to Induce Interlanguage Effects

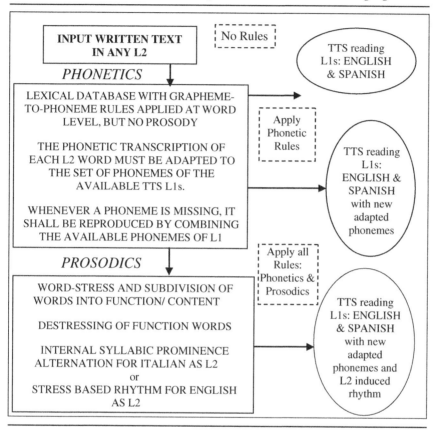

tems. From a pedagogical point of view, this observation confirms the need for learners to study phonetics and prosodics of the L2.

At *Level 2* the TTS is activated by a program that assigns the input word a grapheme-to-phoneme transcription with the appropriate internal phonetics. In this way, the synthesized voice achieves the closest possible approximation to the phonetic system of Italian. The reading is now fully intelligible and in some cases prosodically close to Italian. The impression is of an American at an intermediate level of learning who has still not mastered the prosody of Italian. One hears typical errors in word stress, where stress is placed on the most predictable position—such as the penultimate syllable—when it should be assigned elsewhere. In addition, depending on the L1, one hears vowel reductions misapplied to unstressed syllables; for example, if the L1 (TTS speaking) is English, one hears the unstressed syllables in Italian words like *rivendicano* pronounced without reduced vowels.

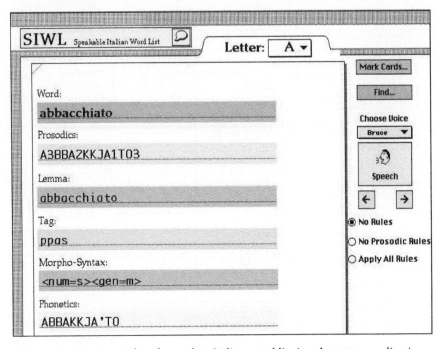

Figure 6.7 Activity window for spoken Italian word list interlanguage application.

At *Level 3* all rules are applied, both phonetic and prosodic. The latter add an Italian-like syllable-based rhythm to the phonetic reading that markedly improves the quality. The auditory impression, in many cases, is of an advanced student of Italian (a native American English speaker) reading with native-like pronunciation. The student's detectable accent lies mainly in vowel quality.

Grapheme-to-phoneme conversion for TTS in Italian is fairly straightforward (e.g., B ->/b/, A ->/a/, R ->/r/, Z ->/ts/; see Delmonte & Stiffoni, 1995; Delmonte, 1998). To produce valid prosody, each syllable fed to the TTS is marked by a duration and amplitude index that captures the alternation of stressed/unstressed syllables at intraword level (Bacalu & Delmonte, 1999; Delmonte, 2000). We used nine different prosodic markers in the SWIL (Table 6.3), which also allow us to differentiate syllable contexts. Thus, *rivendicano* would be represented as RI3V&6NDI3KA5NO3.

Although we have not studied students learning an L2 lexicon from TTS applications, the need for speech synthesis can be argued in case the L2 is a minority language with no stable and institutionally recognized pedagogical role in the local linguistic community (Mercier, Guyomard, & Siroux, 1999). Practicing the words of languages like Breton in a speech technology-enhanced learning environment may be the only available opportunity to learn.

Table 6.3 Prosodic Markers Introduced in the Phonemic Transcription of Italian Words

1 --> primary stress in open syllable or in syllable closed by /r/
2 --> secondary stress in open syllable
3 --> unstressed open or final syllable
4 --> semivowel
5 --> unstressed syllable in postonic position may also alternate with two unstressed syllables
6 --> primary stress in syllable closed by sonorants - /r/ excluded
7 --> primary stress in closed syllable and in truncated words
8 --> secondary stress in closed syllable
9 --> unstressed closed syllable

TTS and Perceptual Phonological Learning

Another goal of first and second language acquisition is phonetic and phonological skills. Concern is growing for addressing these skills in CALL, as suggested by workshops and conferences, such as PTLC (Phonetics Teaching and Learning Conference), MATISSE (http://isca-speech.org/archive/matisse), and InSTIL (Integrating Speech Technology into Language Learning). We shall review one working system and two research prototypes, which can be seen as paradigmatic of applications in which TTS is used fruitfully for phonetics and phonology instruction. Here, the contribution of TTS is essential to the linguistic task, not just ancillary, as in the previously illustrated applications.

Using Speech Synthesis in a Stand-Alone System to Teach Prereading Analytic Skills

The Multimedia Interactive Environment for Literacy Acquisition is the translated name of SIMpA (Sistema Interattivo Multimediale per l'Alfabetizzazione), a software package to facilitate reading created by Umberta Bortolini and her colleagues (Bortolini, 2002, 1993) of the Institute of Phonetics and Dialectology in Padua, under the Italian National Research Council. SIMpA is now available as an interactive CD ROM (see Padua website at http://www.pd.istc.cnr.it/). Its aim is to develop children's prereading skills through auditory and visual perceptual training that enables both normal and impaired children to practice segmental analysis of words and to find rules of correspondence between graphemes and phonemes. Modules address (a) the recognition of a word's sounds and (b) the segmentation of words into phonemes, including decomposition of words into phonemes and graphemes and identification and discrimination of sounds and phonemes within the syllable. A final module is dedicated to "playing with words" by combining drills such as elision, addition, or substitution of sounds or graphemes within words. Speech synthesis underlies parts of all the modules. For example, in the decomposition module, TTS allows the pupil to try out every combination of groups of letters and listen to the result. Being able to hear all possibilities is useful, particularly during practice, and TTS let children get the continuous feedback they need to check the results of applying phonological rules they think they understand but are not yet sure of. TTS also pronounces syllables for the child, who must then identify the syllable heard from a limited number of choices associated with different colors. Also found at the Padua website is Italian TTS that deploys the Festival engine.

Using Speech Synthesis Online to Teach Phonetics, With Extensions to Visualization

More general in scope is a course by Berkovitz, first presented at University College London for the MATISSE workshop (1999; http://isca-speech.org/archive/matisse). The course features rich audio material to be used for speech perception, with the aim of driving students' awareness of their perceptual capabilities. Synthetic speech stimuli are well wrought and permit an analysis of perceptual differences between identification and discrimination. The course allows speech perception experiments to be conducted behind the instructional activity.

Also aimed at simulating perceptual tasks is the WinPitch product originally introduced at EUROCALL by Martin and Germain (1999) and now available online (http://www.winpitch.com/winpitch_ltl.htm). WinPitch lets learners manipulate intonational contours and listen to the synthesized results. The learner may even visually align his or her own contour with the master contour by moving the curve directly on the screen (Martin, 2003). Techniques for this kind of speech visualization and its benefits for learners are discussed in this volume by Mulholt and Hwu as well as by Gómez et al.

A similar tool from KTH (the Royal Institute of Technology), Stockholm, was presented at ICSLP by Sjoelander and Beskow (2000) and at the MATISSE workshop by Sjoelander et al. (1999). Called the SNACK Sound Toolkit, it allows students to work on the web and provides real-time feedback on synthesized speech. It has been extended to serve automatic speech segmentation and alignment (Sjoelander, 2003). The toolkit functions can be freely downloaded (http://www.speech.kth.se/snack/). The exercises in SNACK include changing the identity of a consonant in a synthesized consonant–vowel syllable by manipulating the formant transitions; modifying a word in a minimal pair (e.g., *set–sit*) by manipulating the tone in the first word of the pair to derive the second word of the pair (by changing vowel length, vowel quality, and stress position); and experimenting with prosodic modifications at sentence level, such as changing a statement into a question.

In all exercises, the developers stress the importance of using formant-based synthesis, which, in their words, has significant pedagogical value:

> By using a parametric synthesis paradigm based on a familiar phonetic representation controlled from intuitive graphical interface, exercises can be designed that provide the students with a deeper understanding not only of fundamental speech synthesis techniques, but also about acoustic-phonetic correlates in general. (Sjoelander et al., 1999, p. 144)

This emphasis is consistent with the explanation by Gómez et al. (this volume) for the central role of formants in natural speech production and perception.

CONCLUSION

We close by pointing to a course in speech synthesis from the Technical University of Dresden, first presented at the MATISSE workshop by Hoffmann, Kordon, Kuerbis, Ketzmerick, & Fellbaum (1999). This course is rich in all kinds of teaching materials and is freely available from the web (http://www.ias.et.tu-dresden.de/sprache/lehre/multimedia/tutorial/index.html). We recommend the course as well as TTS products from this group (Hoffman et al., 2003) to anyone with interest in applying synthesized speech to language instruction.

REFERENCES

Bacalu, C., & Delmonte, R. (1999). Prosodic modeling for speech recognition. *Atti del Workshop AI*IA: Elaborazione del Linguaggio e Riconoscimento del Parlato*, 45–55, IRST, Trento.

Bally, C., Benoit, C., & Sawallis, T. R. (Eds). (1992). *Talking machines: Theories, models and designs.* Amsterdam: North–Holland.

Berkovitz, R. (1999). Design, development and evaluation of computer-assisted learning for speech science education. *Proceedings of MATISSE*, 9–16, London.

Bianchi, D., & Delmonte, R. (1999). Reasoning with a discourse model and conceptual representations. *Proceedings of VEXTAL*, 401–411. Padua: Unipress.

Black, A., & Lenzo, K. (2004). Multilingual text-to-speech synthesis. *Proceedings of International Conference on Acoustics, Speech, and Signal Processing (ICASSP04)*, Montreal, Canada.

Black, A., & Tokuda, K. (2005). *Blizzard Challenge 2005.* Special session at Interspeech05, Lisbon. (http://www.festvox.org/blizzard/blizzard2005.html)

Bortolini, U. (1993). *Multimedia integrated environment in literacy acquisition.* Paper presented at 6th International Congress for the Study of Child Language, Trieste. (Also published in *Quaderni del C.S.R.F., 12*, 115–119).

Bortolini, U. (2002). *Sistema Interattivo Multimediale per l'Alfabetizzazione (SIMpA)*, a cura di U. Bortolini, Padua (ISBN: 88-8080-047-7).

Chu, M., Peng, H., & Chang, E. (2001). A concatenative Mandarin TTS system without prosody model and prosody modification. *Proceedings of 4th ISCA Tutorial and Research Workshop on Speech Synthesis*, Perthshire, Scotland.

Cole, R., et al. (2003). Perceptive animated interfaces: First steps toward a new paradigm for human computer interaction. *Proceedings of IEEE, 91*, 1391–1405.

Cole, R., Mariani, J., Uszkoreit, H., Zaenen, A., & Zue, V. (Eds). (1997). *Survey of the state of the art in human language technology*. Cambridge, UK: Cambridge University Press.

Cosi, R., Delmonte, R. Biscetti, S., Cole, R., Pellom, B., & van Vuuren, S. (2004). *Italian literacy tutor: Tools and technologies for individuals with cognitive disabilities*. Paper presented at the InSTIL/ICALL Symposium, Venice, Italy.

CSLU Toolkit (Center for Spoken Language Understanding, Oregon Graduate Institute). http://cslu.cse.ogi.edu/toolkit

Delmonte, R. (Ed.) (1995). How to create SLIM courseware. *Software Linguistico Interattivo Multimediale*. Padua: Unipress.

Delmonte, R. (1997). Learning languages with a "SLIM" automatic tutor. *Asiatica Venetiana, 2*, 31–52.

Delmonte, R. (1998). L'apprendimento delle regole fonologiche inglesi per studenti italiani. *Proceedings of Atti 8 Convegno GFS–AIA*, 177–191, Pisa.

Delmonte, R. (2000). SLIM prosodic automatic tools for self-learning instruction. *Speech Communication, 30*, 145–166.

Delmonte, R., & Bianchi, D. (1998). Dialogues from texts: How to generate answers from a discourse model. *Atti Convegno Nazionale AI*IA*, 139–143, Padua.

Delmonte, R., Bianchi, D., & Pianta, E. (1992). GETA_RUN: A general text analyzer with reference understanding. *Proceedings of 3rd Conference on Applied Natural Language Processing (Systems Demonstrations)*, Association for Computational Linguistics, 9–10.

Delmonte, R., Cacco, A., Romeo, L., Dan, M., Mangilli-Climpson, M., & Stiffoni, F. (1996). *SLIM: A model for automatic tutoring of language skills*. Paper presented at Ed-Media 96, AACE, Boston, MA.

Delmonte, R., & Dolci, R. (1991). Computing linguistic knowledge for text-to-speech systems with PROSO. *Proceedings of EUROSPEECH'91*, 1291–1294, Genoa.

Delmonte, R., Mian, G. A., & Tisato, G. (1984). A text-to-speech system for the synthesis of Italian. *Proceedings of ICASSP'84*, 291–294, San Diego, CA.

Delmonte, R., & Stiffoni, F. (1995). SIWL—Il database parlato della lingua italiana. *Convegno AIA: Gruppo di Fonetica Sperimentale*, 99–116, Trento.

Dutoit, T. (1997). *An introduction to text-to-speech synthesis*. Dordrecht: Kluwer Academic.

Dutoit, T., & Stylianou, Y. (2003). Text-to-speech synthesis. In R. Mitkov (Ed), *Handbook of computational linguistics* (pp. 323–338). Oxford, UK: Oxford University Press.

EULER Project. http://tcts.fpms.ac.be/synthesis/euler/

Hoffmann, R., Kordon, U., Kuerbis, S., Ketzmerick, B., & Fellbaum, K. (1999). An interactive course on speech synthesis. *Proceedings of the MATISSE Workshop*, 61–64, University College, London. (http://ias.et.tu-dresden.de/sprache/lehre/multimedia /tutorial/index.html)

Hoffmann, R., Jokisch, O., Hirschfeld, D., Strecha, G., Kruschke, H., & Kordon, U. (2003). A multilingual TTS system with less than 1 megabyte footprint for embedded applications. *Proceedings of International Conference on Acoustics, Speech, and Signal Processing (ICASSP 03)*, Vol. I, 532–535, Hong Kong.

Hunt, A., & Black, A. (1996). Unit selection in a concatenative speech synthesis system using a large speech database. *Proceedings of ICASSP 96*, Vol. I, 373–376, Atlanta, Georgia.

ICSLP, 2002. *Proceedings of the International Conference on Spoken Language Processing (ICSLP): Interspeech.* 11–13 September, Denver, CO.

IEEE (2002). *Institute of Electrical and Electronics Engineers Workshop on Speech Synthesis.* Santa Monica, CA: IEEE Signal Processing Society.

ISCA (2001). *Proceedings of the 4th International Speech Communication Association Tutorial and Research Workshop on Speech Synthesis,* Perthshire, Scotland.

ISCA (2004). *Proceedings of the 5th International Speech Communication Association (ISCA) Speech Synthesis Workshop,* Carnegie Mellon University.

Klatt, D. (1987). Review of text-to-speech conversion for English. *Journal of the Acoustical Society of America, 82,* 737–797.

Littlemore, J. (2001). Learner autonomy, self-instruction, and new technologies in language learning. In A. Chambers & G. Davies (Eds.), *ICT and language learning: A European perspective.* Lisse, NL: Swets & Zeitlinger.

Martin, P. (2003, July). *Speech analysis and synthesis for WinPitch LingLab, software for language learning.* Paper presented at the 11th ELSNET European Summer School on Language and Speech Communication: Computer Assisted Language Learning, Université de Lille, Villeneuve-d'Asq, France. (http://www.elsnet.org/ess2003site.html)

Martin, P., & Germain, A. (1999). Utilisation d'un logiciel de visualisation pour l'apprentissage de l'oral en langue seconde. *Proceedings of EUROCALL99,* Besançon, France.

Massaro, D. W. (2004). *From multisensory integration to talking heads and language learning.* In G. Calvert, C. Spence, & B. Stein (Eds.), *Handbook of multisensory processes* (pp. 153–176). Cambridge, MA: MIT Press.

Mercier, G., Guyomard, M., & Siroux, J. (1999). Synthèse de la parole en breton: Didacticiels pour une langue minoritaire. *Proceedings of InSTIL: Speech Technology Applications in CALL,* 57–61.

O'Shaughnessy, D. (1998). Review of R. Sproat, 'Multilingual text-to-speech synthesis: The Bell Labs approach.' *Computational Linguistics, 24*(4), 656–658.

Pfister, B., & Romsdorfer, H. (2003). Mixed-lingual text analysis for polyglot TTS synthesis. *Proceedings of Eurospeech03,* Geneva, Switzerland.

Ramakrishnan, A. G., Bali, K., Talukdar, P., & Krishna, N. (2004). Tools for the development of a Hindi speech synthesis system. *Proceedings of the 5th ISCA Speech Synthesis Workshop,* Carnegie Mellon University.

Schröder, M., & Trouvain, J. (2001). The German text-to-speech synthesis system MARY: A tool for research, development and teaching. *Proceedings of 4th ISCA Tutorial and Research Workshop on Speech Synthesis,* Perthshire, Scotland.

Segi, H., & Takagi, T. (2004). A concatenative speech synthesis method using context dependent phoneme sequences with variable length as search units. *Proceedings of 5th ISCA Speech Synthesis Workshop,* Carnegie Mellon University.

Selinker, L. (1992). *Interlanguage.* New York: Longman.

Sjoelander, K. (2003). An HMM-based system for automatic segmentation and alignment of speech. *Proceedings of Fonetik 2003,* Umeå University, Department of Philosophy and Linguistics, *PHONUM 9,* 93–96. (http://www.ling.umu.se/fonetik2003/)

Sjoelander, K., & Beskow, J. (2000). WavcSurfer: An open source speech tool. *Proceedings of the International Conference on Spoken Language Processing (ICSLP2000),* Beijing, China.

Sjoelander, K., Beskow, J., Gustafson, J., Carlson, R., & Granstroem, B. (1999). Web-based educational tools for speech technology. *Proceedings of the MATISSE Workshop,* 141–144, University College, London.

Sproat, R. (Ed.) (1997). *Multilingual text-to-speech synthesis: The Bell Labs approach.* Dordrecht: Kluwer Academic.

van Santen, J., Sproat, R., Olive, J., & Hirschberg, J. (Eds.) (1997). *Progress in speech synthesis.* New York: Springer–Verlag,.

van Santen, J. (2004). Speech synthesis. In W. S. Bainbridge (Ed.), *Berkshire Encyclopedia of Human–Computer Interaction.* Great Barrington, MA: Berkshire Publishing Group.

van Santen, J. (1997). Prosodic modeling in text-to-speech synthesis. *Proceedings of Eurospeech97*, Vol. I, 19–28.

van Santen, J., Shih, C., Möbius, B., Tzoukermann, E., & Tanenblatt, M. (1997). Multilingual durational modeling. *Proceedings of Eurospeech97, V*, 2651–2654.

Warschauer, M., Turbee, L., & Roberts, B. (1996). Computer learning networks and student empowerment. *System, 24*, 1–14.

Webber, B. L. (1981). Discourse model synthesis: Preliminaries to reference. In A. Joshi, B. L. Webber, & I. Sag (Eds.), *Elements of discourse understanding.* Cambridge, UK: Cambridge University Press.

APPENDIX: A SAMPLE OF WEBSITES RELATED TO SPEECH SYNTHESIS

http://cslr.colorado.edu/
http://festvox.org/
http://tcts.fpms.ac.be/synthesis/mbrola.html
http://tcts.fpms.ac.be/synthesis/euler/
http://cslu.cse.ogi.edu/toolkit
http://cslu.ogi.edu/demos/ttsdemos.htm
http://fonsg3.let.uva.nl/Proceedings/IFA-Proceedings.html
http:// www.ias.et.tu-dresden.de/sprache/lehre/multimedia/tutorial/index.html
http:// www.speech.kth.se/snack/
http:// www.speech.kth.se/wavesurfer/
http:// www.cstr.ed.ac.uk/projects/festival/
http:// www.cstr.ed.ac.uk/~awb/synthesizers.html
http://www-a2k.is.tokushima-u.ac.jp/member/kita/NLP/index.html
http://www.ims.uni-stuttgart.de/phonetik/synthesis/
http://lorien.die.upm.es/research/synthesis/synthesis.html
http://mambo.ucsc.edu/psl/speech.html

Developing Prototype Systems

The Examples of Pronunciation Training and Proficiency Testing

INTRODUCTION

Assuming prior work in needs analysis and technology adaptation (Sections II and III), the question becomes how to integrate speech technologies into full-featured computer-assisted language learning (CALL) prototypes. The chapters in Section IV illustrate the processes involved and issues arising in developing prototype systems around speech technologies for training and for testing. Systems for training are represented by Dalby and Kewley-Port, who describe the development of first- and second-language pronunciation tutors that integrate speech recognition as well as visualization schemes. Systems for testing are represented by Bernstein and Cheng, who explain the construction of an automatic assessment instrument for spoken language skill that is based on speech recognition. The chapter authors elucidate the design assumptions and decision methods by which they arrived at activities, scoring methods, feedback, and other system features that effectively exploit speech technologies.

Dalby and Kewley-Port's research shows how a tightly focused application can attain high accuracy and reliability in automatic speech recognition (ASR) performance. Each tutor they develop is intended for a distinct user group with specific misarticulations—hearing impaired children, mentally delayed adults, or speakers of English-as-a-second-language (ESL). Instructional content is primarily minimally contrasting word pairs. Bernstein and Cheng's research shows how the use of acoustic measures can be expanded from measuring pronunciation, as seen in Dalby and Kewley-Port and prefigured in Precoda and Bratt (this volume), to assessing speaking skill more generally, with measures that include latency of response, fluency of utterance, and accuracy of words read or repeated. This composite assessment he calls *speaking facility*.

COMMON PROCESSES IN DEVELOPMENT

Precise Application of Research and Theory to Design

Common to the design of these systems is the researchers' explicit reliance on precise principles from research and theory in linguistics, psycholinguistics, and language learning. Dalby and Kewley-Port call on learning theory to motivate the use of articulation drills, on linguistic analysis to derive phonological contrasts for second language instruction, and on psycholinguistic research to support couplings of speech perception with speech production exercises. Bernstein and Cheng call on psycholinguistics to motivate the measurement of elementary aspects of speaking skill as an indicator of higher-level language facility. In particular, they invoke the pivotal role that psycholinguistic theory assigns to automaticity of elementary skills in achieving discourse proficiency. It is these elementary skills that are well suited to measurement by automatic speech recognition and that the resulting Versant test (formerly, PhonePass SET-10) is designed to tap. The new test construct, speaking facility, is thus grounded in cognitive science and models of human language production.

Rigorous Experimental Validation of Design

Paralleling this theoretical grounding, the development of these systems has in common an exhaustive back-end validation of design features. Dalby and Kewley-Port outline the linguistic studies they conducted to inventory phonetic discriminations and identify training needs, their engineering experiments to select and optimize speech recognition algorithms that make the needed discriminations, and the correlation analyses they performed to validate the feedback given by these algorithms—correlations against discriminations made by human judges, as in Precoda and Bratt (Section II of this volume). Beyond validation, Dalby and Kewley-Port take up the question of instructional effectiveness, reporting on small-scale, laboratory evaluations that reveal improvements in subjects' intelligibility not only for the words trained but also for new words containing the trained contrasts. This work sets the stage for larger scale evaluations that are the subject of Section V in this volume.

Bernstein and Cheng review the experimental procedures used to derive test scores from basic speech recognition measures, to combine and weight scores, to scale and normalize them, and to validate them against human expert scoring as well as against traditional standardized tests that cannot be administered automatically. Bernstein and Cheng draw many of these test construction procedures from the precisely defined methodology of item response theory. The result is a standardized instrument that can be administered and scored easily and automatically and that correlates well with scores on a widely used test of second language speaking skill—the oral proficiency interview (OPI) from the Inter-agency Language Roundtable (ILR)—which requires expert human judges to provide ratings. (The ILR rating scale used in the OPI is described by Clifford and Granoien in Section I.) An obvious advantage of automated oral proficiency testing is cost: automatic scoring is less expensive than methods involving expert humans. Moreover, the Versant test is diagnostic in that subscores on specific elementary skills can be retrieved; whereas the OPI and other expert-judgment instruments are opaque with regard to what aspects of a speaker's performance contribute to a rating.

Both chapters in this section show CALL development as part of a comprehensive research program, exemplifying an approach that goes beyond skillful engineering and imaginative screen design. That approach entails extensive mining of background theory and research, experiments to manipulate and validate speech recognition components, and iterative user studies to ensure the clarity of interface for both primary users (learners, examinees) and secondary users (teachers, therapists, test administrators).

COMMON OUTCOMES: TRANSITIONS TO PRACTICE

The research detailed in both these chapters has transitioned into practice, resulting in commercial products employed in training, remediation, and testing by schools, clinics, and businesses: products from Communication Disorders Technology (www.comdistec.com) in the case of Dalby and Kewley-Port; and from Ordinate Corporation, now under Harcourt Assessment (www.harcourtassessment.com), in the case of Bernstein and Cheng. Furthermore, a version of Versant, customized to assess English language skills for the workplace, is incorporated into assessment services provided by the American College Testing Program (see http://www.act.org/workkeys/index.html). Versant testing has also been cycled back into research as instrumentation for second language learning studies (e.g., by Hincks, 2003, to assess the effect of instructional interventions on pronunciation skills). Finally, we should point to another case of products spun off from prototypes developed through extensive ASR research—the NativeAccent™ tutor for English and the Carnegie Speech Assessment instrument, both from Carnegie Speech Products (http://www.carnegiespeech.com/), based on research at Carnegie Mellon University (Tomokiyo, Wang, & Eskenazi, 2000; Probst, Ke, & Eskenazi, 2002).

REFERENCES

Hincks, R. (2003). Speech technologies for pronunciation feedback and evaluation. *ReCall, 15*, 3–20. (Selected papers from EUROCALL 2002, Jyväskylä, Finland). [http://www.speech.kth.se/~hincks/papers/REcall.pdf]
Probst, K., Ke, Y., & Eskenazi, M. (2002). Enhancing foreign language tutors—in search of the golden speaker. *Speech Communication, 37*, 161–173.
Tomokiyo, M.-L., Wang, L., & Eskenazi, M. (2000). An empirical study of the effectiveness of speech-recognition-based pronunciation training. *Proceedings of ICSLP 2000*, Beijing. [http://www.cs.cmu.edu/~laura/Papers-PS/icslp-fluency.ps]

7 Design Features of Three Computer-Based Speech Training Systems

Jonathan Dalby and Diane Kewley-Port

INTRODUCTION

This chapter describes the design features of speech training systems that we and our colleagues have developed over the course of more than a decade of research. This research began at Indiana University in 1986 and, since 1989, has been continued at Communication Disorders Technology, Inc. Each of the systems described here was developed to serve the training needs of rather different sets of clients. All three systems employ automatic speech recognition (ASR) technology for the purpose of providing feedback to clients about the quality or intelligibility of their speech. It is a basic cognitive assumption underlying all this work that effective training of speech and language structures for persons with disorders of various types, or for second language learners, requires a large amount of individual drill with valid feedback. To the extent that they provide valid feedback about the intelligibility of an utterance, computer-based training systems employing ASR afford amounts of individual training not available in the typical clinical or classroom setting. The first training system is the Indiana Speech Training Aid (ISTRA; Kewley-Port, Watson, Elbert, Maki, & Reed, 1991). This system is designed for use by speech-language pathologists in the treatment of the speech production deficits of normal-hearing, misarticulating, or hearing-impaired children. It uses a speaker-dependent recognizer that provides client feedback based on a numerical score that has been shown to be well correlated with human judgments of speech quality (Watson, Reed, Kewley-Port, & Maki, 1989). The ISTRA system trains clients on their productions of whole words and short phrases.

A second training system, called HearSay, was developed as a speech intelligibility training system for learners of English as a second language. This system employs speaker-independent recognition and provides both speech production and speech perception training using minimally contrasting word pairs. Training curricula that are specific to the English segmental phonological deficits of speakers of specific first languages have been developed (Dalby, Kewley-Port, & Sillings, 1998; Dalby & Kewley-Port, 1999).

The third system that we will describe is currently under development. This system, called You-Said-It, is designed to teach English as a first language to adults with developmental disabilities. You-Said-It uses a speaker-dependent recognizer for pronunciation training that focuses on the segmental intelligibility of words, and it also employs a speaker-independent recognizer for training productions of phrases and sentences. The aim of the following descriptions of these three systems is to show how linguistic analysis has been applied to the problem of speech intelligibility and how the resulting knowledge has been incorporated into computer-based training systems.

ISTRA: EMPLOYING ASR TO AID SPEECH THERAPY

Design of the System

The Indiana Speech Training Aid (ISTRA) is designed to be used under the supervision of speech-language pathologists providing pronunciation training to clients with a variety of speech disorders. The training paradigm in the ISTRA curriculum focuses on contrasting a client's usual "errorful" production of a word or short phrase with an improved version elicited from the client by a speech therapist. The system employs a template-based, speaker-dependent isolated word recognizer combined with graphical game-like speech drill formats (similar to the graphical game formats used in HearSay, described later in this chapter, see Figure 7.1).

Recognition templates in the ISTRA system are made using three tokens of a client's current best productions of a target word as judged by the speech therapist. These good productions are elicited by the therapist using traditional articulation training methods. Before eliciting improved pronunciations, the therapist collects three tokens of the client's errorful utterances. Once a template is made, the client practices the word on the computer without supervision. Feedback to the client is derived automatically from the distance metric of the recognizer.

Use of *speaker-dependent* recognition technology in ISTRA is motivated by the fact that the normative acoustic models used to train speaker-independent recognizers are inappropriate targets for many clients, at least in the early phases of speech therapy. With ISTRA, the training goals can be set and revised to match the progress a client is making on a particular speech error through a cycle of template making, followed by drill, followed by making a better template, more drill, and so forth.

Validating ASR Algorithms in Terms of Accuracy and Effectiveness in Pronunciation Training

The validity of speech training provided by the ISTRA system has been established through two kinds of research results. First, evaluations of the feedback provided to the user by various recognizers has been established through benchmarking of their capability to perform the discriminations required by the training and then by examining the similarity of the feedback they provide to the kinds of feedback that human judges can provide (Watson, et al., 1989; Anderson & Kewley-Port, 1995). Second, training studies have been conducted that used the ISTRA system with clients with a variety of speech disorders (Kewley-Port, et al., 1991). Before automatic speech recognition algorithms are substituted for humans in speech training, it is necessary to verify the accuracy of the recognizer in making the discriminations that are implicit in the training task. This baseline recognition accuracy is established by testing with speech from normal talkers. Second, the recognizer should produce recognition scores that can be used to provide evaluative feedback that is a relevant measure of the quality of the user's speech. Methods we have developed for evaluating how well a proposed recognition technology meets these two requirements are described below.

Accuracy in Phonetic Discrimination:
Comparing HMM and Template-Based Recognizers

The phonetic discriminations that are typically required in word- and segment-level speech training tasks are quite challenging. Anderson and Kewley-Port (1995) evaluated three speaker-dependent recognizers as candidates for use in the ISTRA system. A database of normal and misarticulated English speech was collected. The normal speech included minimal pairs containing the 25 most common substitution errors of misarticulating children. These were word pairs such as "some/thumb, red/wed, then/den, thin/fin" and so on. In all, 500 tokens comprised this corpus. The basic recognition accuracy of one hidden Markov model (HMM) recognizer and two template-based recognizers was evaluated using 20 test tokens per contrast from normal adult speech. For this data set, the HMM recognizer had the best overall accuracy with 90% correct. The best of the two template recognizers was correct on 86% of the trials while the second template recognizer was correct on only 79% of the trials.

The first extensive study of the validity of the speech-quality feedback provided by a computer-based training system was conducted by Watson et al. (1989). In this study, scores from a template-based recognizer, used in the first version of ISTRA, were compared to ratings from a jury of listeners asked to assign ratings in the range of 1–5 to disordered speech. A rating of 1 on this scale meant the speech was unintelligible and 5 meant it was normal speech. Correlation analysis of the jury ratings and recognizer scores showed that the speaker-dependent recognizer in use at the time was almost as good as, and somewhat more consistent than, ratings supplied by human raters. That is, the correlation coefficients computed for the recognizer against the mean of all the human raters compared favorably to coefficients computed for each of the individual raters against the mean ratings of the rest of the group. The ISTRA system has undergone several revisions since this work was first completed. This analysis has been performed on several template-based speaker-dependent recognizers used in these various versions. The correlation coefficient computed for the average of human ratings of a corpus of disordered speech and for the scores produced by the recognizer in the current ISTRA system is .89. Similarly, Anderson and Kewley-Port (1995) used speech from misarticulating children to evaluate the three recognizers in their study for their capability to distinguish between tokens of words rated as "correct" vs. "incorrect" by trained human listeners as well as for their potential in deriving measures of evaluative feedback to be used in speech drill. Tokens of disordered speech were collected from children undergoing speech therapy. Misarticulated tokens were recorded at the beginning of a course of training and improved productions were elicited at the end. The HMM recognizer proved better than the template recognizers in discriminating between the two categories of tokens. However, it was worse than either template recognizer at providing an evaluative score for the speech. Ratings were collected from a jury of five trained listeners on multiple tokens of words from misarticulating children (using a 7-point scale). Templates were made from the three best of these productions, and the recognition scores for the other tokens in the set were collected. Correlation analysis of the recognition scores from the three recognizers with the average of the human listeners was then performed. This analysis showed that the recognition scores for the template-based recognizers were quite similar to interrater correlations, but that this was not the case for the "confidence" score returned by the HMM recognizer.

Effectiveness in Articulation Training

Kewley-Port et al. (1991) reported three articulation training case studies that were conducted with the ISTRA system. These studies involved, respectively, a hearing-impaired child, a profoundly deaf teenager, and a normal-hearing, misarticulating child. Despite the variability in the nature of the phonological disorders of these 3 subjects, all showed improved speech intelligibility following training on the ISTRA system. The hearing impaired child showed a marked improvement in the intelligibility of words containing the affricate /ch/ in both trained and untrained (generalization of training) words. This improvement was evident from ratings of pre- and post-training tokens of the words whether the whole word or only the target segment was judged and whether the judges were trained or naive listeners. Results from the training sessions of the profoundly deaf subject were somewhat different but nevertheless showed the value of ISTRA drill. This subject was a nonoral deaf subject who relied on American Sign Language to communicate but wished to learn to produce a few words in his "personal vocabulary" intelligibly so that he could communicate in a rudimentary way with hearing people. His ISTRA session yielded significantly improved intelligibility for words that he trained but did not show any generalization to untrained words.

The training results for the normal-hearing, misarticulating subject were similar to those for the hearing-impaired subject. Trained words as well as generalization words containing the same phonemes showed significantly improved intelligibility ratings following training. A set of control words containing a different phoneme that this client also produced in error, showed no improvement. These studies together show that effective speech training can be conducted using systems in which the feedback for speech drills is provided by speaker-dependent speech recognition algorithms.

HEARSAY: EMPLOYING ASR IN SECOND LANGUAGE LEARNING

Learning the phonological/phonetic system of a new language is one of the most difficult tasks associated with learning a second language as an adult. We all know someone who speaks English with a strong accent despite years or even decades of residence in an English-speaking environment. The HearSay training system was developed to address the need of English-as-a-second-language (ESL) learners to speak intelligibly. The HearSay curriculum covers both the perception and the production of the phonemes of English.

In Dalby and Kewley-Port (1999) we identified five basic assumptions that underlie the development of the HearSay system. First, we believe that segment-level speech errors (i.e., errors in articulation of phonemes) seriously degrade the intelligibility of nonnative speech (Rogers & Dalby, 1986). Second, we assume that typical pronunciation difficulties in a given target language are specific to the first language of the learner (Kenworthy, 1987; Flege & Wang, 1989; Rochet, 1995). Third, we assume that second language learners have both a perception and a production deficit in the target language (Strange, 1995). Fourth, we assume that explicit training in perception and production using minimally contrasting word pairs can improve second language speech intelligibility (Rogers, Dalby, & DeVane, 1994). Finally, an assumption underlying all our work, and driving the validation of recognizer performance against human judgments, is as follows: To be effective, the feedback provided by computer-based training systems should be similar to the feedback that would be provided by a human trainer (Anderson & Kewley-Port, 1995; Watson et al., 1989). In the following sections we will discuss the first four assumptions and then describe aspects of the design and development methods for HearSay that follow from those assumptions.

Assumption 1: Segmental Errors Degrade Speech Intelligibility

Many acoustic-phonetic properties of nonnative speech can interfere with intelligibility besides inaccurate production of phones, or segmental errors. Tajima, Port, and Dalby (1997) used LPC resynthesis to show that simply adjusting the temporal properties of Mandarin Chinese-accented English, while leaving the spectral properties intact, improved intelligibility significantly. Similarly, native English speech that was modified to be temporally similar to Mandarin-accented English was less intelligible than unmodified English. It seems clear that speech production training aimed at matching the rhythmic properties of native speech would be very useful. It is less clear, however, how such training might be effectively conducted.

Nonphonetic factors also affect the intelligibility of accented speech. Syntactic and semantic context (Morton, 1979), grammaticality, and familiarity of topic (Gass & Veronis, 1984), as well as familiarity with a specific accent or speaker (Brodkey, 1972), all affect how well listeners understand accented speech.

At the same time, basic segmental errors play a major role in impeding the understanding of nonnative speech. Specifically, errors in speech production that lead to initial "bottom-up" errors and uncertainties in a listener's speech processing will have detrimental effects on intelligibility (Marslen-Wilson, 1985). Experiments with synthetic speech have shown that even varieties of such speech that are nearly as intelligible as natural speech in ideal listening conditions still require more cognitive effort to process (Pisoni, Nusbaum, & Green, 1985). This finding suggests that even rather small degrees of accentedness may cost listeners substantially in terms of processing effort and, under suboptimal listening conditions, may cause intelligibility problems.

Rogers and Dalby (1996) studied the effects of segmental errors in Mandarin Chinese-accented English. Segmental errors were evaluated by collecting native English listeners' responses to Mandarin-accented productions of isolated words using minimal pairs (listeners check which word of a pair such as "bead, bid" they heard). This testing method requires knowledge of the expected error (discussed further below) but has the advantage of unambiguous interpretation of the targeted error, even when there are other production errors in the same word (Weismer & Martin, 1992). We also measured errors in sentences and in a short reading passage using a count of words correctly written down by native listeners. Results showed that segmental error scores predicted errors in the sentences and read passages reasonably well (see also Rogers, 1997). Results also showed that certain segmental error types had a greater effect on connected speech intelligibility than did other types. Errors in vowel tenseness, the /i/ and /I/ distinction in "bead, bid," for example, had a greater effect on intelligibility than did other vowel or consonant errors. For consonants, voicing errors (e.g., "pin, bin") reduced intelligibility more than did other types of error.

Assumption 2: Learners' Speech Errors Are Specific to Target and Native Languages

Some of the ways in which the native language (L1) interferes with phonological learning in the target language (L2) are fairly obvious and might even be predicted from a comparison of the two phonologies. The difficulty Chinese speakers have with English word-final consonant clusters can reasonably be attributed to the fact that English has a lot of them and most varieties of Chinese have very few (Kenworthy, 1987; Flege & Wang, 1989; Anderson, 1983). Likewise, an L1 phonological rule such as the Spanish rule that realizes intervocalic stops as fricatives ("lado") may be applied inappropriately, yielding pronunciations of, for example, English "ladder" as "lather" (Flege & Davidian, 1984).

It is not so obvious that phonetic similarities between two languages can cause learning difficulties. Flege (1987) showed that American English learners of French were more accurate in terms of formant frequency values in their productions of the French high front rounded vowel /y/ (tu), which does not occur in English, than they were in their productions of French /u/ (tous), which has a close, but not identical counterpart in English. He hypothesizes that native English speakers fail to learn to produce the phone that is close in formant space to an English phone due to "equivalence classification." That is, the /u/ of English is perceptually close enough to French /u/ that learners use the English phone rather than learn a new sound. The notorious difficulty Japanese learners of English have with the /r/-/l/ distinction may also be due to the existence of similar sounds in Japanese. In this case the two sounds are allophonic variants of a single phoneme in Japanese, rather than separate phonemes, as they are in English (Miawaki, et al., 1975).

It is also not so obvious that the acoustic-phonetic details of encoding the "same" phonological contrasts can vary greatly from language to language. The most compelling examples of these kinds of differences are those in which phonological category boundaries occur at different points on the same acoustic continuum. The voicing contrast in syllable-initial stops in Spanish and English provides an example of this. In both languages the distinction between /p,t,k/ and, respectively, /b,d,g/ is largely cued by differences in voice onset time (VOT) relative to the release of the stop closure (Lisker & Abramson, 1964). But English has "long lag" voiceless and short lag or short lead voiced stops, while Spanish has short lag voiceless and long lead voiced stops in this position. An English-accented Spanish /b/ may well be heard as /p/ by native Spanish listeners just as a Spanish-accented English /p/ can be confused with /b/ by native English listeners (Williams, 1979). Rochet (1995) describes a similar case for a vowel category boundary in the F1 x F2 speech formant space. Fine-grained articulatory and perceptual patterns such as VOT tend to be transferred from the native to the second language (Port & Mitleb, 1983) and since, for adults, they involve well established motor and perceptual habits, they can be difficult to modify. The physiological bases for these difficulties in terms of the development and structure of the human auditory system are explained by Gómez et al. in Section I (this volume).

Assumption 3: Second Language Learners Have Both a Perception and a Production Deficit in the Target Language

The relation of speech production ability to speech perception ability in second language learning is currently not very well understood. Some investigations into the relationship have produced results that are perhaps counterintuitive.

Catford and Pisoni (1970) found that subjects trained to produce a novel speech sound learned to perceive that sound more accurately than subjects who were given only speech perception training on the same sound. Goto (1971) and Sheldon and Strange (1982) showed that some Japanese learners of English were better at producing the English /r/-/l/ contrast than they were at perceiving it. Rochet (1995) cites a study showing that perception training could actually improve speech production skills (see also Bradlow, Akahane-Yamada, Pisoni, & Tohkura, 1996). Native Mandarin Chinese-speaking subjects in this experiment were trained to modify their French VOT boundary for /b/ and /p/ toward native French values using synthetic speech stimuli in a 'bu/pu' continuum. This perception training by itself was shown to improve the subjects' correct productions of words containing these phonemes as measured by native French listener's classification of the words in pre- and post-training testing. Subjects' perception of the French category boundary was also improved, and this result generalized to /b/ and /p/ occurring before different untrained vowels as well as to different voiced/voiceless consonant pairs /g,k/ and /d,t/ occurring before /u/. Importantly, this training did not generalize to different word positions for these phonemes. This fact emphasizes the need to train L2 learners with words containing target contrasts in as many word positions as possible (cf. Lively, Logan, & Pisoni, 1993).

Studies of L2 speech perception training provide results that have led us to include perception training as an essential component of the HearSay system. An important finding relevant to curriculum design is that perception training with natural speech tokens of contrasting phonemes in several phonological environments spoken by multiple talkers is more effective than single-environment or single-talker training (Logan, Lively & Pisoni, 1991). Subjects in this study showed not only improved identification (and lowered response latencies) for the words actually trained, but also generalization of the training to new words containing these sounds spoken by new talkers. Subjects trained on a single talker (Lively, Logan, & Pisoni, 1993) showed no such generalization. It has also been demonstrated that training of this sort can result in changes in adults' L2 perception that persist over time (Lively, Pisoni, Yamada, Tohkura, & Yamada, 1994). Subjects trained using this paradigm who were retested after three months showed that they had retained their improved ability to correctly identify words containing target sounds.

Assumption 4: Training Based on Minimally Contrasting Word Pairs Can Improve Second Language Speech Intelligibility

We believe that the link between segmental errors in isolated words and the intelligibility of sentences or longer utterances, discussed above, validates the use of minimal contrast drill in pronunciation training. Minimally contrasting words are frequently used in speech production training for hearing-impaired and misarticulating children (Kewley-Port et al., 1991). For example, one of the game-like formats used in HearSay for minimal pair speech drill is shown in Figure 7.1 (from Dalby & Kewley-Port, 1999). Minimal pairs have additionally been shown to be effective in speech perception training (Logan et al., 1991).

Minimally contrasting words are also used by second language teachers (Kenworthy, 1987). Rogers, Dalby, and DeVane (1994) showed that computer-based pronunciation training with minimal pairs can be effective for second language learners. The latter study used the ISTRA speech recognizer for training selected English vowel and consonant contrasts. Pre- and post-training intelligibility ratings by a jury of native listeners showed that productions of English vowels (e.g., the /i/ vs. /I/ contrast) and consonants

Figure 7.1 Screen for a speech drill game in the HearSay speech training system. The learner's score for pronouncing the word "rum" is shown as the number of bowling pins knocked down (from Dalby & Kewley-Port, 1999).

(e.g., /th/ vs. /s/) by two Mandarin speakers improved in intelligibility after training, and this improvement generalized to untrained words that contained these contrasts. More recently, this result was extended in a larger study with five Mandarin-speaking subjects (Burleson, 2007). These studies appear to be among only a few that have shown experimentally that second language speech production skills can improve through training that uses speech recognition technology.

Assumption 5: Design and Development Methods for the HearSay Intelligibility Training Curriculum

This section describes the methods used for developing the HearSay pronunciation-training module for Mandarin speakers learning English. The same procedures have been followed in the development of a Spanish/English, a Japanese/English, and an English/Spanish version. There are four primary activities in this development. First, a target-language word list is created containing as inclusive an inventory of syllable onsets, nuclei, and codas as is practical. In the second step, nonnative speakers are asked to read the word list. Broad phonetic transcriptions are made from recordings of these readings, and errors that might cause phonological confusions for native listeners are collated. Next, a set of minimal pairs for each error is constructed and ranked by an estimate of the importance of the error to overall intelligibility. These minimal pairs are incorporated into a set of game-like drills that can be run in either speech perception or speech production mode. A fourth activity is evaluation of the performance of the speech recognizer on the challenging minimal pairs discrimination task. These development steps are detailed in the following sections.

Step 1: Segmental Inventory Test

A list is created of L2 words that inventory target sounds. American English has 67 possible syllable-initial consonant clusters ("cheat"), about 173 possible syllable-final clusters ("beach"), and very many more possible word-medial clusters ("teacher"). We have developed a word list of about 360 words containing all the initial and final clusters of the language. It is impractical to include all the medial clusters in the list. We have rationalized this necessary economy by noting that all medial clusters are composed of a possible syllable final cluster followed by one of the possible syllable initial clusters. A similar list for Spanish contains about 230 words.

Step 2: Error Analysis

Digital audio recordings are collected of native L1 speakers reading the target L2 segmental inventory test, with speakers selected to represent different levels of ability. A consensus method of transcription by several phoneticians assures that the transcriptions are reliable. To help ensure that the errors are representative of the group of speakers, errors that occur only once are eliminated. The error analysis of Mandarin Chinese-accented English yielded an inventory of 45 consonantal and 13 vocalic errors.

Step 3: Development of the Pronunciation Training Sequence

Following the error analysis, lists of minimal pairs of words containing the segmental contrasts of the analysis are created. To speed this process, software has been developed that searches machine-readable dictionaries that include phonemic transcriptions. Pairs containing extremely infrequent words are eliminated by hand. Next, the importance of each error is estimated. This estimate is based on the frequency of the phonemes in the error pair and the relative number of minimal pairs for that pair in the lexicon. Contrast word pairs are included in the curriculum in numbers that are roughly proportional to the estimate of the contrast's importance. The pairs are read by four (or more) native speakers to provide the models used in perception training and as auditory prompts in production training. This speech corpus is also used for evaluating the speech recognizer used in the system.

The minimal pairs training drills are incorporated into a multimedia system that evaluates and records performance on both of these tasks continuously. In addition to keeping current scores for each task and all contrasts in the curriculum, the system also keeps a global score that is a weighted sum of the scores by task. By maintaining this global training score, the system has the capacity to adapt automatically to differential learning difficulty for the various contrasts. This unique aspect of HearSay training provides a mechanism derived from linguistic principles for steering the student efficiently through the curriculum. Users may choose which contrast and which types of drills they wish to practice, but their overall intelligibility profile will improve more if they show improvement on the phonetic contrasts that are more highly valued by the global training score.

Step 4: Recognizer Evaluation

The speech recognizer is evaluated on ability to discriminate minimal pairs. Recognizer evaluation for the HearSay system has been conducted following procedures similar to those described above for the ISTRA system. A database of digitized speech has been collected from 14 male and 14 female speakers of American English. These speakers pronounced the contrast drill word pairs derived from the error analysis of Mandarin-accented English. Baseline speaker-independent recognition rates on a subset of these data for a template-based recognizer and an HMM recognizer show a similar pattern of relative performance. While the overall recognition accuracy for the HMM recognizer is highest, its scores are lower than the template recognizer for vowel and nasal contrasts. To date, neither recognizer has produced scores with acceptably high correlations with human judgments of speech quality (>.80) when tested in speaker-independent mode. While some investigators report deriving valid intelligibility rating measures from a speaker-independent recognition technology (Neumeyer, Franco, Digalakis, & Weintraub, 2000), HearSay has been implemented using the HMM recognizer. Since pronunciation training is conducted using the minimal pairs target/error paradigm derived from L1-specific error analyses, we can assume that the correct/incorrect feedback of the system is valid.

YOU-SAID-IT: EMPLOYING ASR TO IMPROVE SPEECH OF THE DEVELOPMENTALLY DISABLED

Communication disorders, more than any other single characteristic, typify persons with mental retardation and other developmental disabilities. Delayed or deviant development of language and communication are "implicit in our definitions of mental retardation and autism" (Warren & Abbeduto, 1992, p. 125). Despite progress in public school special education programs in recent years, it is clear that many people with developmental disabilities enter adult life poorly prepared to cope with the demands of independent living. Moreover, despite intensive research aimed at improving communication skills training conducted over the last two decades or so (Warren & Reichle, 1992), it is also clear that many young adults leave school with communication deficits. These communication deficits often include articulation errors (Rosenberg & Abbeduto, 1992) as well as morpho-syntactic errors.

You-Said-It is a multimedia system designed to provide a training environment that can address both articulation and morpho-syntactic disorders. For articulation training, the system includes a version of ISTRA. The language training curriculum in the system is a series of animated scenarios, called simulations, which depict scenes in which oral communication skills can be practiced. These simulations are familiar to anyone who has studied a second language using the audio-lingual method of dialogues. The simulations are designed to be pragmatically useful situations such as a trip to the doctor's office or the bank, taking the bus to the recreation center, and so forth, in which oral communication is necessary. Each simulation has a set of drills that target specific points of English grammar. Feedback in the language training module is provided by a large-vocabulary, speaker-independent hidden Markov model recognizer. In our development system we have followed the HearSay feedback model by including the expected errors in the recognition vocabulary. Since morpho-syntactic errors can create a great deal of variability in the sentences that disordered talkers might actually say, this method is not as precise as the segment errors accounted for in HearSay. To provide data on which to base this method, we have conducted an extensive language sample analysis of the speech of 30 subjects drawn from our client population.

We conducted two studies to determine whether moderately mentally retarded adults could benefit from speech intelligibility training using the training system. In the first study, 3 adults diagnosed as having articulation disorders trained using ISTRA. In the second study, 5 adults diagnosed as having morpho-syntactic deficits were trained using a prototype of You-Said-It. Both studies were conducted under the supervision a speech-language pathologist at Stone Belt Center in Bloomington, Indiana, a provider of employment and habilitation services to adults with developmental disabilities.

Segmental Intelligibility Training

Procedure

Three volunteer adult males with articulation disorders, ages 19 (JV), 21 (JY), and 33 (BP), were selected from the Stone Belt Center consumer population for the study. Criteria for selection included classification as moderately mentally retarded, presence of an articulation disorder, availability for training several times a week, and what is referred to as *stimulability*. Two of the three subjects had mild high-frequency hearing loss.

The picture-prompted survey of isolated word articulation was administered from the Arizona Articulation Proficiency Scale (Fudala & Reynolds, 1986). Subjects' error inventories were compared to lists of functional, everyday vocabulary items selected for each client. Training targets for 2 of the subjects included word-initial consonant clusters /kl/ as in "clean, clock" (subjects JV, JY). The third subject deleted unstressed syllables, pronouncing "computer" as "puter," and "envelope" as "enlope."

Three tokens of each of three training words and three tokens of each of three similar untrained words were tape-recorded in pre- and post-training conditions for each subject. Two subjects (JV and JY) participated in 24 training sessions of 45 minutes each. The third subject (BP) reached criterion after 17 sessions. Training for all subjects was conducted on the ISTRA system.

Pre- and post-training recordings of the subjects' productions of their three training and three generalization words were digitized, randomized, and presented binaurally over headphones to listeners. Seven students enrolled in graduate speech and hearing sciences class at Indiana University served as listeners. All had completed at least one semester of training in transcribing disordered speech. Listeners were asked to rate the intelligibility of the words on a 6-point scale from unintelligible to completely intelligible. Raters judged each of 108 tokens five times except for two listeners who completed only four repetitions of the word list. None of the listeners was familiar with the speech of any of the talkers.

Intrarater reliability was estimated by calculating the mean of four correlation coefficients for each rater (three for the two raters with only four repetitions). In this calculation the first and second, second and third, third and fourth, and fourth and fifth ratings of the 108 tokens were paired, and the mean of the four (or three) correlation coefficients was computed. These means for the seven listeners are as follows: .84, .75, .83, .75, .79, .73, .66. Interrater reliability was estimated by calculating the correlation coefficients for the mean token-by-token rating of each listener paired with the means for all other raters combined. These coefficients are as follows: .78, .73, .81, .79, .75, .78, .59. With the exception of Listener 7, all listeners performed the task quite consistently. All raters were included in the analysis of results.

Results

Mean listener ratings for the pretraining tokens were paired with mean ratings for the posttraining tokens of the adult trainees. Two-sample *t*-tests were performed on these pairings. As seen in Table 7.1, all three subjects showed significant improvement in their posttraining productions for the trained words ($p < .00001$), while two subjects also showed significant improvement in the generalization words ($p < .0001$). In general, these results are encouraging. We might infer that Subject BP should not have been released from training early.

Sentence Intelligibility Training

Procedure

The lesson employed in the sentence intelligibility study of You-Said-It is a multimedia training scenario that includes a "mentor," a model talker, and a silent robot character named Bumper. Clients are prompted by the mentor to instruct Bumper to perform an action. If the client's response is recognized as correct by the speech recognizer, Bumper performs the action.

Table 7.1 Mean Listener Ratings for Pronunciations of Trained and Untrained Words by Subjects JY, JV, and BP (Note: Rating scale is 0–5, with 5 being fully intelligible; means are in bold, followed by standard deviations.)

Ss	JY		JV		BP	
	Trained	*Untrained*	*Trained*	*Untrained*	*Trained*	*Untrained*
Pre	**2.8**, 1.1	**2.2**, 1.1	**2.7**, 1.1	**2.0**, 1.3	**3.2**, 1.1	**3.5**, 0.9
Post	**4.3**, 1.0	**2.6**, 1.4	**4.1**, 0.9	**3.1**, 1.1	**4.3**, 0.7	**3.4**, 0.8
p	.0000	.0001	.0000	.0000	.0000	.12

If not, the mentor prompts the client to try again. The model talker is a digitized waveform of a normal talker saying the expected response to the mentor's prompt. The model can be turned off as the client's skills improve. For example, the You-Said-It lesson reported here involves putting away groceries in the kitchen. It teaches clients to ask WH-questions such as "Where does the ice cream go?" and to make polite requests as in "Please put it in the freezer." The recognizer vocabulary that is active for this frame of the scenario also includes strings such as "Please put it in freezer," "Put in freezer," "Put freezer," etc. These error strings have a subjective score attached to them, with the first being rated better than the last. Neumeyer et al. (2000) have published methods for deriving numerical scores for phrases and sentences from HMM recognizers; these methods may offer an improvement to our current scoring method.

Five volunteers at Stone Belt Center participated in training whole utterances using the simulation software described above. Four of the subjects were males, one female. Subjects were in their late-teens to mid-20s. Four subjects had moderate mental retardation, while one subject (RM) had mild retardation. Two subjects had mild high-frequency hearing loss. Selection criteria were similar to those described for the articulation training study above, except that subjects had language rather than speech impairment. This was determined through administration of the Oral and Written Language Scales test (Carrow-Woolfolk, 1995). All 5 subjects had expressive language scores in the lower 0.1 percentile on this test. An age-equivalency measure based on these scores ranged from 3 years, 5 months to 5 years, 6 months.

Subjects received varying amounts of training on the simulation, with 30-minute sessions held two to three times a week over an 8-week period. The average total training time was about 5 hours; the range was 3 hours to 6 hours. Pre- and post-training tokens of 10 client-response sentences of the lesson were tape recorded, digitized, and randomized for playback to listeners for rating. These utterances were elicited using still pictures extracted from the simulation.

Six listeners, all linguistics students at Indiana University, rated the utterances of lesson one on a 7-point scale. A rating of 1 was labeled "completely unintelligible" and 7 was labeled "completely intelligible." None of the listeners was familiar with the training subject's speech. Each listener judged each sentence from each talker once. Half the listeners heard the sentences in the original randomization and half in reverse order. Interrater reliability was estimated following the procedures of the articulation test described above. The correlation coefficients for the six raters were .78, .80, .72, .79, .83, .74. Ratings for all six listeners are included in the analysis of results.

Results

The ratings were z-transformed to normalize variance between subjects. Pooled across the five talkers, the ratings showed a significant improvement in intelligibility in the posttraining sample (t = 9.35, df = 579, p < .01). Results of paired-sample t-tests on untransformed ratings for individual talkers are shown in Table 7.2.

The data show that 4 of the 5 subjects were rated higher in intelligibility from pre- to post-test conditions. While the effects for DH and JV were not significant, these subjects show a trend toward improvement. Only subject JY showed no improvement at all.

In summary, two separate clinical evaluations suggest that speech and language skills improve with computer-based training. Although future studies must evaluate the generalization and maintenance of these skills in the context of daily life, it appears that adults with moderate mental retardation can improve their speech communication skills through supervised practice using the ASR-based systems described here.

CONCLUSIONS

We believe that the speech intelligibility training methods described here are most effective at the segment (phone) and word level of analysis. For intelligibility problems that are largely phonological, the kinds of training that our ASR-based systems offer appear to be both appropriate and adequate.

However, there are aspects of language training that are currently not fully addressed in any computer-based system that we know of. Many, perhaps most, speech disorders involve not only segmental errors but also suprasegmental errors (i.e., involving prosodic features like intonation and rhythm). This is true of many of our clients with developmental disabilities and also of those with severe hearing impairments. It is also certainly true that second language learners need training in aspects of speech and language production beyond those involved in the production and perception of phonological segments. We view the methods implemented in You-Said-It for evaluating morpho-syntactic errors as more rudimentary than those that address segmentals.

Table 7.2 Mean Listener Ratings for Pronunciations of Trained and Untrained Words by Subjects DH, JV, JY, RM, and TB (Note: Rating scale is 0–7, with 7 being fully intelligible; means are in bold, followed by standard deviations.)

Ss	DH	JV	JY	RM	TB
Pre	**4.0**, 2.0	**3.2**, 1.7	**2.1**, 1.4	**4.3**, 1.6	**2.1**, 1.3
Post	**4.7**, 1.7	**3.8**, 1.8	**1.8**, 1.0	**6.0**, 1.2	**3.6**, 1.5
p	.11	.10	.15	.0000	.0000

Rather than apologizing for this, however, we ask the reader to consider the complexity of a human judgment of the intelligibility of sentences. Errors that shape this judgment may occur at the level of phonetic implementation, phonological implementation, and the implementation of both word- and sentence-level prosodics. Each of these levels affects the spectral and the temporal properties of speech, and it is almost certain that deviations from native norms at each level influence intelligibility. We are a long way from having machines that can not only provide an analysis of all these potential deviations but also advise clients on what to do to correct them.

ACKNOWLEDGMENTS

This work was supported by National Institutes of Health–National Institute on Deafness and other Communication Disorders SBIR grants DC00893 and DC02213, NIH–National Institute of Child Health and Human Development SBIR grant 35425 and Army Research Institute contract DASW01-96-C-044 to Communication Disorders Technology, Bloomington, Indiana. We thank Doreen Devitt, CCC–SLP for conducting the training of the Stone Belt Center consumers, and Daren Swango and Keiichi Tajima for their help with the analysis of the data in that study. We would also like to acknowledge the contributions of William Mills and Roy Sillings to the development of the CDT speech training systems.

REFERENCES

Anderson, J. I. (1983). The difficulties of English syllable structure for Chinese ESL learners. *Language Learning and Communication, 2*(1), 53–61.

Anderson, S., & Kewley-Port, D. (1995). Evaluation of speech recognizers for speech training applications. *IEEE Proceedings on Speech and Audio Processing, 3*(4), 229–241.

Bradlow, A., Akahane-Yamada, R., Pisoni, D. B., & Tohkura, Y. (1996). Three converging tests of improvement in speech production after perceptual identification training on a nonnative phonetic contrast. *Journal of the Acoustical Society of America, 100*(4), Pt. 2, 2725(A).

Brodkey, D. (1972). Dictation as a measure of mutual intelligibility: A pilot study. *Language Learning, 22*(2), 203–217.

Burleson, D. F. (2007). *Training segmental productions for second language intelligibility.* Unpublished Ph. D. dissertation, Indiana University Department of Linguistics.

Carrow-Woolfolk, E. (1995). *Oral and written language scales.* Circle Pines, MN: American Guidance Service.

Catford, J. C., & Pisoni, D. B. (1970). Auditory versus articulatory training in exotic sounds. *The Modern Language Journal, 54,* 477–481.

Dalby, J., Kewley-Port, D., & Sillings, R. (1998). Language-specific pronunciation training using the HearSay system. *Proceedings of the European Speech Communication Association conference on Speech Technology in Language Learning,* 25–28.

Dalby, J., & Kewley-Port D. (1999). Explicit pronunciation training using automatic speech recognition technology. In M. Holland (Ed.), Tutors that Listen: Speech Recognition for Language Learning, *Special Issue of the Journal of the Computer Assisted Language Learning Consortium, 16*(5), 425–445.

Flege, J. E. (1987). The production of "new" and "similar" phones in a foreign language: Evidence for the effect of equivalence classification. *Journal of Phonetics, 15,* 47–65.

Flege, J. E., & Davidian, R. D. (1984). Transfer and developmental processes in adult foreign language speech production. *Applied Psycholinguistics, 5,* 323–347.

Flege, J. E., & Wang, C. (1989). Native-language phonotactic constraints affect how well Chinese subjects perceive the word-final /t/-/d/ contrast. *Journal of Phonetics, 17,* 299–315.

Fudala, J. B., & Reynolds, W. M. (1986). *Arizona Articulation Proficiency Scale* (2nd ed.). Los Angeles: Western Psychological Services.

Gass, S., & Veronis, M. (1984). The effect of familiarity on the comprehensibility of nonnative speech. *Language Learning, 34,* 65–90.

Goto, H. (1971). Auditory perception by normal Japanese adults of the sounds "l" and "r". *Neuropsychologia, 9,* 317–323.

Kenworthy, J. (1987). *Teaching English Pronunciation.* New York: Longman

Kewley-Port, D., Watson, C. S., Elbert, M., Maki, D., & Reed, D. (1991). The Indiana Speech Training Aid (ISTRA) II: Training curriculum and selected case studies. *Clinical Linguistics and Phonetics, 5*(1), 13–38.

Lisker, L., & Abramson, A. (1964). A cross-language study of voicing in initial stops: Acoustical measurements. *Word, 20,* 384–422.

Lively, S. E., Logan, J. S., & Pisoni, D. B. (1993). Training Japanese listeners to identify English /r/ and /l/ II: The role of phonetic environment and talker variability in learning new perceptual categories. *Journal of the Acoustical Society of America, 94,* 1242–1255.

Lively, S. E., Pisoni, D. B., Yamada, R. A., Tohkura, Y., & Yamada, T. (1994). Training Japanese listeners to identify English /r/ and /l/ III: Long-term retention of new phonetic categories. *Journal of the Acoustical Society of America, 96,* 2076–2087.

Logan, J. S., Lively, S. E., & Pisoni, D. B. (1991). Training Japanese listeners to identify English /r/ and /l/: A first report. *Journal of the Acoustical Society of America, 89,* 874–886.

Marslen-Wilson, W. D. (1985). Aspects of human speech understanding. In F. Fallside & W. A. Woods (Eds.), *Computer speech processing.* Englewood Cliffs, NJ: Prentice Hall.

Morton, J. (1979). Word recognition structure and process. In J. Morton & J. Marshall (Eds.), *Structure and process.* Cambridge, MA: MIT Press.

Miawaki, K., Strange, W., Verbrugge, R., Liberman, A., Jenkins, J., & Fujimura, O. (1975). An effect of linguistic experience: The discrimination of [r] and [l] by native speakers of Japanese and English. *Perception and Psychophysics, 18*(5), 331–340.

Neumeyer, L., Franco, H., Digalakis, V., & Weintraub, M. (2000). Automatic scoring of pronunciation quality. *Speech Communication, 30,* 83–93.

Pisoni, D. B., Nusbaum, H., & Greene, B. (1985). Perception of synthetic speech generation by rule. *Proceedings of the IEEE, 73,* 1665–1676.

Port, R., & Mitleb. F. (1983). Segmental features and implementation in acquisition of English by Arabic speakers. *Journal of Phonetics, 11,* 219–229.

Rochet, B. L. (1995). Perception and production of second-language speech sounds by adults. In W. Strange (Ed.), *Speech perception and linguistic experience.* Timonium, MD: York Press.

Rogers, C. L. (1997). *Segmental intelligibility assessment for Chinese-accented English.* Unpublished Ph.D. dissertation, Indiana University Department of Linguistics.

Rogers, C. L., & Dalby, J. M. (1996). Prediction of foreign-accented speech intelligibility from segmental contrast measures. *Journal of the Acoustical Society of America, 100*(4), Pt. 2, 2725(A).

Rogers, C. L., Dalby, J. M., & DeVane, G. (1994). Intelligibility training for foreign-accented speech: A preliminary study. *Journal of the Acoustical Society of America, 96*(5), Pt. 2, 3348(A).

Rosenberg, S., & Abbeduto, L., (1992). Linguistic communication in persons with mental retardation. In S. Warren & J. Richle (Eds.), *Causes and effects in communication and language intervention.* Baltimore, MD: Paul H. Brooks.

Sheldon, A., & Strange, W. (1982). The acquisition of /r/ and /l/ by Japanese Learners of English: Evidence that speech production can precede speech perception. *Applied Psycholinguistics, 3,* 243–261.

Strange, W. (1995). Cross-language studies of speech perception a historical review. In W. Strange (Ed.), *Speech perception and linguistic experience.* Timonium, MD: York Press.

Tajima, K., Port R., & Dalby, J. (1997). Effects of temporal correction on intelligibility of foreign-accented English. *Journal of Phonetics, 25,* 1–24.

Warren, S., & Abbeduto, L. (1992). The relation of communication and language development to mental retardation. *American Journal on Mental Retardation, 97*(2), 125–130.

Warren, S., & Richle, J., (Eds.). (1992) *Causes and effects in communication and language intervention.* Baltimore, MD: Paul H. Brooks.

Watson, C. S., Reed, D., Kewley-Port, D., & Maki, D. (1989). The Indiana Speech Training Aid (ISTRA) I: Comparisons between human and computer-based evaluation of speech quality. *Journal of Speech and Hearing Research, 32,* 245–251.

Weismer, G., & Martin, R. (1992). Acoustic and perceptual approaches to the study of intelligibility. In R. D. Kent (Ed.), *Intelligibility in speech disorders: Theory, measurement and management.* Amsterdam: J. Benjamins.

Williams, L. (1979). The modification of speech perception and production in second-language learning. *Perception and Psychophysics, 26*(2), 95–104.

8 Logic and Validation of a Fully Automatic Spoken English Test

Jared Bernstein and Jian Cheng

INTRODUCTION

Skillful performance in a human language often involves a composite of elementary skills, such that language skills, cognitive skills, and social skills can be conflated in the judgment of a human listener. A recent, computer-based method (Versant for English) provides an estimate of spoken language skills that is relatively independent of the speaker's other social and cognitive skills. The Versant system has been implemented using interactive voice response to administer a standardized spoken English test that measures speaking and listening during a 12-minute telephone call. The system calculates scores on five performance subscales from a set of more basic measures that are produced by automatic speech recognition of examinee responses. Item response theory is used to analyze and scale aspects of examinee performance. The scores are also related to performance rubrics used in criterion-based human scoring of similar responses. This chapter outlines the test construct and describes the scaling methods and validation process with reference to experimental procedures used in developing the test.

BACKGROUND

Computational and applied linguists have developed various methods for evaluating the performance of different elements and agents in speech communication. These elements include the spoken message source, the transmission medium or system, and the spoken message receiver. The spoken message source and receiver are most often human beings, but they can be speech synthesizers or speech recognizers. The testing methods used to evaluate message sources and message receivers differ by tradition (e.g., applied linguistics or spoken language engineering) and depend also on the population being tested (e.g., automatic systems, or second language learners, or deaf children).

This chapter presents an automatic method for evaluating the spoken language skills of second language learners. In particular, we describe a proficiency test called Versant for English, developed by Ordinate Corporation. This test, originally called the PhonePass test or the SET–10, measures a person's facility in spoken English.

A proficiency test, as such, assumes a domain of knowledge or skill that is independent of any particular instructional curriculum but that measures a construct. The construct of a test is a hypothesis about the attribute (or trait) that the test is designed to measure, for example, "mechanical aptitude" or "language proficiency." The construct of a test is important because it indicates what the test scores should mean; that is, what inference(s) can be drawn from the test scores. The validation of a test is the compilation of evidence that the test is reliable and that the scores do, in fact, reflect the intended construct and do not reflect construct-irrelevant characteristics of the candidates or of the test itself.

Spoken Language Proficiency Tests

Tests of reading, grammar, or vocabulary can be administered quite efficiently. However, traditional speaking/listening tests have been administered by skilled examiners who usually interact with the test-takers one on one, or, at best, listen to tapes one by one. If the assessment of speaking/listening can be automated or even partially automated, then these skills can be tested more often and more reliably across time and place. The end result will be a more accurate and timely evaluation of examinees.

Over the past several decades, human performance in spoken language has traditionally been measured in an oral proficiency interview (OPI) that is judged by the interviewer and, often, by a second human rater. Starting in the 1960s, efforts began to define a construct that would satisfactorily represent general proficiency with the spoken forms of language. Wilds (1975) and Sollenberger (1978) describe the development and use of oral proficiency interviews (OPIs), which were designed by the U.S. Government to measure an examinee's production and comprehension of spoken language during participation in a structured interview with trained interlocutor/raters. The oral proficiency construct was analyzed into a set of level descriptors within each of five subskill areas: comprehension, fluency, vocabulary, grammar, and pronunciation. The level descriptions used in the OPI scale are presented by Clifford and Granoien in this volume. In the 1980s and 1990s, as those authors point out, this general method of interview and level descriptions was adapted and refined for use by other bodies, including the American Council on the Teaching of Foreign Languages (ACTFL) and the Council of Europe. The oral proficiency interview has also been taken as an important validating criterion measure in the development of "indirect" standardized tests that intend to encompass an oral component, for example the Test of English as a Foreign Language (TOEFL), TSE, and TOEIC tests from the Educational Testing Service. Thus, all these tests rely, at least partly or indirectly, on the OPI oral proficiency construct.

Since the mid-1980s, several experiments have shown that the pronunciation quality of spoken materials can be estimated from direct acoustic measurement of select phenomena in recorded speech samples. Early studies by Molholt and Pressler (1986), by Major (1986), and by Levitt (1991) supported the idea that particular acoustic events in nonnative speech could be used to order sets of speech samples by pronunciation. Bernstein, Cohen, Murveit, Rtischev, and Weintraub (1990) demonstrated that some aspects of pronunciation can be scored reliably by completely automatic methods (see also Neumeyer, Franco, Weintraub, & Price, 1996). These measures of pronunciation quality have some further predictive power, because, in a population of nonnatives, the pronunciation of a sample of speakers is a good predictor of overall oral proficiency (Bejar, 1985). The development of Versant for English is an attempt to go beyond this convenient, predictive relation of pronunciation to proficiency and attempt to define automatic procedures that offer a more convincing measurement of the several performance elements that comprise speaking skill (as discussed by Bernstein, De Jong, Pisoni, & Townshend, 2000).

The remainder of the paper describes an automatically scored 10-minute spoken language test that is delivered by the Ordinate's testing system. First, the target construct of the 12-minute Spoken English Test (Versant for English) is described. Next, the test structure is described in relation to an underlying psycholinguistic theory of speaking and listening. Finally, evidence is presented to establish the valid use of this test as a measure of speaking and listening.

The Facility Construct

Facility in Spoken English

Versant for English was designed to measure "facility in spoken English." We define facility in spoken English to be the ability to understand spoken language and respond intelligibly at a conversational pace on everyday topics. Assuming normal intelligence and basic social skills, this facility should be closely related to successful participation in native-paced discussions—that is, the ability to track what's being said, extract meaning in real time, and then formulate and produce relevant responses at a native conversational pace. The Versant test measures both listening and speaking skills, emphasizing the candidate's facility (ease, accuracy, fluency, latency) in responding to material constructed from common conversational vocabulary. The test focuses on core linguistic structures and basic psycholinguistic processes.

In Contrast to OPI Oral Proficiency

The Versant construct "facility in spoken English" does not extend to social skills, higher cognitive function, or world knowledge. Nor is the Versant for

English test intended to differentiate between examinees' performance on elements that characterize the most advanced range of communicative competence, such as persuasiveness, discourse coherence, or facility with subtle inference and social or cultural nuances. Thus, Versant for English is not a direct test of "oral proficiency" as measured by an oral proficiency interview (OPI), but it shares some key construct elements with such interview tests and will account for much of the true variance measured by oral proficiency interviews. Because the test measures basic linguistic skills, with emphasis on ease and immediacy of comprehension and production, scores should be appropriate in predicting how fully a candidate will be able to participate in a discussion or other interaction among high-proficiency speakers.

Processing Capacity Hypothesis

If a test measures only spoken language facility, distinct from other social and cognitive abilities, why should it also be a strong predictor of oral proficiency scores that are designed explicitly to include these other abilities (see the section, "Concurrent Validity with Tests of Related Constructs")? An analogy may be found in the literature on comprehension of synthetic speech. Bernstein and Pisoni (1980) measured students' comprehension of paragraphic material when the paragraphs were read aloud and the students were asked to answer multiple choice questions on the content of the paragraph. The paragraphs were read aloud in two conditions—either by a human talker or by a speech synthesizer. Results suggested that there was no significant decrement in comprehension when students listened to synthetic speech relative to natural human speech. In a later experiment Luce, Feustel, and Pisoni (1983) ran a parallel study but required students to perform a concurrent memory-load task involving visually presented digits that students were asked to recall later. Results from the second study showed a large and significant decrement in comprehension when students listened to synthetic speech in comparison to natural human speech. The authors hypothesized a processing capacity limit to explain the difference in the two experimental results. With no concurrent task, the listeners used as much cognitive capacity as was needed to comprehend the speech samples, and they could extract the words and meanings in the paragraphs adequately in either the human-read or synthesized rendition. However, with the concurrent digit memory task, the listeners still had enough capacity to understand the human speech but did not have the extra capacity required to decode the synthetic speech. Thus, their comprehension of the synthetic speech suffered.

We hypothesize a similar processing capacity limit relevant to speaking. When a person has limited English skills, the cognitive resources that might be spent on planning a discourse or attending to subtle aspects of the social situation are instead used to find words and expressions that will convey the basic information to be communicated. As a person's command of a language becomes more complete and automatic, more cognitive capacity will be available to apply to the construction of complex argument and/or to the expression of social nuance.

Similarly, in listening, if a person can immediately and completely understand every word and every sentence spoken, then that person will have time to consider the rhetorical tone and the intellectual and social setting of the material. When a person with limited proficiency in a language listens to a connected discourse (even on a familiar topic), that person spends much more time in reconstructing what has been said; thus, there is less time to consider the finer points of the message. Thus, in both listening and speaking, if a person's control of the language is not automatic and immediate, there will likely be a corresponding decrement in the person's ability to use the language for a full range of communication tasks. This hypothesis is consistent with the findings of Verhoeven (1993) that discourse analysis and rhetorical skills will transfer from one language to another. For this reason, over a range of language proficiencies from beginner to advanced intermediate levels, automaticity in reception and production of basic linguistic forms is a key construct.

VERSANT FOR ENGLISH TEST STRUCTURE

General Structure

The Versant for English test is an examination of speaking and listening in English that is administered over the telephone by a computer system. Candidates' spoken responses are digitized and judged by specially modified, automated speech recognition (ASR) system. The test presents the examinee with a set of interactive tasks (e.g., to repeat a sentence or answer a question) that require English oral comprehension and production skills at conversational speeds. The test was designed to be particularly appropriate for screening or placement decisions when large numbers of students or candidates are tested and when the examinees are not conveniently available in a single location. The test is intended for use with adult nonnative speakers and incorporates fluency, pronunciation, and alacrity in speaking, reciting, and reading aloud; it also incorporates productive control of common vocabulary and of basic sentence structure in repeating sentences and answering short questions. The adult Versant test has been validated with populations as young as 15 years, and newer "junior" forms of the test have been developed for school children.

The Versant for English test, schematized in Table 8.1, has five parts: Readings, Repeats, Short-Answers, Sentence-Builds, and Open Questions. The first four parts (A–D) are scored automatically by machine, while the fifth part (E) collects three 20-second samples of the examinee's speech that can be reviewed by score users. General instructions are printed on the back of the test paper, and specific instructions for the five parts of the test are spoken by the examiner voice and printed verbatim on the face of the test sheet. Items are presented in various item voices that are distinct from the examiner voice that introduces the sections and provides instructions.

Versant tasks are designed to be simple and intuitive both for native speakers and for proficient nonnative speakers of English. Items cover a broad range of skill levels and skill profiles. They are designed to elicit examinee responses that can be analyzed by machine to produce measures that underlie facility with English, including fluency, listening, vocabulary, sentence mastery, and pronunciation.

Item Design Specifications

All item material was crafted specifically for the test, but it follows lexical and stylistic patterns found in actual conversation. The items themselves are recorded utterances that are presented in a specified task context. To ensure conversational content, all materials use vocabulary that is actually found in the spontaneous conversations of North Americans.

Vocabulary

Versant for English vocabulary is taken from a list of 7,727 word forms that occurred more than eight times in the Switchboard corpus, a 3-million word corpus of spontaneous American conversation available from the Linguistic Data Consortium (http://www.ldc.upenn.edu). Items may include any regular inflectional forms of the word; thus, if "folded" is on the word list, then "fold," "folder," "folding," and "folds" may be used.

Voices

The audio item prompts are spoken by a diverse sample of educated native speakers of North American English. These voices are clearly distinct from

Table 8.1 Versant for English Test Design

Part	Item Type	Target Skills	Item Count
A	Read aloud	Basic listening, reading fluency, pronunciation	8
B	Repeat sentence	Listening, vocabulary, syntax, fluency	16
C	Short answer	Vocabulary in syntactic context	24
D	Sentence build	Listening, vocabulary, syntax, fluency	10
E	Open response	Discourse, fluency, pronunciation, vocabulary	3

the examiner voice that announces the general instructions and the task-specific instructions.

Speaking Style

The Repeat and Short Question items are written in a nonlocalized but colloquial style, with contractions where appropriate. Thus, a prompt will be written out (for the item speaker to recite) in a form such as, "They're with the contractor who's late," rather than "They are with the contractor who is late." The people who speak the items are instructed to recite the material in a smooth and natural way; however, normally occurring variation is permitted in speaking rate and pronunciation clarity between speakers and items.

World Knowledge and Cognitive Load

Candidates should not need specialized world knowledge or familiarity with local cultural referents to answer items correctly. Versant for English items are intended to be within the realm of familiarity of both a typical North American adolescent and an educated adult who has never lived in an English-speaking country. The cognitive requirement to answer an item correctly should be limited to simple manipulations of time and number. Operationally, the cognitive limit is enforced by requiring that 90% of a norming group of native speakers can answer each item correctly within six seconds. Versant for English items should not require unusual insight or feats of memory.

PSYCHOLINGUISTIC PERFORMANCE THEORY

Psycholinguistic research has provided evidence for the operation of internal processes that are used when people speak and listen. Some of these processes have a parallel in linguistic theory while others do not. Adapting from the model proposed by W. J. M. Levelt in his book *Speaking* (1988), we can posit the psycholinguistic processing steps shown in Figure 8.1. A speaker encodes declarative, social and discourse information into spoken utterances, and the listener needs to decode this information with reference to a common set of language structures.

To understand what is said in a conversation, a listener needs to hear the utterance, extract lexical items, identify the phrase structures manifest in the words, decode the propositions carried by those phrases in context, and infer from them the implicit or explicit demands. When speaking, a person has to perform a similar set of operations but in approximately the reverse order. Note that the experimental evidence is equivocal about the exact order (or interleaving) of these operations and their modularity. However,

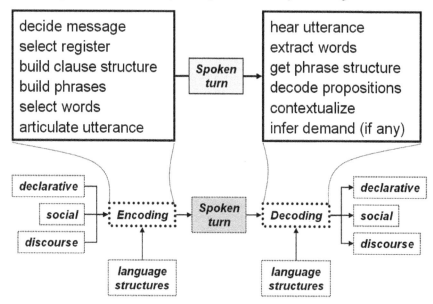

Figure 8.1 Internal processing flow in a model of speaking and listening.

all these operations must be accomplished in order to speak and understand speech. During a conversation, every active participant is performing either the understanding processes or the speaking processes or some of both.

If a test measures a candidate's facility in grasping spoken utterances in real time and producing relevant, intelligible responses at a native conversational pace, then it should be covering the basic components of psycholinguistic processing. Because the task items in the Versant for English test present decontextualized voice recordings to the candidate, each of which elicits a spoken response, each task item exercises the processing elements shown in Figure 8.1 except for register selection and the contextualization.

Versant for English is a direct test of facility with spoken English materials. Performance on the Versant tasks provides evidence of ability to participate in English conversation to the extent that those tasks require many of the same skills used in natural conversation. Following the theoretical framework of Levelt (1988), the corresponding skills include the following:

Generation/Speaking Elements	Sampled in Versant Items
1. decide message	all items
2. select register	—
3. build clause structure	long repeats, questions, sentence builds
4. build phrases	questions
5. select lexical items	repeats, questions, sentence builds
6. articulate utterance	all items

Listening/Understanding Elements	Sampled in Versant Items
1. hear utterance	all items
2. recognize lexical forms	repeats, questions, sentence builds
3. extract linguistic structure	long repeats, questions, sentence builds
4. decode propositions	questions
5. contextualize	—
6. infer demand	all items

It can be seen from this list that the Versant for English items exercise all the processing steps in listening and speaking except register selection and contextualization. The ability to select an appropriate register and to accommodate material for current context could be tapped in Versant for English, but these functions would require more elaborate items than are now included in the test.

SCORING

General Approach to Scoring

The Versant for English Score Report gives an overall score and four component subscores. The Overall score represents a measure of the examinee's facility in spoken English. It is calculated as a weighted average of the four subscores, as follows:

30%: *Sentence Mastery*—understand, recall, and produce phrases and clauses in complete sentences
20%: *Vocabulary*—understand words spoken in sentence context
30%: *Fluency*—rhythm, phrasing and timing, as evident in constructing, reading and repeating sentences
20%: *Pronunciation*—intelligible consonants, vowels, and lexical stress

These four subscores are relatively independent of each other, although some of them represent different measures derived from the same responses, as suggested above in the aligned list of process elements and item types. For example, the Pronunciation subscore is based on responses to the Reading, the Repeat, and sentence build sections.

The subscores are of two logical types, categorical and continuous. The first type, categorical, is based on the correctness of the content of the response. That is, the subscore reflects the number of found in the exact words spoken in the responses. This type of score shows how well the candidate understood the item and provided a complete and correct response to it. Scores of this type (Sentence Mastery and Vocabulary) comprise 50% of the Overall score. The second type of score, continuous, is based on the manner in which the response is spoken (pronunciation and fluency); these scores comprise the remaining 50% of the Overall score.

Criterion Scoring by Human Listeners

The continuous subscores (pronunciation and fluency) were developed with reference to human judgments of fluency and pronunciation. The rubrics for these criterion scores and the level descriptions of the skill components were developed by expert linguists who are active in teaching and evaluating spoken English.

Three master graders were asked to develop, apply, and refine the definitions of two scoring rubrics: fluency and pronunciation. The rubrics include definitions of these skills at six levels of performance as well as criteria for assigning a "no response" grade. The master graders scored a large, random sample of examinee responses and tutored other human graders in the logic and methods used in the criterion grading.

Human graders assigned over 129,000 scores to many thousands of responses from hundreds of different examinees. Item response analysis of the human grader scores indicates that human graders produce consistent fluency and pronunciation scores for the Versant materials, with single-rater reliabilities between .82 and .93 for the various subskills.

Machine Scoring

All Versant for English reported scores are calculated automatically using speech recognition technology. ASR in Versant for English is performed by an HMM-based speech recognizer built with Cambridge University Engineer Department's HTK toolkit (Young et al., 2004; http://htk.eng.cam.ac.uk/). The acoustic models, pronunciation dictionaries, and expected-response networks were developed at Ordinate Corporation using data collected during administration of Versant for English.

The acoustic models consist of tristate triphone models using seven Gaussian mixtures that specify the likelihood of 26-element Cepstral feature vectors. These models were trained on a mix of native and nonnative speakers of English using speech files collected during administration of Versant for English. The expected response networks were formed from observed responses to each item over a set of over 370 native speakers and 2,700 nonnative speakers of English. The speech data from one quarter of the speakers was reserved for testing only.

As outlined above, subscores are calculated by two main techniques: analysis of correct/incorrect responses and function approximation using statistical output from the speech recognizer.

First, each utterance is recognized and categorized. In the Repeat and Sentence Build section of Versant for English, the accuracy of the response can be determined by reference to the number of words inserted, deleted, or substituted by the candidate. These item-level scores are then combined to give a "Sentence Mastery" component measure. This combination is done using Item Response Theory (IRT) such that both the difficulty of the item and the expected recognition performance of the item contribute to its weight. For example, very difficult items will have a small effect on the measure of a low-level examinee but a larger effect on more proficient examinees. Similarly, items that are often misrecognized will have lower weight. Using the same method, a correct/incorrect decision for each item in Parts C (see Table 8.1) contributes to the "Vocabulary" component measure. These correct/incorrect decisions are based partly on observed responses to the item by native and nonnative speakers.

In the Reading, Repeat, and Sentence Build parts of the test, the responses consist of a complete phrase or sentence. Thus, in addition to the accuracy of the response, we can also make use of the alignment and other properties of the speech signal to further judge the speaker's ability. Signal analysis routines perform a set of acoustic base measures on the linguistic units (segments, syllables, and words) and return these base measures.

Different base measures are combined in different ways into the two continuous measures—Pronunciation and Fluency. The combination is achieved by a parametric function optimized against judgments from human raters on these same criteria. The goal of the function is that for each examinee, the expected difference between the human-judged ability and the component measure should be minimized. An overall summary grade, representing facility in spoken English, is calculated as a weighted combination of the continuous measures and the categorical measures.

EVIDENCE OF VALIDITY

An assertion that scores from a given test are valid for a particular use can be supported by many kinds of evidence. We have gathered seven kinds of evidence for the assertion that the Versant for English instrument provides a valid measure of facility in spoken English:

1. Test material samples key aspects of the performance domain.
2. Human listeners can estimate candidate skills reliably from the recorded responses.
3. Machine subscores and the Overall score are reliable.
4. Uniform candidate groups get similar scores.
5. Different subscores are reasonably distinct from each other.
6. Machine scores correspond to criterion human judgments.

7. Scores correlate reasonably with concurrent scores from tests of related constructs.

Test Material Samples the Performance Domain

As outlined in the sections above, the items of Versant for English are designed to conform to the vocabulary and register of colloquial American English. The items present a quasi-random sample of phrase structures and phonological styles that occur in spontaneous conversation, while the vocabulary is restricted to the high-usage sector of the vernacular lexicon. In particular, the requirement that at least 90% of educated adult native speakers perform correctly on every item suggests that the tasks are within reasonable expectations for all performance elements, including underlying abilities like memory span. The Reading, Repeat, Short Question, and Sentence Build items offer an opportunity for candidates to demonstrate their English skills in integrated performances that exercise most basic psycholinguistic components of speaking and listening.

Human Listeners Estimate Candidate Skills Reliably

As introduced above (see Criterion Scoring by Human Listeners), human listeners judged over 129,000 individual item responses and produced orthographic transcriptions of 247,000 responses during the original development and validation of the Versant for English test. Applying item response theoretic analyses (Wright & Stone, 1979) to these human judgments and transcriptions, we see from the reliability data that human listeners do make consistent judgments of the elemental abilities represented in the Versant for English subscores (see Table 8.2).

We sampled a set of 50 speakers whose test responses were completely transcribed by human listeners and whose responses had human ratings of fluency and pronunciation. We used these human-generated data to derive scores that are parallel to the machine-generated scores of Versant for English. These ratings were reduced to ability subscores for each individual using a single-dimensional IRT analysis with a Rasch model. In addition, each individual's responses to the Vocabulary, Repeat, and Sentence Build items on the test were transcribed by a human listener, and the number of word errors was calculated. These results were also analyzed using IRT to give a "human-based" ability in vocabulary and sentence mastery. Finally, the four scores for each individual were combined (using the same linear weighting as for the Versant Overall facility score) to give a "human" Overall grade for each individual.

Reliability of the human subscores is in the range of that reported for other human-rated language tests, while the reliability of the combined human Overall score is greater than that normally found for most human-rated tests. These results support the presumption that candidate responses to the items in a single 10-minute test administration provide an adequate sample of spoken data upon which to base meaningful and reliable skill estimates.

Machine Scores Are Reliable

It is not too surprising that a machine will score a single item response consistently, but we want to know whether the Versant system will score many responses from a given candidate in a manner reflecting the relative consistency of those performances. The machine score reliabilities displayed in Table 8.2 suggest that the speech processing technology used in Versant can transcribe the short utterances elicited from nonnative speakers by Versant for English nearly as well as a human listener can transcribe them. Further, the data suggest that the machine's pronunciation and fluency judgments are generally similar in reliability to that observed with a highly trained human listener. The human and machine Overall scores show a reliability of .98 and .97, respectively. The reliability is equally high whether the tests are hand transcribed and judged by a human listener or whether the system operates without human intervention.

Uniform Candidate Groups Get Similar Scores

A common form of test validation is to check whether the test produces expected score distributions for familiar populations with well-understood ability levels in the target construct. One may presume that there are relatively uniform groups of candidates who have very distinct levels of the construct being measured. One would expect that the distribution of scores from a test of proficiency in algebra, for example, would be different for

Table 8.2 Human and Machine Score Reliability for Four Subscores and the Overall Score (*n* = 50)

Subscore	One Human Rater	Machine
Sentence Mastery	.96	.93
Vocabulary	.85	.88
Fluency	.98	.95
Pronunciation	.98	.97
Overall	.98	.97

different groups, such as 8-year-old children, high-school students, and professional mathematicians.

Figure 8.2 show the cumulative density distribution of Versant for English Overall scores for four groups of candidates. The score range displayed on the abscissa extends from 10 through 90, as the Overall scores are calculated inside the Versant system. (Note that scores are reported only in the range from 20 to 80, with scores below 20 reported as 20 and scores above 80 are reported as 80.)

The thick black line, rightmost in Figure 8.2, shows the data for a balanced set of 775 native speakers. The native group consisted of approximately 33% speakers from the U.K. and 66% speakers from the USA. The female/male ratio was 55/45, and ages ranged from 18 to 75. Seventy-nine percent (79%) got a score of 80 and only 5% got a score lower than 70.

The thick gray line in Figure 8.2 displays the cumulative score distribution for a norming group of 606 nonnative speakers, ages 12 to 56, balanced in gender, and representing 40 different native languages. Scores from the norming group form a quasi-normal distribution over most of the score range, with a median score of 41.

The two thin lines (black and gray) show two approximately homogeneous populations. The thin black line, leftmost in Figure 8.2, shows a group of 90 first-year students at a Japanese university. They are all the same age and all studied the same English curriculum for five years; their scores range from 20 to 60. The thin gray line is a group of 170 international graduate students seeking qualification to work as university teaching assistants. Their scores range from 40 to 80.

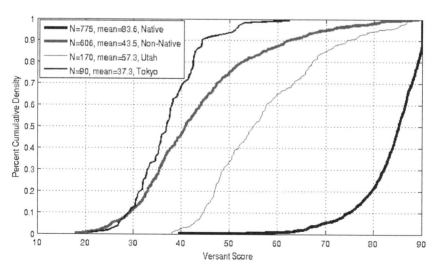

Figure 8.2 Cumulative distribution of Versant overall score for various populations.

Subscores Are Reasonably Distinct

Versant for English was designed to measure an array of subskills that, when taken together, will provide a reasonable estimate of a more general "facility" in spoken English. The subskill scores are based on distinct aspects of the candidate's performance, and they are identified by names that reflect the performance criteria they are intended to measure. Thus, the Vocabulary score is derived only from items wherein the response task principally involves the immediate recognition and understanding of spoken words and the production of related words. The Fluency score is derived only from measures of a candidate's rhythm, pace, and phrasing while producing complex material, as in Repeat and Sentence Build responses.

Over many candidate populations, various measures of second language abilities will correlate to some degree, often with coefficients in the range .5 to .9. If subscores correlate too highly, it might indicate that they are two different labels for a common ability. Yet, in some special populations the correlation between certain language skills may be very low, as between reading fluency and repeat accuracy in a group of illiterate native speakers.

Table 8.3 shows that the machine subscores correlate with each other, with coefficients in the range .61 to .92; they correlate with the Overall score in the range .84 to .92. An interesting case appears in Figure 8.3, a scatter plot of the Sentence Mastery and Fluency scores for a nonnative norming set of 603 candidates. For each candidate, these two scores are measured from the same utterances exactly, but the correlation, as shown in Table 8.3, is only .67.

Just as there are candidates who can read aloud but cannot speak fluently, so there are candidates who can repeat a long, complex sentence but cannot do so fluently. There are also candidates who can repeat a short utterance quite fluently, but cannot grasp, understand, and reproduce a longer, more complex sentence. The different subscores reflect these differences.

Machine Scores Correlate With Human Judgments

Scores must be reliable to be valid, but reliability alone will not establish validity. A reliable test score could be a consistent measure of the wrong

Table 8.3 Correlation Coefficients Between Versant for English Subscores

	Voc.	SentM	Fluency	Pron	Overall
Vocabulary	1.00	.73	.61	.65	.84
Sentence Mastery		1.00	.67	.71	.88
Fluency			1.00	.92	.90
Pronunciation					.92

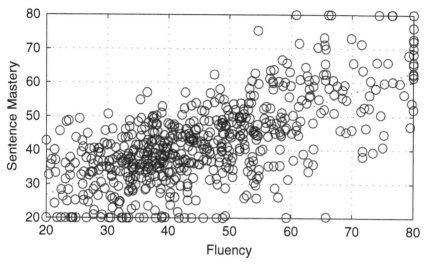

Figure 8.3 Sentence Mastery versus Fluency (*n* = 603; *r* = .67).

thing. The human scores for the Overall facility construct exhibit a reliability of .98, and it is .97 for the machine scores, but we need to know whether the machine scores actually match the human listener scores. Correlations between machine and human subscores in Table 8.4 show a consistent close correspondence between human judgments and machine scores. The correlation coefficients for the two categorical scores (Sentence Mastery and Vocabulary) are .93, .94, indicating that the machine recognition algorithms that count for 50% of the score produce measures in close accord with the human-derived scores. Both the algorithmic fluency and pronunciation measures match the human judgments with correlation coefficients of .89.

We selected a balanced subset of 50 Versant testing candidates whose data had sufficient coverage of human transcriptions and human fluency

Table 8.4 Correlations Between Machine and Human Scores for Overall Score and Subscores

Score	Correlation
Overall	.97
Sentence Mastery	.93
Vocabulary	.94
Fluency	.89
Pronunciation	.89

and pronunciation grades to provide a fair comparison between the human and machine grades for the Overall scores.

Figure 8.4 shows a scatter plot of the Overall human grades against the Versant Overall grade. The correlation coefficient for this data is .97, which compares well with the single-rater reliability we observed for the human-rated Overall score of .98. That is, the machine grades agree with the aggregate human judgments about as well as single human raters agree with the aggregate human judgment.

It is interesting to note that the close score correspondence extends over the whole range of scores. Candidates in the 20–40 range have difficulty producing a sentence of four words length, while candidates in the 65–80 range are usually quite fluent and able to generate spoken English at a native or near native pace in paragraphic chunks. The next section presents correlations of Versant scores with other human-graded tests that have somewhat divergent target constructs.

Scores Correlate With Concurrent Scores From Related Tests

The predictive validity of Versant testing as a measure of "oral proficiency" has been studied at several sites. A group of 51 technical visitors to a U.S. Government training program in Texas took oral proficiency interviews (ILR OPI conducted by U.S. government examiners) and also took Versant for English. The correlation between the ILR OPI speaking scores and the Versant Overall scores was .75. Because the OPI's interrater reliability is about .76, a correlation of .75 with a two-rater average suggests that

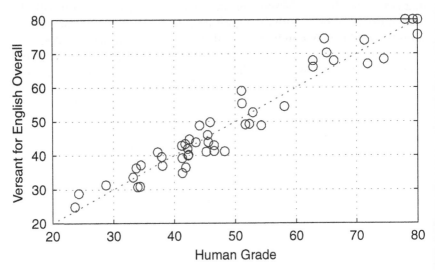

Figure 8.4 Versant overall facility in spoken English vs. human-rater overall grade ($n = 50$; $r = .97$).

Versant Overall scores match the OPI scores about as well as the individual expert human ratings match each other.

We have also examined the correlation between the Versant scoring and scores from other well-established tests of English. These results are shown in Table 8.5. Cascallar and Bernstein (2000) conducted a study of Versant scoring for a New York State agency. The Versant test was administered concurrently with the Test of Spoken English (TSE) scored at the Educational Testing Service. The subjects were a balanced group of Spanish, Chinese and Russian native speakers.

TSE is delivered in semi-direct format, which maintains reliability and validity while controlling for the subjective variables associated with direct interviewing. The TSE score should be a reflection of an examinee's oral communicative language ability on a scale from 20 to 60 (from "No effective communication" to "Communication almost always effective"). Human raters evaluate speech samples and assign score levels using descriptors of communicative effectiveness related to task/function, coherence and use of cohesive devices, appropriateness of response to audience/situation, and linguistic accuracy.

A raw correlation of .88 was measured between the TSE and Versant for English over a sample of subjects relatively evenly spread over the TSE score scale. A corrected validity coefficient of .90 was found with respect to TSE as a criterion measure. These results, coupled with the measured reliability of Versant for English, indicate that Versant for English can produce scores that measure a similar underlying construct to that of TSE. Furthermore, Versant scores can be used to infer TSE scores for the same subject with a mean square error of 5.1 TSE scale points. Since the TSE scale is quantized in 5-point steps, this indicates that a Versant score can predict a subject's TSE score within one score step in most cases.

The TOEFL correlation shown in Table 8.5 was calculated from a pool of Versant for English candidates who also reported a TOEFL score. These 418 candidates were repeatedly resampled according to the reported distribution of TOEFL scores, to establish a correlation estimate that would be consistent with the range and distribution of TOEFL scores as actually

Table 8.5 Correlation With Concurrent Scores From Tests With Related Constructs

Test	Correlation with Versant Scores	N
TSE	.88	59
ILR OPI	.75	51
TOEFL	.73	418
TOEIC	.71	171

observed worldwide. Because TOEFL is a test of reading comprehension, English structure, and listening (with no speaking component), a correlation such as .73 may be expected, as would be expected between any two tests of related but different language skills over most populations.

The study of Versant for English in relation to TOEIC was performed in Japan at the Institute for International Business Communication (IIBC). IIBC selected a stratified sample of 171 adults who had recently taken the TOEIC. The sample of candidates fairly represented the range and approximate distribution of TOEIC candidates that are tested in Japan. The correlation of .71 between Versant for English and the TOEIC is in the expected range, in that the TOEIC is primarily a reading and listening test, and there is a strong reading component even in the listening section of the test.

Notably, the Versant scoring predicts the scores of the two concurrent tests (TSE and ILR OPI) that are primarily speaking tests and predicts these as well as or better than do the trained, expert raters on those tests. This is true even though the scoring rubrics for both the TSE and the ILR OPI include rhetorical and sociolinguistic aspects of speaking performance that are clearly outside the realm of the scoring algorithms used in Versant for English.

DISCUSSION

The Versant for English test has been designed to exercise and measure the performance of basic psycholinguistic processes that underlie speaking and listening in spontaneous conversation. The test is delivered and scored completely automatically. Yet its scores seem to correspond closely to human judgments of communicative effectiveness as measured in traditional direct and indirect speaking tests.

We have proposed a hypothesis to explain this close correspondence. The hypothesis posits that limits on cognitive processing capacity may explain this extension of the scoring to rhetorical and sociolinguistic properties of speaking performance. It seems that this hypothesis could, in principle, be tested by following the lead of Luce et al. (1983), and measuring the decrement in discourse cohesion that results when a highly skilled talker is burdened with a difficult collateral task while speaking. Another approach to testing the hypothesis, in principle, would be to measure language independent aspects of discourse cohesion, for example, in two spoken performances on the same topic by the same person in two languages in which the speaker has widely different levels of speaking facility.

In the time since this chapter was drafted and its publication, Ordinate has also built Versant tests for Spanish (Bernstein, Barbier, Rosenfeld, & De Jong, 2004) and Dutch (Reed Elsevier, 2005). These tests have been validated with much more thorough comparison to concurrent human-scored interview tests, and the strong relation between machine scores of *facility* and human ratings of interview performance are consistently high.

Finally, it may be noted that the Versant for English test has been available for several years now by telephone for use from anywhere in the world, 7 days a week, at any time of the day. Test results are available, on the Ordinate website (www.ordinate.com), within about a minute after a test is completed. In operation, the Versant for English scores are more reliable than those from any operational human-scored tests, and thus the Versant testing service may offer a convenient alternative to traditional spoken language testing methods.

REFERENCES

Bejar, I. (1985). *A preliminary study of raters for the test of spoken English.* Research Report RR-85-5, Princeton, NJ: Educational Testing Service, Princeton.

Bernstein, J., Barbier, I., Rosenfeld, E., De Jong, J. (2004). Development and validation of an automatic spoken Spanish test. *Proceedings of InSTIL/ICALL 2004 Symposium*, Paper 034, Venice. [http://www.isca-speech.org/archive/icall2004/iic4_034.html]

Bernstein, J., Cohen, M., Murveit, H., Rtischev, D., & Weintraub, M. (1990). Automatic evaluation and training in English pronunciation. *Proceedings of 1990 International Conference on Spoken Language Processing*, 1185–1188, Kobe, Japan, Acoustical Society of Japan.

Bernstein, J., De Jong, J., Pisoni, D., & Townshend, B. (2000). Two experiments on automatic scoring of spoken language proficiency. In P. Delcloque (Ed.), *Proceedings of InSTIL2000: Integrating Speech Technology in Learning* (pp. 57–61), University of Abertay Dundee, Scotland.

Bernstein, J., & Pisoni, D. (1980). Unlimited text-to-speech device: Description and evaluation of a micro-processor-based system. *Proceedings of 1980 IEEE International Conference Record on Acoustics, Speech, and Signal Processing*, 576–579.

Cascallar, E., & Bernstein, J. (2000). *Cultural and functional determinants of language proficiency in objective tests and self-reports.* Paper presented at the American Association for Applied Linguistics (AAAL-2000) Annual Meeting, Vancouver, British Columbia.

Levelt, P. (1988). *Speaking.* Cambridge, MA: MIT Press.

Levitt, A. (1991). Reiterant speech as a test of non-native speakers' mastery of the timing of French. *J. Acoustical Society of America, 90*, 3008–3018.

Luce, P., Feustel, T., & Pisoni, D. (1983). Capacity demands in short-term memory for synthetic and natural word lists. *Human Factors, 25*, 17–32.

Major, R. (1986). Paragoge and degree of foreign accent in Brazilian English. *Second Language Research, 2*, 53–71.

Molholt, G., & Pressler, A. (1986). Correlation between human and machine ratings of English reading passages. In Stansfield, C. (Ed.), *Technology and Language Testing* (a collection of papers from the Seventh Annual Language Testing Research Colloquium, held at ETS, Princeton, NJ, April 6–9, 1985), TESOL, Washington D. C.

Neumeyer, L., Franco, H., Weintraub, M., & Price, P. (1996). Automatic Text-independent pronunciation scoring of foreign language student speech. In

Bunnell, T. (Ed.), *Proceedings ICSLP 96: Fourth International Conference on Spoken Language Processing, 3*, 1457–1460.

Reed Elsevier (2005, press release). Ordinate Corp. and CINOP complete automated test of spoken Dutch (07 February 2005). [http://www.reed-elsevier.com/index.cfm?Articleid=1217]

Sollenberg, H. (1978). Development and current use of the FSI oral interview test. In Clark, J. (Ed.), *Direct testing of speaking proficiency:Theory and application.* Princeton, NJ: Educational Testing Service.

Verhoeven, L. (1993). Transfer in bilingual development: The linguistic interdependence hypothesis revisited, *Language Learning, 44*, 381–415.

Wilds, C. (1975). The oral interview test. In R. Jones & B. Spolsky (Eds.), *Testing Language Proficiency.* Arlington, VA: Center for Applied Linguistics.

Wright, B., & Stone, M. (1979). *Best Test Design.* Chicago, IL: MESA Press.

Young, S., Evermann, G., Kershaw, D., Moore, G., Odell, J., Ollason, D., et al. (2004). *The HTK book (for HTK Version 3.2).* Cambridge, UK: Cambridge University Engineering Department. [http://htk.eng.cam.ac.uk/]

Section V
Evaluating Systems
The Case of a Reading Tutor

INTRODUCTION

The final stage along the path from research toward practice is evaluation of computer-assisted language learning (CALL), the topic of Section V. In speech-based CALL, as in other areas of instructional technology, evaluation effort tends to be outweighed by development effort. This disparity is due in part to the complexity of developing advanced technology prototypes, as seen in earlier sections of this book, requiring slow and measured movement toward full-scale evaluation. While prototypes may undergo small, snapshot tests in the research lab, and thereby demonstrate learning gains, the question remains whether these prototypes will scale up to practical use and what value they will yield over time (as Garrett, 1995, remarked early on). As characterized by Wang & Munro (2004), studies of speech-interactive CALL have lacked significant "impact on pedagogy" because they often address selected theoretical points in language learning, employ limited instructional content, and apply strict procedures that may not reflect real-world dynamics. It is not clear, therefore, whether their results will generalize to classrooms, language labs, web-based courses, or other instructional venues. Needed are system evaluations with realistic content in authentic settings.

FORMATIVE AND SUMMATIVE PHASES OF EVALUATION

In one sense, evaluation is assumed by instructional technology research as an intrinsic part of development. Evaluation in that sense involves user tests, often with small groups of users, to identify problems in evolving designs and to examine alternative solutions. We saw this kind of testing in the work on adaptation and development presented in Sections III and IV, where user experiments and informal observations helped researchers adjust speech technologies to instructional purpose and shape exercises and interfaces for usability and clarity. For example, Dalby and Kewley-Port used small-scope experiments to compare different technical approaches to speech recognition to determine the best recognizer for rating articulation of minimal pair differences. Similarly, Bernstein and Cheng applied progressive tests to validate the scaling methods in the Versant test. Other research programs in speech-based CALL, such as the Tactical Language Trainer, point to iterative user testing as a key to determining how to detect errors, and how and when to correct them (Sethy, Mote, Narayanan, & Johnson, 2005).

Iterative user testing is part of formative evaluation as distinct from summative evaluation of a developed system or program—a formal assessment designed to inform decisions about implementation. Details on the methodologies of formative and summative phases of evaluation and associated issues can be found in the educational research literature (e.g., Chatterji, 2005; Haertel & Means, 2003; Weston, 2004). To promote generalizability and utilization of results, summative evaluation of a system should meet a range of criteria: use of authentic settings, significant instructional content, statistically sufficient samples of the learner population, externally valid measures of effectiveness, and reliable experimental controls. Valid measures of effectiveness, for example, require selection of practically important and widely accepted (preferably, standard) measures. These measures should address not just immediate learning but transfer to new material and retention over time. Reliable experimental controls require comparisons of the treatment (system) under consideration against no treatment as well as against competing treatments (e.g., a CALL system without speech interaction). Evaluations that meet these criteria are complicated and costly to execute and typically apply at the end of a development cycle. While rare in the relatively young field of speech-interactive CALL, they can be found in some longer term programs. A notable example is Project Listen at Carnegie Mellon University.

EVALUATION IN PROJECT LISTEN

The course of Project Listen has led from research prototypes in the early 1990s to comparatively long-term classroom evaluations now going on in Pittsburgh public schools, evaluations designed systematically to meet the criteria for generalizability and impact set forth above. The goal of Project Listen is to develop computer-based tutors and coaches that use speech recognition to listen to children read aloud and to diagnose and treat their difficulties. These tutors are being evaluated on measures important to schools, such as gains in reading grade level based on nationally normed reading tests. The evaluations to date suggest that for this application, it is no longer a question of whether speech recognition can be usefully integrated into CALL but rather, given that it can, what are the most effective designs for tutoring, what impact do these designs have on learning to read, and what can the tutoring data reveal about the learning process.

Reflecting the role of Project Listen in providing a model for CALL assessments, this book includes two chapters from that project to shed light on questions significant to CALL research: When and how should prototypes be evaluated in real-world settings? What is an appropriate control group? How can we move from measuring acceptance and usability to the more challenging step of measuring effectiveness? What user and design variables should be considered in evaluation? What practical problems are encountered in the less controlled environments of classrooms and language labs and how might these problems be mitigated? What can assessment results tell designers about how to refine aspects of interface, lesson content, and core technologies? What can the results tell researchers about the acquisition of reading skill?

Pretest–Posttest Evaluation of Learning Gains

The chapter by Mostow et al. describes a formal assessment of the Project Listen reading tutor compared not only with conventional instructional activities but also with commercial software that lacks speech recognition. Of general interest to CALL is the selection of an instrument to measure tutoring effectiveness, a choice Mostow et al. based on the sensitivity of that instrument to change as well as its credibility as a national standardized test. Of further interest is the authors' inclusion of measures of efficiency, such as time on task, to balance measures of effectiveness in interpreting the impact of the tutoring treatment. Having found greater gains in reading scores via the reading tutor with no loss in efficiency, the authors go on to show how an analysis of submeasures on the reading test permits inferences about the cognitive processes that underlie the observed reading gains.

In chronicling this evaluation, the authors depict a range of methodological challenges in structuring and monitoring a study of several months' duration outside the research lab. For example, one challenge is measuring tutoring efficiency in terms of the length of a tutoring session, given that students can leave the computer for any number of reasons and that software crashes inevitably occur. Moreover, instructor attitudes toward the treatment, which may vary widely, influence effectiveness measures in ways long acknowledged in educational research but that are difficult to quantify or control, especially in public schools. The Mostow et al. study can be taken as a pioneer that predicts some of the difficulties likely to arise in classroom-based CALL evaluations and that, furthermore, illustrates how to mine assessment data to interpret what is being learned and how those processes are affected by technology.

Comparative Evaluation of Design Variations

The logical successor to a pretest–posttest evaluation of speech-interactive CALL is the study of design variables within a CALL system and how these affect learning—a kind of apples-with-apples comparison that is possible with mature systems (MacWhinney, 1995). Comparative evaluations are important not only to refine the system in question but also to discover general principles that can be applied to other systems. The final chapter in this volume, by Aist and Mostow, reports this kind of study. Aist and Mostow employ classroom contexts to assess major interface features of the reading tutor. Their results point to the primacy of menu design and interactional policy in getting the best effects from speech-interactive CALL.

Interactional policy in Project Listen refers to the issue of learner control that has proved fertile in instructional technology research within and outside of CALL (e.g., Bertin, 2001). Whereas many CALL approaches presuppose the merits of learner autonomy (Delmonte, this volume; Littlemore, 2001; Wang & Munro, 2004), research in educational technology indicates that for certain kinds of learners—those with mixed ability and young learners—guided navigation through a lesson yields better learning than does undirected exploration (e.g., Aleven, Stahl, Schworm, Fischer, & Wallace, 2003). In essence, letting learners always choose their path may result in very little exploration as learners stick to what they know, a circumstance predicted for CALL by Schacter (1974). This is indeed the finding of Aist and Mostow, who arrive at a mixed-initiative policy that lets system and student take turns choosing what story to read next. Their study charts a process for converting a prototype into a practical tool for learning. In fact, both chapters in this section suggest that interface, usage policy, and implementation strategy can be just as important to success as the technology itself and that both iterative observation and full-scale in-situ evaluation are required to resolve design questions and prove effectiveness.

The speech recognition technology underlying the reading tutor is not elaborated in these chapters but has been covered elsewhere (e.g., Tam, Banerjee, Beck, & Mostow, 2003; Mostow, 2004; Mostow & Aist, 1999). Readers interested in that aspect can refer to the Project Listen website (http://www-2.cs.cmu.edu/~listen/) for articles on experiments with and adaptations of the component speech recognition algorithms.

EVALUATION BY ATTITUDE QUESTIONNAIRES AND EXPERT OPINION

Evaluations of instructional effectiveness are expensive, requiring controlled comparisons of systems or approaches with valid assessment instruments and sizable samples of students. Lacking these, we can get an idea about utility and quality of a system from measures of attitude and acceptance by teachers and students, gained through questionnaires and interviews (a framework for which is offered by Hubbard, 1998). We can also consult expert reviews of software provided in periodicals like *The CALICO Journal* (http://calico.org/CALICO_Review/) and *Language Learning and Technology* (http://llt.msu.edu/). Here, language professors with experience in developing or employing CALL offer critiques of commercial software, including those that integrate speech technologies (e.g., Lafford, 2004; Sanchez & Obando, 2005).

Although expert reviews can be locally useful, they do not inform the scientific base for CALL. Although attitude surveys can be revealing, they do not yield the data about learning and retention needed to enrich theory and stimulate further research in CALL.

SCALING UP TO PRACTICE

A common finding in the field of educational technology is that successful pilot innovations fail to scale up (Cuban, 2001; Fishman, 2002; Roschelle, Pea, Hoadley, Gordin, & Means, 2000; Wallace, 2004; Zhao, Pugh, Sheldon, & Byers, 2002). Systems deemed effective in evaluation, even when evaluation is authentically situated, cannot be assumed to move smoothly to practice. To predict the effects of learning technology in its implementation, and to promote its potential benefits, requires thorough investigation and understanding of variables that affect practice, from the computer to the institution (Cuban, 2001; Dede, Honan, & Peters, 2005; Zhao & Frank, 2003). The chapters in Section V shed light on some of these variables for speech-interactive CALL.

REFERENCES

Aleven, V., Stahl, E., Schworm, S., Fischer, F., & Wallace, R. M. (2003). Help seeking and help design in interactive learning environments. *Review of Educational Research, 73*(2), 277–320.
Bertin, J. (2001). CALL material structure and learner competence. In A. Chambers & G. Davies (Eds.), *ICT and language learning: A European perspective.* Lisse, NL: Swets & Zeitlinger.
Chatterji, M. (2005). Evidence on "what works": An argument for extended term mixed-method (ETMM) evaluation designs. *Educational Researcher, 34*, 14–24.
Cuban, L. (2001). *Oversold and underused: Computers in classrooms.* Cambridge, MA: Harvard University Press.
Dede, C., Honan, J. P., & Peters, L. C. (Eds.) (2005). *Scaling up success: Lessons learned from technology-based educational improvement.* San Francisco: Jossey–Bass.
Fishman, B. J. (2002). *Linking the learning sciences to systemic reform: Teacher learning, leadership, and technology.* Presented at the Annual Meeting of the American Educational Research Association, New Orleans.
Garrett, N. (1995). ICALL and second language acquisition. In V. M. Holland, J. Kaplan, & M. Sams (Eds.), *Intelligent Language Tutors.* Mahwah, NJ: Lawrence Erlbaum Associates.
Haertel, G., & Means, B. (Eds.). (2003). *Evaluating educational technology: Effective research designs for improving learning.* New York: Teacher's College Press.
Hubbard, P.L. (1998). An integrated framework for CALL courseware evaluation. *CALICO Journal, 15*, 51–72.

Lafford, B.A. (2004). Review of "Tell Me More Spanish." *Language Learning and Technology, 8*, 21–34. [http://llt.msu.edu/vol8num3/pdf/review1.pdf]

Littlemore, J. (2001). Learner autonomy, self-instruction, and new technologies in language learning. In A. Chambers & G. Davies (Eds.), *ICT and language learning: A European perspective*. Lisse, NL: Swets & Zeitlinger.

MacWhinney, B. (1995). Evaluating foreign language tutoring systems. In V. M. Holland, J. Kaplan, & M. Sams (Eds.), *Intelligent language tutors*. Mahwah, NJ: Lawrence Erlbaum Associates.

Mostow, J. (2004). Advances in children's speech recognition within an interactive literacy tutor. In A. Hagen, B. Pellom, S. van Vuuren, & R. Cole (Eds.), *Proceedings of the Human Language Technology Conference 2004*, North American Chapter of Association for Computational Linguistics: Boston, MA.

Mostow, J., & Aist, G. (1999). Giving help and praise in a reading tutor with imperfect listening—Because automated speech recognition means never being able to say you're certain. *CALICO Journal, 16*, 407–424.

Roschelle, J. M., Pea, R., Hoadley, C., Gordin, D., & Means, B. (2000). Changing how and what children learn in school with computer-based technologies. *The Future of Children, 10*, 76–101.

Sanchez, A., & Obando, G. (2005). Fonix iSpeak version 3.0. *CALICO Journal, 22*, 741–750. [http://calico.org/CALICO_Review/review/fonixispeak30.htm]

Schachter, J. (1974). An error in error analysis. *Language Learning, 24*, 205–214.

Sethy, A., Mote, N., Narayanan, S., & Johnson, W. L. (2005). Modeling and automating detection of errors in Arabic language learner speech. *Proceedings of EUROSPEECH 2005*, Lisbon.

Tam, Y.-C., Beck, J., Mostow, J., & Banerjee, S. (2003). Training a confidence measure for a Reading Tutor that listens. *Proceedings of EUROSPEECH 2003*, Geneva. [http://www-2.cs.cmu.edu/~listen/pdfs/cm_euro03.ps]

Wallace, R. M. (2004). A framework for teaching with the internet. *American Educational Research Journal, 41*, 447–488.

Wang, X., & Munro, M. (2004). Computer-based training for learning English vowel contrasts. *System, 32*, 539–552.

Weston, T. (2004). Formative evaluation for implementation: Evaluating educational technology applications and lessons. *American Journal of Evaluation, 25*, 51–64.

Zhao, Y., & Frank, K. (2003). Factors affecting technology use in schools: An ecological perspective. *American Educational Research Journal, 40*, 807–847.

Zhao, Y., Pugh, K., Sheldon, S., & Byers, J. (2002). Conditions for classroom technology innovations. *Teachers' College Record, 104*, 482–515.

9 4-Month Evaluation of a Learner-Controlled Reading Tutor That Listens

Jack Mostow, Gregory Aist, Cathy Huang,
Brian Junker, Rebecca Kennedy, Hua Lan,
DeWitt Latimer IV, Rollanda O'Connor,
Regina Tassone, and Adam Wierman

INTRODUCTION

Project LISTEN at Carnegie Mellon University has developed a Reading Tutor that employs automatic speech recognition (ASR) to listen to children read aloud and help them learn to read. In particular, the Sphinx-II continuous speech recognizer (Huang et al., 1993; available since 2000 as open source software, http://cmusphinx.sourceforge.net/) was adapted to analyze the student's oral reading (Mostow, Roth, Hauptmann, & Kane, 1994). The ASR techniques in this tutor have been discussed previously (Mostow et al., 1994), as has the design of reading activities and tutoring strategies (Mostow & Aist, 1999). A companion chapter by Aist and Mostow (this volume) details the rationale behind this design and subsequent improvements in it. Here we report on a formal evaluation of the Reading Tutor in classrooms, measuring its effect on standardized reading scores. Although research and development in Project LISTEN have continued (e.g., Mostow, 2004), the initial classroom evaluation of the Reading Tutor has not been previously reported.

Educational research has observed widespread difficulties in scaling up technology that succeeded in the pilot phase, difficulties ascribed to a range of factors (Becker, 2000; Zhao & Cziko, 2001; Zhao & Frank, 2003). We intend this report not only to demonstrate methodological issues in assessing speech-interactive CALL, such as designing control conditions, but also to anticipate factors that influence whether and how well the benefits of systems like the Reading Tutor will scale up to practice.

MOTIVATION FOR EVALUATION IN CLASSROOMS

A pilot study of the Reading Tutor (Mostow & Aist, 1997) evaluated the progress of six low-reading third graders in a low-income urban elementary school. At the outset, they averaged 3 years below grade level. Using a pilot version of the Reading Tutor, these children averaged 2 years of progress in only 8 months. However, they used the Tutor under the individual supervision of a school aide, who played an important role by taking children out of class to use the Tutor, helping them choose what to read, and keeping an eye on their behavior. Although these results were promising, it was not clear how much credit belonged to the Reading Tutor. Also, individual adult supervision is seldom cost-effective for educational software use. This chapter reports the first controlled study, done in 1998, to evaluate the Reading Tutor's effectiveness in regular classrooms. The purpose of this study was to determine whether the dramatic results observed in the 1996–1997 study would scale up to regular classrooms, where teachers are too busy teaching to spend much time supervising software use. In 1997, the Reading Tutor was redesigned for children to use on their own. For example, talking menus were added to let nonreaders log in and pick stories to read (Aist & Mostow, this volume).

DESIGN FEATURES AND TUTORING STRATEGIES

Figure 9.1 (from Aist & Mostow, 1997) shows the 1998 version of the Reading Tutor, which is described in detail elsewhere (Mostow & Aist, 1999). That version let the child choose a story to read and displayed it one sentence at a time. The Reading Tutor intervened when the reader encountered a difficult word, clicked for help, hesitated for a few seconds, made a reading mistake serious enough for the Reading Tutor to detect, or finished the sentence. These problems were detected and diagnosed by ASR, adapted for this purpose over a series of experiments and user trials (Mostow et al., 1994, Aist & Mostow, 1997, Mostow & Aist, 1999). The Reading Tutor's spoken and graphical feedback, modeled in part after expert reading teachers, helped the reader identify words. This help included reading all or part of a sentence aloud, sounding out or spelling a word, or giving a hint such as a rhyming word, a word that starts with the same sound, or the sound made by some letter(s) in a word. Other responses included backchanneling, advancing to the next sentence, occasional praise, and help on using the Tutor.

EXPERIMENTAL METHOD

To prove that an educational intervention is effective, it is not enough to show that children learn; the question is whether they learn more than they would have otherwise. We therefore compared children using the Reading Tutor against a control group that did not use the Reading Tutor. To reduce variability due to differences among teachers, we compared within classrooms. To reduce variability due to differences among students, we matched students based on their pretest scores.

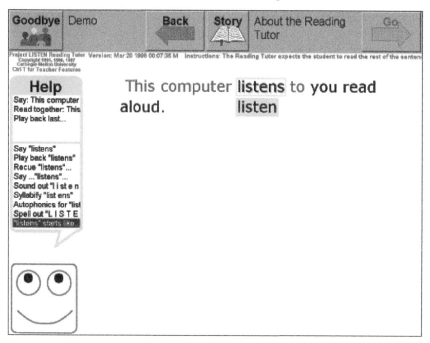

Figure 9.1 Reading Tutor used in spring 1998 study.

To prove that educational software is effective, it is not enough to compare against a baseline control; the results might be due simply to using a computer. We therefore also compared against grade-appropriate commercial reading software that speaks but does not listen; that is, it does not employ ASR. We installed this software on one of the two Macintosh computers already installed in each classroom.

To prove that a reading intervention is effective, it is important to control time on task. Reading is learned largely by doing, and time on task is a key predictor of improvement in reading (Cunningham & Stanovich, 1991). Getting children to use software in schools is a genuine challenge, similar to patient compliance with medication schedules in health care (e.g., van Berge Henegouwen, van Driel & Kasteleijn-Nolst Trenite, 1999). Our goal was to test the Reading Tutor's efficacy *if used as prescribed*. Therefore we specified a nominal fixed time (20–25 minutes) and frequency (every day) for Reading Tutor use.

Measures

To measure the Reading Tutor's effectiveness in helping children learn to read, we needed a good pre- and post-test. We chose the Woodcock Reading Mastery Test-Revised (WRMT; Woodcock, 1987), used by many reading researchers for its reliability and sensitivity to reading growth. The WRMT is an individually administered reading test with multiple subtests, norm-referenced by grade and month, scaled with mean 100 and standard deviation 15 in the national norming sample.

Specifically, we used three WRMT subtests appropriate to the study:

- Word Attack, which measures the ability to decode unfamiliar words;
- Word Identification, which measures word recognition; and
- Passage Comprehension, which measures understanding of text.

Two forms of each subtest make it easy to test and retest. We also measured oral reading fluency, defined as the number of words read correctly per minute in a passage at the child's grade level, and measured as the median for three such passages. Reading rate is a sensitive measure of reading progress (O'Connor & Jenkins, 1999) and has a striking .9 correlation with silent comprehension (Deno, 1985).

Design

In January 1998, 72 students in three classrooms at a low-income urban elementary school in Pittsburgh, Pennsylvania, were pretested by graduate students in education, using WRMT-R Form G. These classrooms—a second-grade room, a fourth-grade room, and a fifth-grade room—had not used the Reading Tutor. We excluded third-grade rooms because they were already using the Reading Tutor.

We ordered the students in each controlled-study class by the average of their three Woodcock subtests. We then blocked them into matched triples—the three lowest-scoring students in the class, the next lowest three, and so on. To avoid bias, we assigned students to treatments randomly within each block of three.

The study design called for each student to spend 20–25 minutes daily on his or her assigned treatment—the Reading Tutor, commercial reading software, or other classroom activities, including other computer use. Each classroom had one 200 MHz, 128MB Pentium™ for the Reading Tutor group of 8–10, plus two school-owned Macintosh™ computers—one for the commercial reading software group and another with other software. Children took turns using these computers during the class day, as a complement to regular instruction. Teachers were responsible for maintaining the treatment schedule. They set up charts and trained students to take turns on their own. We provided kitchen timers for end-of-session reminders.

Procedure

A project member enrolled students on the Reading Tutor, showed how to use it, and visited weekly (11 times) to fix technical problems and write

Tutor-captured data onto CDs. The data included students' recorded utterances, their associated speech recognizer output, and detailed logs of Tutor interactions.

Treatment lasted from February to May, when 63 children were posttested using WRMT-R Form H. The testers were not told who was in which treatment group. Of the 9 other children, 5 had moved and 4 were absent. In addition, 3 of the posttested children were not available for fluency tests.

Effectiveness Results

Based on the Reading Tutor's emphasis on word identification and letter-to-sound mappings, we expected the Reading Tutor group to improve more than the control group(s) in Word Attack and possibly Word Identification. We did not expect effects on Passage Comprehension because the Reading Tutor did not target comprehension other than through reading aloud. Mostow et al. (1994) had shown that such assistance helped children comprehend a *given* text, not that it helped them learn to comprehend *new* text.

Analysis

We performed a repeated-measures analysis of variance (ANOVA) for Word Attack, Word Identification, Passage Comprehension, and Fluency. In each case the factors were BLOCK (to take account of statistical matching) and STUDY_GROUP (to look for significant effects of treatment). For each test, Table 9.1 shows the F value and significance results for effect of STUDY_GROUP and post hoc group differences calculated with Bonferroni corrections for multiple comparisons.

Results

The results are summarized in Table 9.1. It includes the mean pre- and post-scores of the three study groups (Reading Tutor, Baseline control, and commercial reading software) on the three WRMT subtests and oral reading fluency.

The only significant effect was a main effect of STUDY_GROUP for Passage Comprehension. Table 9.1 shows results for all 63 posttested subjects; however, the three groups were affected differentially by dropouts. Consequently, paired comparisons are more informative or at least more dramatic.

We computed gains on each subtest as posttest minus pretest. For each two treatments, we compared subtest gains by students in the same block, excluding unpaired students so as to exploit pairing with paired T-tests. Only one difference was significant: The 17 students who used the Reading Tutor gained significantly more on Passage Comprehension than their paired block-mates in the baseline control. A 2-tailed paired T-test gave $p = .0023$,

Table 9.1 Summary of Pre- and Post-tests for 3 Study Groups

Test	Study Group	Pretest mean	Posttest mean	F	Post hoc gain differences: 16–17 intact pairs	Post hoc differences: 13 intact blocks
Word Attack (normed score)	Reading Tutor— Baseline control— Commercial software—	77.0 75.0 72.9	82.2 80.3 80.5	0.01	None significant	None significant
Word Identification (normed score)	Reading Tutor— Baseline control— Commercial software—	73.3 75.1 71.7	74.9 76.4 74.2	0.05	None significant	None significant
Passage Comprehension (normed score)	Reading Tutor— Baseline control— Commercial software—	74.5 75.5 71.8	76.6 72.3 72.9	4.77 (significant at .05)	Reading Tutor > baseline ($p =$ .02 after Bonferroni correction for (9) multiple comparisons)	Reading Tutor > baseline ($p =$ .1 after Bonferroni)
Fluency (words read correctly per minute)	Reading Tutor— Baseline control— Commercial software—	59.3 49.6 53.6	67.1 62.3 63.7	0.51	None significant	None significant

Note: Results are shown for all posttested subjects.

or $p = .02$ after correcting for (9) multiple comparisons. Gains averaged +4.6 for the Reading Tutor and –4.7 for the baseline control. (Table 9.1 shows somewhat different results because it includes the unpaired subjects as well.) WRMT scores are normed by grade and month, so positive gains correspond to rising percentiles. As their classmates fell further behind, the Reading Tutor students were catching up with their national cohort.

How large was this effect? Effect size is defined as difference between group means divided by the standard deviation in the control group, which was 7.1 for the baseline condition students in the 17 intact pairs used in this comparison. Thus the 9.3-point difference in gains corresponds to an effect size of 1.3—quite large in educational research. However, 17 students are not many, and their pretest scores fell far below the national average. If, instead, we use the norm-referenced standard deviation of 15 points, we get an effect size of 0.62—still quite healthy.

To see whose comprehension the Reading Tutor improved the most compared to the baseline control, we stratified by grade and by pretest. Gains were 14.0 points higher in grade 2, 10.5 points higher in grade 4, and 2.4 points higher in grade 5. Gains were 14.1 points higher for students whose averaged WRMT scores put them in the bottom half, yielding $p < .0003$ (before correcting for multiple comparisons) even with only 8 pairs. (This effect is not regression to the mean, which would affect the control group just as much.) Gains were 5.1 points higher for the top half. The data suggest that the Reading Tutor helped younger and weaker students more, but the sample was too small to make either correlation statistically significant.

Analysis of the 13 intact blocks showed the same pattern for Passage Comprehension gains: Reading Tutor +5.2, baseline –4.0, and commercial software +3.2. These gains differed significantly from the baseline, at $p = .01$ for the Reading Tutor and $p = .02$ for the commercial software. Neither difference was significant after correcting for multiple comparisons, and no other differences were significant even before correcting.

Results differed if we included unpaired students. Some students were unpaired to begin with (top-scoring students left over after blocking within classes of sizes not divisible by 3). Other students became unpaired due to dropouts. Gains by unpaired students in the control group averaged +5 points, in contrast to –4.7 for the paired ones.

ANALYSIS OF READING TUTOR USAGE

Measuring Usage

Before publishing these results, we wanted to see how well the actual experiment had conformed to the study design. How close had we come to 20–25 minutes of daily usage? This simple question proved surprisingly tricky to answer.

Usage in Terms of Sessions

At first we tried analyzing the logs captured by the Tutor to determine session duration and frequency. One problem was conceptual—how to define a session? To keep students from reading as someone else, the Reading Tutor asked for birth month as a simple password and timed out after prolonged inactivity if the student failed to click *Goodbye*. Did a "session" start when a student began to log in to the Reading Tutor, or only after the student selected his or her correct birth month? Did it end if the Tutor timed out, even if the student was still there and logged back in? What if the student left for lunch or a fire drill? We decided to call the time from login to *Goodbye* or to timeout a "mini-session," and call a student's consecutive mini-sessions a single session if the hiatus between them did not exceed 20 minutes.

Analysis based on this criterion found 1,131 mini-sessions totaling 620 sessions from January 12 to June 12, because children continued to use the Reading Tutor after the study. Session duration averaged 12 minutes, only half our goal. This average is approximate due to the inclusion of 79 sessions by the "Demo" reader (used for technical support) plus other sessions too long to be credible, such as a 165-minute session from 9:52 a.m. to 12:38 p.m., with the last 2 hours spent on the story "If the Reading Tutor is Slow." Sometimes headphones were loud enough to trigger speech detection, making the Reading Tutor keep listening to itself after a student left in mid-story without clicking *Goodbye*.

Another problem was computational. Analysis of logs not designed for the specific analysis can be hard to program. For example, analysis would have been easier if the Reading Tutor logged the current student for each event. Instead, we had to parse student-changing events—a task complicated by cases such as logins that failed due to wrong passwords or that succeeded via an unlogged "back door" (*Cancel*) implemented for convenience in demos.

Usage in Terms of Stories

We also wanted to know how many stories students read and how long it took. Here we faced similar difficulties due to incomplete logging. For example, not all exit paths from a story got logged, so analysis code had to infer some exit paths. Table 9.2 shows the result of this analysis. Of 3,055 stories started, only 942 ended with the student's finishing the story. However, 1,045 of the 3,055 readings were tutorial stories that the Reading Tutor chose randomly at login and read to the student. Students left 633 tutorials to read other stories. They finished 813 of 1,990 regular stories, timed out of 226, left 527, clicked Goodbye from 398, and crashed out of 26. Tutorial stories consumed 1,302 of 6,067 total minutes.

Log analysis was too messy to trust by itself, so we complemented it with a simpler "weigh the data" approach: We computed the amount of

Table 9.2 Story Readings on 3 Reading Tutors, Spring 1998

How Kid Got Out of Story	Regular Story Readings			Tutorial Story Readings			All Story Readings		
	# Times Started	Total Mins	Average Duration	# Times Started	Total Mins	Average Duration	# Times Started	Total Mins	Average Duration
Finished	813	2127.85	2.62	129	344.43	2.67	942	2472.28	2.62
Paused	226	570.62	2.52	97	226.28	2.33	323	796.90	2.47
Opened another	527	925.05	1.76	633	524.30	.83	1160	1449.35	1.25
Goodbye	398	1010.93	2.54	176	194.88	1.11	574	1205.82	2.10
Crashed	26	130.32	5.01	10	11.97	1.20	36	142.28	3.95
Total	1990	4764.77	2.39	1045	1301.87	1.25	3035	6066.63	2.00

recorded speech. To bypass the pitfalls of analyzing logs, we analyzed the simpler files recorded by the Reading Tutor for each utterance. One file contained the recorded speech. Another file contained the time-aligned word sequence "heard" by the Reading Tutor. A third file contained the sentence the student was to read. Utterance files were stored in separate student directories. Filenames included the recording date and the time to the nearest second. The utterance data recorded only students' oral reading, not their other actions (such as clicks) or the Reading Tutor's actions; yet the utterance data proved useful despite—or because of—its simplicity.

Usage in Terms of User-Days

To sidestep the issue of "what is a session," we adopted "user-day" as a simpler measure. That is, how many days did each student produce at least one recorded utterance?

Students used the Reading Tutor much less than planned. The number of days on the Reading Tutor averaged 20.5 for the second and fourth graders, or only 1 school day in 4, and only 9.67 for the fifth graders—barely 1 day in 8! The box plot in Figure 9.2 shows how students' days of use varied.

Recorded oral reading averaged about 6 minutes per student for days on which the student did any oral reading, with about two utterances per sentence on average. Thus, student speech occupied half of an average

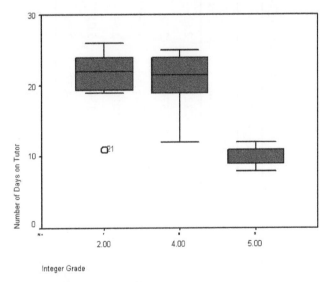

Figure 9.2 Days on Reading Tutor, by grade.

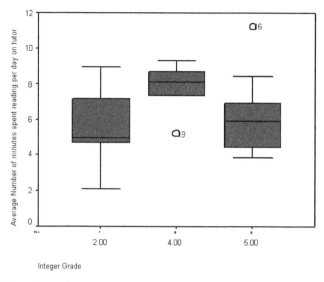

Figure 9.3 Read speech per session (minutes spent reading), by grade.

12-minute session, with silence and Reading Tutor speech for the other half. Figure 9.3 shows how speech varied by and within grade.

Figure 9.4 shows students' differing percentages of sentences read only once. Lower percentages reflect more rereading. The figure indicates that the percentage of unique sentences rises, or rereading drops, from second to fourth and from fourth to fifth grades.

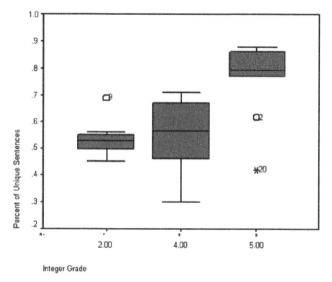

Figure 9.4 Percent of unique sentences (read once), by grade.

Factors Affecting Usage

Why was usage so much lower than planned? A range of factors were involved, commonly observed to affect the move from laboratory to classroom.

Technical Problems

One reason for less-than-expected usage is that technical problems reduced availability. Hardware problems included broken or misplugged headset microphones and unplugged or powered-off machines. Software problems included outright crashes and subtler problems that degraded functionality or performance, such as memory leaks that gradually slowed down response time.

How reliable was the Reading Tutor? The Reading Tutor was left running because it took minutes to relaunch. So one index of reliability is how often it crashed. The Reading Tutor starts a new log file each time it is launched. The logs for the spring 1998 controlled study span 257 machine-days. Of these logs, 30 ended in normal exits (28 of them with Demo as the last user). The other 184 ended in crashes (15 of them as Demo). To average over a day between crashes, or 184 crashes in 257 days, sounds good for artificial intelligence applications.

However, this analysis is deceptive because most of the time, such as weekends and after school, the Reading Tutor wasn't being used. Staying up without being used is easy. Mean time of actual use between crashes tells us more. If we divide 620 total user sessions by 184 crashes, we find that the Reading Tutor averaged one crash per 3.4 sessions, or 41 minutes of actual use. We had wanted each Reading Tutor to be used 20–25 minutes by 8–10 students—3 hours daily, which is the most to expect due to lunch, gym, specials, and so forth. Three hours' use averaged four to five crashes. Fast recovery mattered.

Our experience suggests that crash frequency matters less than recovery speed. People will use a program that crashes often if recovery is quick and easy. Outright crashes are obvious—the program vanishes off the desktop—and easy to fix—just double-click on the program icon. However, subtler bugs, such as memory leaks and broken microphones, are harder to diagnose and fix, and they may deter usage. In fall 1997, we had added stories such as "If the Reading Tutor is Slow" to teach children about such bugs. The spring 1998 Reading Tutor read one of these tutorials (chosen at random) each time a student logged in. If a student learned the tutorial well enough to fix the bug on the spot, it could avoid days of wait for a tech support visit.

Teacher Variables

A second factor involves teachers' role as gatekeepers. Mean days of use per student turned out to be representative of the corresponding populations because the teachers tended to control the number of days on the Reading Tutor for each student. For example, for ease of classroom management, computers were not used when student teachers taught or when standardized tests were being administered. When teachers did allow computer use, their concern for fairness led them to equalize computer time for all three treatment groups. Consequently, children in the baseline control condition got more (nonreading) computer time than they would have without a Reading Tutor in their classroom.

Student Variables

An obvious third factor involves student variability. Student absenteeism or refusal obviously limits frequency. Figure 9.2 shows that students' total days of use varied more between classes (by more than 2) than within class (typically by less than 2). Teachers may have reduced variation by giving priority to absentees after they returned.

Student attitude is an obvious influence on session duration. Session duration shows much greater variation in read speech, a proxy for session duration, within than between classes. Session duration is much harder for teachers to control than session frequency: It is easier to send students to use a computer or to set up a regular rotation than to remember exactly when to stop them. We provided kitchen timers to control session duration, but this mechanism depended on students to set the timer for the prescribed time. Students sometimes reset the timer to shorten or lengthen a session.

DISCUSSION

Careful analysis revealed that actual sessions averaged one fourth the frequency and one half the duration we had aimed for, or an order of magnitude less total usage. Mostow and Aist (1997) reported similar usage in the pilot study, ranging from 30 to 60 sessions in 8 months, averaging 14 minutes.

Why, then, did a student who used the Reading Tutor gain significantly more in Passage Comprehension than a classmate with similar pretest scores and the same teacher? Presumably the gain differences in Passage Comprehension but not Word Identification or Word Attack imply a gain in something else that enhances comprehension. But what? Candidate hypotheses are as follows:

- Comprehension may require the *ability to identify words in the context of connected text*, not just isolated words as in the WRMT's Word Identification and Word Attack subtests. Accuracy on fluency passages should reflect this ability.

- *Automaticity in word identification* frees up cognitive resources for comprehension. Fluency reflects automaticity, and our data do not support this compelling explanation.
- Comprehension may require the *confidence to try*. Many teachers said that their poorer readers gained in confidence.
- Comprehension takes *sustained attention to connected text*. The Reading Tutor gave students practice in looking at text.
- *Habitually rereading sentences* may aid in comprehension. Utterances per sentence averaged more than two.
- Comprehension might take a *conceptual breakthrough* that it is possible to make meaning from text. The Reading Tutor read many sentences using expressive human speech—yet so did the commercial reading software.
- Reading to students may improve *listening comprehension* and thus their reading comprehension (Gough, Juel, & Griffith, 1992).
- *Asking if a sentence makes sense* helps comprehension. The Reading Tutor may have improved this metacognitive skill by reading aloud, by getting students to read, or by contextual hints (recuing) to stimulate semantic processing.

To shed light on these hypotheses, we used linear regression to test how well gains in word attack, word identification, and fluency predicted comprehension gains in each treatment group. None of these factors was a statistically significant predictor of passage comprehension gains in any of the three treatment groups. However, gain in word identification was suggestive both in the commercial software group ($n = 21$, $p = .123$) and in the Reading Tutor group ($n = 23$, $p = .120$).

To investigate this trend further, we turned to a larger sample from a related study. The within-classroom comparison necessarily excluded seven classrooms where the whole class had been using the Reading Tutor since September 1997. These seven "uncontrolled" rooms included a first-grade room, a second-grade room, all three third-grade rooms, and two fourth-grade rooms. The uncontrolled rooms were pretested in December 1997 and posttested in May 1998. Analysis of these other data exhibited the same pattern: Gains in word identification strongly predicted gains in passage comprehension ($n = 134$, $p < .001$).

Illustrating the pattern are scatterplots of gains in passage comprehension versus other gains. Figure 9.5 shows a clear linear relationship between comprehension gains and gains in word identification. The partial regression plots in Figures 9.6 and 9.7 show no obvious relationship of comprehension gains with gains in word attack or in fluency, respectively. Of course, these associations do not necessarily imply causality.

Finally, the uncontrolled study rooms differed from the controlled study rooms in multiple respects. They spanned Grades 1–4, versus Grades 2, 4, and 5. They started using the Reading Tutor a full semester before they were

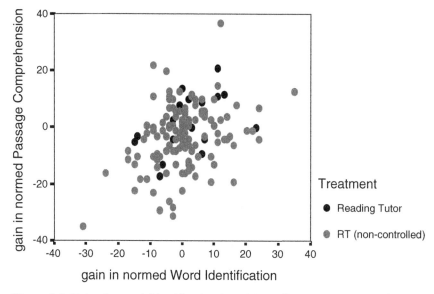

Figure 9.5 Gains in word identification (x-axis) predict gains in comprehension (y-axis) (*n* = all 157 kids who used the Reading Tutor, *p* < .001).

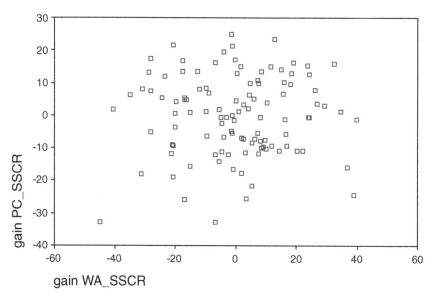

Figure 9.6 Gains in comprehension not clearly related to gains in word attack (*n* = 157).

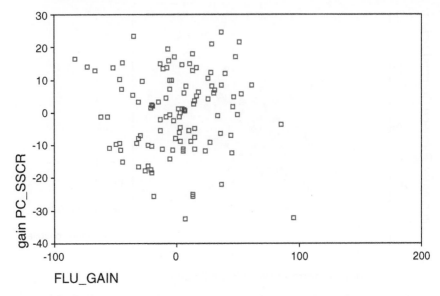

Figure 9.7 Gains in comprehension not clearly related to gains in fluency (*n* = 157).

pretested, versus after. They had about 25 children use each Reading Tutor, versus 8. The classroom teacher, versus the study design, set policy for who was to use the Reading Tutor.

Whatever skills affect comprehension, the question arises as to what factors might explain between-group differences in development of these skills? Time on task is generally a strong predictor of improvement in reading skills. Certainly the Reading Tutor treatment involved more time reading than the baseline condition. But so, presumably, did the commercial reading software. Although usage of the commercial reading software was not instrumented, we assume that it matched or exceeded Reading Tutor usage, because it was less prone to software problems and not vulnerable to microphone breakage. Indeed, the commercial software group gained almost as much in Passage Comprehension as the Reading Tutor group did, but not enough to achieve statistical significance compared to the baseline group. It would be instructive to analyze children's actual use of Reading Tutor and commercial reading software in terms of how much time they spend reading or being read to, as opposed to other activities such as logging in or playing with animations.

SUMMARY

In review, we evaluated an automated, speech-interactive Reading Tutor that let children pick stories to read and listened to them read aloud. All 72 children in three classrooms (Grades 2, 4, and 5) were independently tested on the nationally normed Word Attack, Word Identification, and Passage Comprehension subtests of the Woodcock Reading Mastery Test, as well as on oral reading fluency. We split each class into three matched treatment groups: Reading Tutor, commercial reading software, or other activities. In four months, the Reading Tutor group gained significantly more in Passage Comprehension than the control group ($p = .002$), even though actual usage was a fraction of the planned daily 20 minutes. To help explain these results, we analyzed gains by 134 additional children who used the Reading Tutor in other classrooms (Grades 1–4). Gains in Word Identification predicted gains in Passage Comprehension ($p < .001$), but gains in Word Attack and fluency did not.

CONCLUSION

Children in the Reading Tutor group improved in passage comprehension more than the baseline control group and more than a national cohort, leading the eloquent school principal to note that they were "closing the gap." On the other hand, passage comprehension results for the commercial software group, lacking ASR, were ambiguous—statistical significance depended on whether we included students whose counterpart(s) in another condition had dropped out of the study. No other differences were significant.

Surprisingly, these results were achieved with an order of magnitude less usage than the daily 20-minute sessions we aimed for. The control treatment also departed from our study design. Within-classroom comparison to control for teacher effects turned out to increase the control group's computer access. The lesson is that side effects of treatment can distort within-classroom comparisons against prior practice.

Measuring usage turned out to be unexpectedly difficult. One idea that helped was replacing the slippery concept of "session" with the much simpler "user-day." We also found sequences of simple utterance files easier to analyze than more detail-rich logs yet surprisingly informative.

We realized that further research was needed to understand the Reading Tutor and the role of ASR in helping children read: What skills does the Reading Tutor benefit? How much? Whom does it help? For example, the data suggest that younger and weaker students are helped more, but the sample was too small to make the correlation statistically significant. Which features of the Reading Tutor affect learning? Why? How can this tutor improve? For example, while the version of the tutor described here let the child choose a story to read, the revised version described by Aist and Mostow (this volume) uses mixed-initiative story choice, which they show gives students more exposure to stories that will improve their skills. Does that policy have a significant effect on reading gains? Studies to address these questions have been guided by lessons reported here. Additional features of the Reading Tutor have been investigated, such as predicting reading miscues (Banarjee, Beck, & Mostow, 2003) and using confidence measures (Tam, Beck, Mostow, & Banerjee, 2003).

Finally, the classroom experience of Project Listen confirms observations from the broader field of research in educational technology: Expectations from pilot studies do not necessarily bear out in larger evaluations. The advantage of the Reading Tutor seen in our pilot study did extend to the larger study, but gains were more selective than expected and tutor usage was lower. Our report has identified some of the variables affecting scale-up; these might be expected to increase in range and complexity with further moves toward practice (Zhao & Frank, 2003).

REFERENCES

Aist, G. S., & Mostow. J. (1997). Adapting human tutorial interventions for a reading tutor that listens: Using continuous speech recognition in interactive educational multimedia. *Proceedings of CALL'97 Conference on Multimedia*, Exeter, England.

Banerjee, S., Beck, J., & Mostow, J. (2003). Evaluating the effect of predicting oral reading miscues. *Proceedings of EUROSPEECH 2003*, Geneva. [http://www-2.cs.cmu.edu/~listen/pdfs/Eurospeech2003_Evaluating_predicted_miscues.pdf]

Becker, H.J. (2000). Who's wired and who's not: Children's access to and use of computer technology. *Future of Children, 10*, 44–75.

Cunningham, A. E., & Stanovich, K. E. (1991). Tracking the unique effects of print exposure in children: Associations with vocabulary, general knowledge, and spelling. *Journal of Educational Psychology, 83*, 264–274.

Deno, S. L. (1985). Curriculum-Based Measurement: The emerging alternative. *Exceptional Children, 52*, 219–232.

Gough, P. B., Juel, C., & Griffith, P. L. (1992). Reading, spelling, and the orthographic cipher. In P. Gough, L. Ehri, & R. Treiman (Eds.), *Reading Acquisition* (pp. 35–48). Hillsdale, NJ: Lawrence Erlbaum Associates.

Huang, X. D., Alleva, F, Hon, H. W., Hwang, M. Y., Lee, K. F., & Rosenfeld, R. (1993). The SPHINX-II speech recognition system: An overview. *Computer Speech and Language, 7*(2), 137–148.

Mostow, J. (2004). Advances in children's speech recognition within an interactive literacy tutor. In A. Hagen, B. Pellom, S. van Vuuren, & R. Cole (Eds.), *Proceedings of the Human Language Technology Conference 2004*, North American Chapter of Association for Computational Linguistics, Boston, MA.

Mostow, J., & Aist, G. S. (1997). When speech input is not an afterthought: A reading tutor that listens. *AAAI Workshop on Perceptual User Interfaces*, Banff.

Mostow, J., & Aist, G. S. (1999). Giving help and praise in a reading tutor with imperfect listening—because automated speech recognition means never being able to say you're certain. *CALICO Journal 16*(3), 407–424. Special issue (M. Holland, (Ed.), *Tutors that Listen: Speech recognition for Language Learning*.

Mostow, J., Roth, S., Hauptmann, A. G., & Kane, M. (1994). A prototype reading coach that listens. *Proceedings of the Twelfth National Conference on Artificial Intelligence* (AAAI-94), Seattle, (Outstanding Paper).

O'Connor, R. E., & Jenkins, J. R. (1999). Prediction of reading disabilities in kindergarten and first grade. *Scientific Studies of Reading, 3*, 159–197.

Tam, Y.-C., Beck, J., Mostow, J., & Banerjee, S. (2003). Training a confidence measure for a reading tutor that listens. *Proceedings of EUROSPEECH 2003*. Geneva. [Retrieved December 8, 2006, from http://www-2.cs.cmu.edu/~listen/pdfs/cm_euro03.ps]

van Berge Henegouwen M., van Driel H., & Kasteleijn-Nolst Trenite, D. (1999). A patient diary as a tool to improve medicine compliance. *Pharmacy World and Science, 21*(1), 21–4.

Woodcock, R. W. (1987). *Woodcock Reading Mastery Tests—Revised.* American Guidance Service, Circle Pines, MN 55014. Available at http://www.agsnet.com.

Zhao, Y., & Cziko, G. (2001). Teacher adoption of technology: A perceptual control theory perspective. *Journal of Technology and Teacher Education, 9*, 5–30.

Zhao, Y., & Frank, K. (2003). Factors affecting technology use in schools: An ecological perspective. *American Educational Research Journal, 40*, 807–047.

10 Balancing Learner and Tutor Control by Taking Turns

Faster and Better Mixed-Initiative Task Choice in a Reading Tutor That Listens

Gregory Aist and Jack Mostow

INTRODUCTION

An important task in tutoring is choosing which task the student should attempt next (Corbett, Koedinger, & Anderson, 1997; Kalchman, & Koedinger, 2005). This decision should be *efficient* for whomever makes it—the tutor or student, especially a young student. Its outcome should be *effective* in educational terms. To summarize with a pun, the "choice task" of deciding what to work on should efficiently yield a "choice task" in the sense of helping the student learn. This paper analyzes the efficiency and effectiveness of task choice in the context of a tutor that listens to children read aloud: specifically, the Reading Tutor from Project LISTEN, further described in the chapter by Mostow et al. (this volume). This tutor uses automated speech recognition (ASR) to detect and diagnose the reading problems of children as they read stories aloud from the computer screen. The ASR techniques, and the methods by which we developed and tested them, have been covered elsewhere (e.g., Mostow & Aist, 1999a; Mostow, Roth, Hauptmann, & Kane, 1994). Here, we describe design features added to successive versions of the Reading Tutor to improve efficiency and effectiveness of choosing stories, defining efficiency as the time to pick a story and effectiveness in terms of exposing students to new material. We follow with a quantitative evaluation of the resulting versions of the tutor, making use of data collected through the speech recognizer, and conclude with lessons learned en route.

The companion chapter by Mostow et al. presents the methodology and results of a controlled classroom evaluation of the Reading Tutor before we varied story choice options. That chapter shows that the basic version of the Reading Tutor, which let the child choose what stories to read, led to greater gains in reading scores than did control conditions without speech recognition. The question addressed here is whether, given the demonstrated success of the speech-interactive tutor, we can optimize these gains by revising policies for story choice.

Research on the Reading Tutor has continued (e.g., Aist et al., 2001; Mostow, et al. 2001; Mostow, Beck, & Bey, 2004), but the results and implications of the original investigation of story choice have not before been presented. These implications are important for the continuing issue of locus of control—whether with the learner or with the tutor—in computer-based instruction (Aleven & Koedinger, 2000; Corbett & Anderson, 2001; Koedinger & Corbett, 2006; Lepper, Woolverton, Mumme, & Gurtner, 1993; Littlemore, 2001; Niemiec et al., 1996; Schnackenberg & Hilliard, 1998).

EFFICIENT TASK CHOICE IN THE READING TUTOR

First, we describe how children chose stories to read in the version of the Reading Tutor used in the first extended elementary school deployment: a low-income urban school during the 1996–1997 school year (Mostow & Aist, 1997). Figure 10.1 shows that version of the Reading Tutor. It displayed a story on the screen one sentence at a time and, using ASR techniques, listened to the child read it aloud. The Tutor responded with spoken and graphical feedback. When a sentence was finished, the Tutor grayed it out and went on to display the next sentence. Included in the system was a

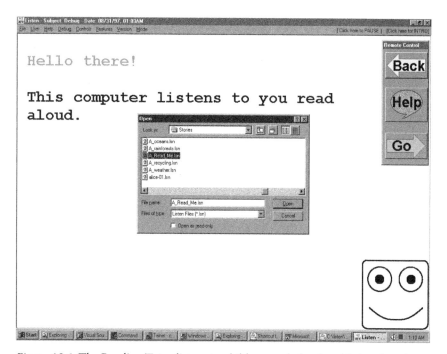

Figure 10.1 The Reading Tutor listens to children read aloud and helps them learn to read.

set of stories that children could choose to read with adult assistance. Task choice consisted of picking what story to read next.

Evaluation was conducted with eight low-reading third graders under the supervision of a Title I-funded school aide (Ms. Lovelle Brooks). The aide escorted one child at a time out of class to use the Reading Tutor in a small room. The aide helped the child use the generic file picker mechanism to pick stories, represented as files. For example, the file A_Read_Me.lsn highlighted in the menu contains the "Read Me" story shown on the screen. The prefix "A_" identifies the story level as Grade 1. (We substituted "A, B, C" for "gr1, gr2, gr3" at the advice of teachers, to avoid embarrassing students who read below their grade level.)

As evident from Figure 10.1, the mechanism for story choice was not designed for children to use by themselves. The numerous icons and menu items are bewildering, the mouse targets are too small for young hands, the file picker does not identify or explain the choices to nonreaders, and nothing prevents the user from moving (inadvertently or deliberately) to some directory other than Stories. We used the generic file picker purely for expedience, so as to start testing extended use of the Reading Tutor as early as possible without waiting to implement a more child-usable mechanism. In fact, the pilot study succeeded spectacularly: the 6 children who were pre- and post-tested had started out 3 years below grade level but averaged 2 years' progress in the 8 months they used the Reading Tutor (Mostow & Aist, 1997). Our next goal was to scale up to classroom use instead of relying on one-on-one adult supervision.

We redesigned story choice in 1997–1998 to accommodate nonreaders. Figure 10.2 shows the result of considerable user testing and design iteration. This version of the Reading Tutor displayed prompts for what to do and spoke them aloud. When a child clicked on a story title, the Reading Tutor highlighted it, read it aloud, and estimated its difficulty from the percentage of words the student had not seen before, for example, "might be a little hard," "may be about right," or "probably way too easy." The child could then click Okay to read the story. Children often clicked on several titles to hear them before selecting one. If the child remained inactive, the Reading Tutor said, "If that's what you want to read, then click Okay." The child could use the large Up and Down buttons on the right to scroll through the story list or click on an index tab at the left to scroll directly to the corresponding story level.

Once the child clicked Okay to confirm a story choice, the Reading Tutor displayed the story a sentence at a time, listening to the child read it and intervening as described elsewhere (Mostow & Aist, 1999a). At the end of the story, the Tutor asked, "Was that story easy, hard, or just right?" and used a multiple-choice mechanism to get the answer.

The 1997–1998 story picker proved fairly usable for children, at least in Grade 2 and above. However, young children have difficulty with two-step plans—such as clicking on a story to hear its title and then clicking Okay

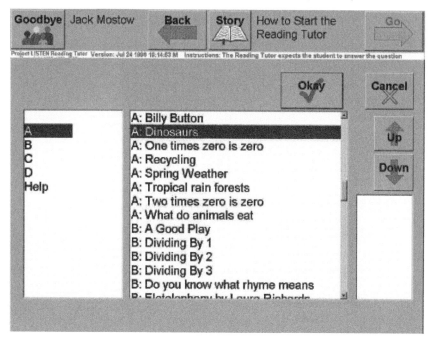

Figure 10.2 Story picker used in 1997–98 school year: click title to hear it; click Okay to read that story.

(personal communication, David Klahr, 1998). Just-in-time prompts helped considerably by reminding the student to click Okay. However, we wanted to eliminate the need for reminders.

In 1998–1999 we designed, implemented, tested, and refined the simplified "one-click pick" menu, as shown in Figure 10.3. This menu is designed for a spectrum of reading ability. To pick a story, students who can read the menu for themselves simply click on its title. Otherwise, the Reading Tutor gives spoken assistance. It speaks the prompt shown above the menu, then successively highlights each title in the menu and reads it aloud. If the student fails to select an item, the Tutor reads the menu again, then reprompts the student if there is no response within a few seconds. Finally, the Tutor logs the student out, saying, "Ask your teacher for help on what to do next." On the other hand, if the student does click on a title, the tutor displays that story and prompts the student to read it aloud. To pick a different story, the student can click Back to return to the story picker. Thus, the one-click picker replaces the two-click "select and confirm" with "select, then optionally repeat."

The revised story picker is designed to reduce complexity. It introduces no new buttons; the Goodbye, Back, and Go buttons at the top of the screen appear throughout the Reading Tutor, and the small Fix button is for teachers. The picker lists only six titles at a time, shown on the left. Each story

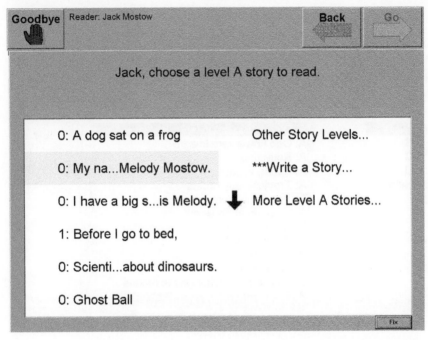

Figure 10.3 "One-click" story picker used in Fall 1999: Reading Tutor speaks the list; child clicks item to pick it.

title is preceded by number of times the child has read that story before. The items on the right let the student move to other story levels, add their own stories (Mostow & Aist, 1999a, 1999b), or see another screenful of stories at the current story level.

EFFECTIVE TASK CHOICE IN THE READING TUTOR

Learner control has been found important for motivation (Lepper et al., 1993; Littlemore, 2001). Accordingly, the 1996–1997 version of the Reading Tutor was designed to let the student choose what story to read next, with adult assistance to operate the generic file picker. However, the aide noticed (and told us about) the children's tendency to keep rereading the same easy stories. She played an important role in encouraging them to try new, more challenging stories, thereby increasing the effectiveness of the Tutor. In the transition to independent operation under regular classroom conditions, however, this influence was lost except to the limited extent that teachers told students what stories to pick.

This observation points to locus of control as a complicated issue: Despite its motivational benefits, learner control of tutoring events can reduce learning effectiveness (Aleven & Koedinger, 2000). Children, in particular, have their own agenda when it comes to software use, which may or may not match the desired educational outcome. Children typically want to explore a simulation or to win a game, not learn arithmetic or the alphabet (Hanna, Risden, Czerwinsky, & Alexander, 1999). The Reading Tutor's goal is to help students learn to read. A student's goal may be reading a story or exploring the story menus.

To build fluency and vocabulary, however, students must encounter new words in natural in-context use; accordingly, students must read stories they have not read before. Students may not always challenge themselves by reading material hard enough to contain new words. Not only did teachers note that some students read the same story over and over (either a favorite story such as an excerpt from Martin Luther King's "I Have a Dream" speech or an easy story such as a nursery rhyme), but also the experimenters observed that some students consistently chose stories that were too easy or too hard.

To make shared reading effective, the Reading Tutor should help children choose appropriate material. How can this be done? One possibility is to establish individual reading lists: each student has his or her own list of stories to read, and the teacher or an administrator can adjust a student's list. However, we have found it difficult to involve teachers in using the Reading Tutor directly for such things as entering student data. Teachers are busy; they seem to prefer interacting with the Reading Tutor indirectly by guiding students towards productive behaviors and (occasionally) checking on student activity or progress. For example, one teacher put a list of stories to read on an index card and set the card on top of the computer monitor. To support such indirect use, we could have the Tutor filter the list of stories to restrict student access to stories at an appropriate level; or have the Tutor sort the stories to guide students. This approach would have to be balanced to allow teachers to use the computer "indirectly" through influencing students' choices, if desired.

Policies for Involving the Student in Choosing Stories

We did not want to take away student choice altogether. Some of the less drastic options we considered were the following:

1. *Sorting the story list:* arranging the list so that students are more likely to choose new stories. This policy is not guaranteed to be effective: a student could ignore the suggestion and choose the same story over and over.
2. *Restricting the story list:* restricting the list of stories that students choose from. However, such a restriction would have to be explained to both the student and the teacher—and any nontrivial restriction could be difficult to explain. Also, how would the student get to choose

an old favorite some of the time without being able to choose it all of the time?

3. *Providing different lists:* having the student alternately choose from two separate lists of stories. For example, we could show one list of new and one list of old stories. This policy has advantages: it guarantees that students read new material, is simple to describe, lets the student reread favorite stories, seems fair in letting the student make the choices, and should take no more time than choosing from a single list. Although technically easy, this solution might not be easy to use because students would have to make choices from two very different lists. Also, why require student to pick an old story if they would rather read something new?

4. *Taking turns:* having the student choose some stories and the Reading Tutor choose some, with the Tutor always choosing new ones. This policy guarantees that every student will read some new material. Taking turns is easy to describe to students and teachers, and it (sometimes) lets students choose an old favorite. Is it fair? Students don't get all the choices, but the choices given are not restricted. Is it quick? Assuming the computer takes negligible time, this policy should take about half the time of the 1997–1998 Tutor. Is it easy to use? Each decision of the student is from the same list of stories, which should be simpler to remember than different lists.

Of these policies, providing different lists and taking turns had the most advantages and fewest drawbacks. We decided to implement a policy of taking turns. We felt it would be slightly easier to explain than different lists, and it (sometimes) provides students with an unfiltered free choice of what to read. Finally, taking turns should take less time than providing alternate lists, giving the student more time to read.

Implementing "Taking Turns": The Reading Tutor and the Student Alternate Choosing Stories

We revised the story choice procedure for the 1999–2000 Reading Tutor as follows. First, we introduced a mechanism to let the Tutor and the student take turns choosing stories instead of always allowing the student to choose. Second, we added features to encourage students to choose appropriately challenging material. The idea is for Tutor and student to take turns and for the decision about who picks first to be made randomly each day. However, implementing this policy was a bit tricky. On the one hand, we wanted to give students another chance if they didn't like the story. On the other, we needed to keep them from circumventing the policy altogether.

We now detail the solution we adopted. When a student logs in, the Reading Tutor checks whether the student has previously logged in that day, in which case the cached value of a "who chooses next" variable is used for who chooses the next story. If the student has not logged in that day, then half the time (randomly) the student chooses the first story; the other half, the Tutor chooses. The result of this decision is stored as "who chooses next." The randomization prevents systematic bias from defeating the goal of a 50–50 split. (A simpler alternative is for the Tutor always to choose first, but some teachers have students read just one story a day.) When the student finishes a story, the "who chooses next" variable is updated. For example, if the student just chose the story, the variable is set to the Tutor. By making the value of this variable persist until either the student finishes a story or at least 1 day has passed, we prevent students from "cheating the system"—such as getting around the Tutor's story choice by logging out and then back in. Students may still escape from a story they don't like via the Back button, without losing their turn to pick or without the Tutor's losing its turn. Some students use this mechanism to explore the set of available stories before committing to one.

Implementing "Taking Turns": The Reading Tutor Chooses Story by Student's Reading Level

It is important to match task difficulty to the level of the student. Each story in the Reading Tutor is graded K, A, B, C, D, or E for kindergarten through fifth grade; U for unleveled (student-authored stories); or Help. The story levels K through E are ordered in difficulty. The Tutor sorts the stories (around 200 in fall 1999) into five categories, shown in Figure 10.4: previously read; below, at, or above recommended level, and at a noncomparable level. The Tutor tries to pick new stories at the recommended level. If no story is available there, the Tutor chooses a harder story.

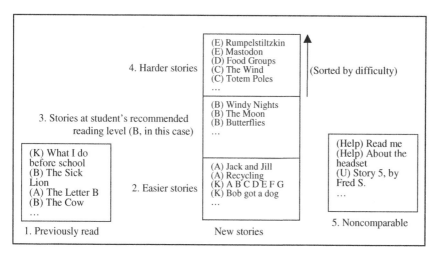

Figure 10.4 Sorting the stories for Reading Tutor story choice.

The Reading Tutor estimates a student's reading level based on age, entered upon enrollment. Teachers can override this estimate, but we do not want to rely on input that teachers may be too busy to provide. The age-based heuristic is a deliberate underestimate to avoid frustrating children with stories at too high a level. To keep difficulty reasonable, the tutor adjusts recommended reading level as the student progresses. The adjustment criterion for fall 1999 was based on the number of words accepted as correct per minute (WAPM) of assisted reading, a policy further described in Table 10.1. WAPM was calculated from speech recognition algorithms adapted for the tutor (e.g., Mostow & Aist, 1999a). Teachers could override the recommended level. Our experience suggests that level-independent thresholds are inflexible; promotion and demotion thresholds should be story-level specific.

We assessed the "take turns" story choice policy for usability and acceptance at various sites: first, in several 1-day trials held at Fort Pitt; second, with children in the CHIkids program at the 1999 Computer–Human Interaction Conference in Pittsburgh; third, with several dozen students at Fort Pitt's 1999 Summer Reading Clinic.

These tests generated a number of concerns. First, some students were frustrated because the Reading Tutor chose material that was too hard for them. We changed the level-choosing mechanism to be more cautious about adjusting the recommended reading level. Second, some students were frustrated because they wanted to read a different story than the one the Tutor picked. We responded by cushioning Reading Tutor turns with comments such as "Here's a story chosen just for you" and "Read this story, and then you'll choose one." Third, the Tutor sometimes picked a story that was actually the middle of a multipart story. For example, Cinderella is split into

Table 10.1 Adjusting Recommended Reading Level After Student Finishes a Previously Unfinished Story, Using Adapted Speech Recognition Results (Accepted Words per Minute)

Last Story Completed Compared to Recommended Reading Level	AWPM < 10 (AWPM: Accepted Words per Minute)	10 ≤ AWPM < 30	AWPM ≥ 30
Easier	Move down one level	Stay same	Stay same
At level	Move down one level	Stay same	Move up one level
Harder	Stay same	Stay same	Move up one level
Noncomparable	Stay same	Stay same	Stay same

several pieces to make each piece a reasonable length. Project LISTEN programmer Andrew Cuneo defined a prerequisite for each piece of a multipart story and modified the program to choose a piece only if the student had finished its prerequisite. This incident exposed a common sense rule ("read multipart stories in sequence") that students supplied in the learner control condition but that we had to program into the automated choice condition.

EVALUATION

We compared the efficiency and effectiveness of three versions of the Reading Tutor. The pilot version was used in 1996–1997 by eight low-reading third graders at a low-income urban school under the supervision of a school aide. The 1997–1998 version was used in spring 1998 at the same school by 24 second, fourth, and fifth graders of varying levels. The fall 1999 version was used at a different school by 60 second and third graders in the bottom half of their class.

Efficiency of Story Choice

The "one-click" mechanism seems easier than its two-step predecessor to select an item from a list, not only for children but also for adults. To confirm this impression, we quantified the efficiency of the story choice mechanisms in the successive tutors. How long did each one take to pick a story?

Method

To measure time to pick a story, we analyzed data captured in the three time periods by the respective versions of the Reading Tutor. Although all three versions logged details of the interactions, the complex and time-varying form of the logs made them hard to analyze. Therefore, we used a simpler form of data that remained stable across versions—the successive oral reading utterances recorded by the Tutor. Specifically, we used data from the speech recognizer to measure the time interval between the start of the last sentence of one story and the start of first two sentences of the next story read the same day (so as not to count story choices that were immediately abandoned). For each version of the Tutor, we randomly selected 10 such transitions and analyzed them by hand, referring to log files as needed. This approach let us identify behaviors (e.g., reading the same story twice in a row) and anomalies (e.g., timeouts) that we might not otherwise have noticed. We used utterance start times rather than end times because utterance start times were easier to retrieve. Thus, the computed time interval includes duration of the last utterance.

Predictions

We expected that adult-assisted story choice would be faster than the child-operated two-click picker because the aide would keep children from getting stuck or spending too much time picking. We expected that the one-click picker would be faster than the two-click picker because it was both simpler and encouraged the student to read the first story chosen.

Findings

Based on this preliminary analysis, story choice time averaged 3 minutes for the human-assisted condition in 1996–1997, with a range of 1 to 4 minutes. The two-click picker used in 1998 averaged 2 minutes, with our sample of 10 transitions ranging from 40 seconds to 2 minutes, 40 seconds. The 1998 sample included one 6-minute, 36-second interval where a student looked at the first sentence of several different stories without going on to the second sentence (a browsing behavior that reflects reduced supervision). The one-click, turn-taking picker used in 1999 averaged a mere 26 seconds, with our sample of 9 transitions ranging from 13 seconds to 1 minute. This survey suggests that the combination of turn-taking and one-click picking is dramatically more efficient than the mechanism it replaced, at least for students who accept the resulting choice.

Effectiveness of Story Choice

To confirm that "take turns" gets students to see relatively more new stories, sentences, and words, we compared story choice data for 1999–2000 (the "take turns" Reading Tutor) against story choice data from the 1996–1997 and 1997–1998 version of the Tutor.

Method

Using the same data as in the efficiency evaluation, we conducted a more automatic and comprehensive analysis, treating over 144,000 utterances recorded by the three versions of the Tutor. We computed the fraction of sentences new to each student by analyzing all the sentences read by that student. Counting sentences gave us a finer-grained measure than counting the number of new stories read. Also, unlike counting new vocabulary, counting sentences gave credit for seeing the same words in new contexts. To calculate how often an average student read new material, we analyzed the distribution of these per-student fractions rather than pooling all the data.

Predictions

We expected the analysis to show that students using the 1996–1997 pilot Tutor saw higher percentages of new sentences than those using the 1997–1998 version, thanks to the aide who helped them pick stories and encouraged them to try new ones. We predicted that students using the 1999–2000 Tutor would read higher percentages of new sentences than those using the 1997–1998 version because of the redesigned story choice features, especially turn taking.

Findings

Tables 10.2–10.4 show the results of this analysis in terms of students' new-sentence percentages for each version of the Reading Tutor. These percentages averaged 43% for the eight low-reading third graders in the 1996–1997 version (Table 10.2), 61% for the 22 second, fourth, and fifth graders in the 1998 version (Table 10.3), and 64% for the 58 second and third graders in the 1999 version (Table 10.4). As Table 10.4 shows, the fall 1999 version has the highest floor (37%) although, with the largest number of students, one would expect just the opposite. This result reflects the success of turn taking at exposing every student to new material. The 1999 figure is artificially low because the first utterances for each session consisted of students' reading their name as a microphone test, thus inflating the number of reread "sentences." The fact that the 43% figure for the pilot version of the Reading Tutor is much *lower* than the other versions is surprising and may reflect various factors, including the aide's tendency to have students read stories twice in a row or the fact that the eight pilot subjects initially averaged three years below grade level.

The data from Tables 10.2–10.4 can also be summarized as a scatter plot. This summary is shown in Figure 10.5 and discussed following the presentation of the tables.

Table 10.2 Story Choice Effectiveness in 1996–1997 Pilot Reading Tutor

Student	Sentences	New Material Rate	S.E. Mean
MGT	244	0.30	0.03
MCR	287	0.39	0.04
MTW	163	0.39	0.05
MDC	306	0.40	0.04
MRT	331	0.43	0.04
MMD	209	0.44	0.05
FBW	471	0.48	0.03
MJT	222	0.60	0.05
Average		**0.43**	

Table 10.3 Story Choice Effectiveness in Spring 1998 Reading Tutor

Student	Sentences	New Material Rate	S.E. Mean
FSMR	212	0.26	0.03
MKJ	115	0.36	0.05
FTLM	345	0.47	0.04
MEE	179	0.49	0.05
MJC	276	0.50	0.04
MOH	175	0.51	0.05
FSG	178	0.52	0.05
FKVB	374	0.55	0.04
FCH	185	0.56	0.05
FKK	580	0.56	0.03
FJMF	312	0.58	0.04
MJT	295	0.59	0.04
MNJ	49	0.62	0.11
MARW	335	0.63	0.04
FJLB	251	0.64	0.05
MAC	470	0.66	0.04
FLH	523	0.69	0.03
FLB	169	0.73	0.06
MBP	233	0.74	0.05
FSB	228	0.75	0.05
FAW	244	0.76	0.05
FCR	197	0.79	0.05
FJO	205	0.80	0.05
MCD	219	0.84	0.05
Average		**0.61**	

The scatter plot of the data from Tables 10.2–10.4 is shown in Figure 10.5. Each point in the plot represents one student (the shape of the point shows the version of the Reading Tutor used by that student). The x-coordinate represents the total number of sentences read by that student, so that more prolific readers appear toward the right. The y-coordinate represents the percentage of new sentences, so that more adventurous readers appear higher. These data suggest that the fall 1999 version of the Reading Tutor encourages readers to be both more prolific and more adventurous, again pointing to the advantage of the turn taking feature in fostering more reading.

RELATION TO OTHER WORK

Task choices pervade human–computer interaction, not to mention life itself! This paper focuses on a task choice for a particular population (children), activity (ASR-assisted reading), object (story), and goal (literacy). In computer tutors where the student learns by doing, a key dimension of task choice is the division of labor between tutor and student.

At one extreme, the tutor always chooses what task to perform next. A good example is Anderson et al.'s Algebra Tutor (Corbett, Trask, Scarpinatto, & Hadley, 1998; now produced by Carnegie Learning, at http://www. carnegielearning.com/). The Algebra Tutor uses a model of what the student knows (Corbett & Anderson, 1995) to select a problem-solving task designed to develop the rule(s) that the student needs to learn. Tutor control requires a tutor sophisticated enough to know what task to choose and a learner motivated enough to accept that choice (Aleven et al., 2003; Aleven & Koedinger, 2000). The Reading Tutor lacks a strong enough student model to know which specific story is best for the student to read next, and even if it had such a model, depriving the student of the choice would reduce motivation (e.g., Littlemore, 2001).

At the opposite extreme are programs that always let the student choose the task. For example, an edutainment program such as Jumpstart Kindergarten lets the child choose what activity to do (e.g., coloring) and for how long. Another example is a program that lets the student choose a book to read. To be educationally effective, learner control requires learners who understand the choices, can operate the mechanism needed to make a choice, and are mature enough to choose an appropriate task. In the Reading Tutor, nonreaders need help to understand the choices, so the Tutor reads titles aloud. Because we found that some younger children had trouble using the story picker, we redesigned it. Because we also saw that many children chose stories too easy or (occasionally) too hard, we adopted a hybrid solution.

Various forms of mixed-initiative task choice lie between pure tutor control and pure learner control. For example, the Piano Tutor (Dannenberg

Table 10.4 Story Choice Effectiveness in Fall 1999 Reading Tutor

Student	Sentences	New Material Rate	S.E. Mean
MJC	114	0.37	0.06
MBR	164	0.41	0.05
MLD	139	0.45	0.06
MAG	322	0.50	0.04
MMW	408	0.50	0.03
MSK	218	0.50	0.05
MDS	501	0.51	0.03
FAS	590	0.52	0.03
FCD	633	0.52	0.03
FJP	458	0.52	0.03
MBE	440	0.53	0.03
MDM	564	0.53	0.03
FSK	476	0.54	0.03
FDR	353	0.55	0.04
FTA	266	0.55	0.05
MLF	483	0.56	0.03
FQB	369	0.58	0.04
FAM	279	0.59	0.05
FDL	546	0.60	0.03
MCR	364	0.60	0.04
MDB	570	0.60	0.03
MMH	286	0.60	0.04
MTR	261	0.60	0.05
MJT	118	0.61	0.07
MDH	352	0.62	0.04
FJE	202	0.63	0.05
MJH	515	0.64	0.03
MKB	546	0.64	0.03
FBC	496	0.65	0.03
FJB	390	0.65	0.04
FNC	335	0.65	0.04

Table 10.4 Story Choice Effectiveness in Fall 1999 Reading Tutor *(Continued)*

Student	Sentences	New Material Rate	S.E. Mean
MTB	485	0.65	0.03
MGB	460	0.66	0.04
FTB	431	0.67	0.04
FTH	216	0.67	0.05
MAJ	348	0.67	0.04
MRM	208	0.67	0.05
FAE	373	0.68	0.04
MGP	406	0.68	0.04
FMG	414	0.69	0.04
MTP	466	0.69	0.04
FAS	591	0.70	0.03
FSB	452	0.70	0.04
FJP	465	0.71	0.04
FLG	503	0.71	0.03
FSW	556	0.71	0.03
FKG	418	0.72	0.04
MJP	609	0.72	0.03
FNC	456	0.73	0.04
MJC	419	0.74	0.04
FBG	562	0.75	0.03
FPO	681	0.75	0.03
FSO	507	0.75	0.03
MJK	459	0.75	0.03
MLG	525	0.75	0.03
MSF	463	0.78	0.03
MJA	393	0.80	0.04
FCP	450	0.81	0.03
FMW	80	0.87	0.07
MOB	24	0.96	0.08
Average		**0.64**	

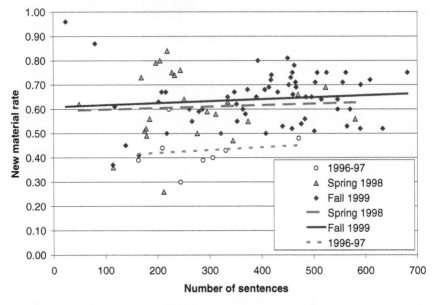

Figure 10.5 Scatterplot showing new material rate by number of sentences for 3 versions of Reading Tutor (1996–97, Spring 1998, Fall 1999). Each data point represents one student's performance over the course of the respective study.

et al., 1990) computes which lessons the student is ready for and invites the student to choose one of them. Similarly, the Reading Tutor estimates the student's reading level and lets the student pick a story at that level. In Edmark's Let's Go! Read, the student picks a form of activity and the program chooses content, such as which letter sound to drill next. Similarly, the Reading Tutor lets the student pick the story, but it decides what assistance to give. Finally, to keep students from rereading the same stories, the Reading Tutor takes turns picking stories.

We have not seen turn-taking in other tutorial programs but would not be surprised to find it. One direction for future work would be for the Reading Tutor to monitor the student's choices and make choices of its own only when the student makes choices not conducive to learning. For example, the Reading Tutor could intervene to choose a new story only if the student chose an old story last time—but otherwise leave the student to his or her own choices. A challenge of this approach is to operationalize "choices not conducive to learning," automate the detection of such choices, and respond to them in ways that the student is likely to accept as fair—or at least unable to be circumvented. Experience with children's creativity in pursuing their own goals—sometimes at the sacrifice of their learning needs—has taught us to value simplicity of design over attempts to outwit children, because they tend to beat us every time.

CONCLUSION: LESSONS LEARNED
FROM STORY CHOICE EXPERIMENTS

Having developed and tested ASR methods that can detect and diagnose difficulties of early readers, we want to be sure that students get the most benefit from these methods. We want to guide students to the set and sequence of stories that will optimize their learning. How can tutors steer students to tasks they will learn from? More specifically, how can the Reading Tutor get students to read aloud stories that will improve their fluency and vocabulary? The process of developing and analyzing solutions to this problem has exposed several desiderata for story choice:

- Ease: Are choices clear and unambiguous to the student? To help, the Reading Tutor reads titles aloud.
- Speed: Every minute spent choosing a story is a minute not spent reading. Our data suggest that turn taking and one-click choice make story choice much faster.
- Simplicity: Is story choice policy simply described to students and teachers? To set clear expectations, the Reading Tutor introduces a Tutor-chosen story with appropriate recorded phrases (e.g., Read this story, and then you'll choose one.)
- Fairness: Does the policy seem fair? Does it treat the student as (at least!) an equal to the computer? Taking turns is a concept familiar to children.
- Motivation: Does the policy sometimes let the student reread favorite stories? Students may get frustrated when they want to do this but must instead read a Tutor-chosen story. Setting the proper expectations for story choice at the outset seems important for student acceptance.
- Cheat-resistance: The Reading Tutor is designed to prevent various methods of circumventing tutor story choice, such as logging out and logging back in again.
- Fault-tolerance: Students should not be forced to read a story that is too hard or that they just don't like, whether they picked it by accident or the Reading Tutor picked it. The Back button affords another chance.
- Appropriateness: Is story choice matched to the student's reading level? The Reading Tutor uses its estimate of the student's reading level both to choose stories and to suggest to the student which stories to choose from. The Tutor adjusts this estimate based on the student's oral reading fluency measured by ASR.
- Teacher-friendliness: Does story choice avoid burdening busy teachers yet allow them control when they want? The Tutor's heuristics for adjusting students' reading level and choosing stories are designed to make reasonable choices without teacher input while letting teachers fix the level of an individual student or story.

- Effectiveness: Does story choice policy ensure that every student will read appropriate new material regularly, yet permit some rereading? Taking turns keeps children from rereading easy stories all the time. Analysis of over 144,000 utterances recorded by three versions of the Reading Tutor shows that turn taking yielded an increase in average percentage of new sentences seen per student and in the minimum percentage of new sentences seen by even the lowest student.

In review, we designed and implemented a child-friendly menu in the Reading Tutor with two improvements over previous versions: The new menu spoke all items on the list to support use by nonreaders and it required just one click to select an item. Second, we combined this child-friendly menu with a mixed-initiative policy where the tutor and the student took turns choosing stories. These improvements resulted in measurably more efficient and effective story choice over previous versions.

This chapter has examined effectiveness defined as exposing readers to new language samples. Not addressed directly is pedagogical effectiveness: How well does the Reading Tutor help children learn to read? This question is taken up in the chapter by Mostow et al. (this volume), reporting a 4-month controlled evaluation of the Reading Tutor with learner control (1997–1998), and by Mostow et al. (2001), summarizing an 8-month evaluation of the Reading Tutor that takes turns (1999–2000).

What remains? Goals of Project Listen include increasing the lowest performing students' motivation to read, to better take advantage of the diagnostic speech recognition algorithms we have adapted for teaching reading. The project also seeks to improve the interfaces that allow students, teachers, administrators, and researchers to track students on story choice and reading performance, thereby allowing us to gather data about how children learn to read.

ACKNOWLEDGMENTS

This paper is based upon work supported in part by the National Science Foundation under Grant Nos. MDR-CDA-9616546 and REC-9979894, and by the first author's National Science Foundation Graduate Fellowship and Harvey Fellowship. Any opinions, findings, conclusions, or recommendations expressed in this publication are those of the authors and do not necessarily reflect the views of the National Science Foundation or the official policies, either expressed or implied, of the sponsors or of the United States Government.

We thank current and previous members of Project LISTEN who have made substantive contributions to this work. Dan Barritt participated in the design process for the story choice menu and helped supervise the summer reading clinic where the menu was refined and tested. Professor David Klahr gave an insightful analysis of menu choice for children and pointed out that children have trouble following two-step plans.

REFERENCES

Aist, G., Burkhead, P., Corbett, A., Cuneo, A., Junker, B., Mostow, et al. (2001). Computer-assisted oral reading helps third graders learn vocabulary better than a classroom control—about as well as one-on-one human-assisted oral reading. *Proceedings of Artificial Intelligence and Education (AI-ED 01)*, 267–277.

Aleven, V., & Koedinger, K. R. (2000). Limitations of student control: Do students know when they need help? In G. Gauthier, C. Frasson, & K. VanLehn (Eds.), *Proceedings of the 5th International Conference on Intelligent Tutoring Systems, ITS 2000* (pp. 292–303). Berlin: Springer Verlag.

Corbett, A., & Anderson, J. (1995). Knowledge tracing: Modeling the acquisition of procedural knowledge. *User Modeling and User-Adapted Interaction, 4*, 253–278.

Corbett, A., & Anderson, J. R. (2001). Locus of feedback control in computer-based tutoring: Impact on learning rate, achievement and attitudes. *Proceedings of ACM CHI'2001 Conference on Human Factors in Computing Systems*, 245–252.

Corbett, A., Koedinger, K., & Anderson. J. (1997). Intelligent tutoring systems. In M. G. Helander, T. Landauer, & P. Prabhu (Eds.), *Handbook of human computer interaction, 2nd edition* (pp. 849–874). Amsterdam: Elsevier.

Corbett, A., Trask, H., Scarpinatto, K. C., & Hadley, W. (1998). A formative evaluation of the PACT Algebra II Tutor: Support for simple hierarchical reasoning, In B. Goettl, H. Halff, C. Redfield, & V. Shute (Eds.), *Intelligent tutoring systems: Fourth international conference, ITS '98* (pp. 374–383). New York: Springer.

Dannenberg, R. B., Sanchez, M., Joseph, A., Capell, P., Joseph, R., & Saul, R. (1990). A computer-based multi-media tutor for beginning piano students. *Interface—Journal of New Music Research, 19*(2–3), 155–173.

Hanna, L., Risden, K., Czerwinsky, M., & Alexander, M. (1999). The role of usability research in designing children's computer products. In A. Druin (Ed.), *The design of children's technology*. San Francisco: Morgan Kaufmann.

Kalchman, M., & Koedinger, K. (2005). Teaching and learning functions. In S. Donovan & J. Bransford (Eds.), *How students learn*. Washington, D.C.: National Academy Press.

Koedinger, K. & Corbett, A. (2006). Cognitive Tutors: Technology bringing learning science to the classroom. In K. Sawyer (Ed.), *The Cambridge Handbook of the Learning Sciences*. Cambridge, UK: Cambridge University Press.

Lepper, M., Woolverton, M., Mumme, D., & Gurtner, J. (1993). Motivational techniques of expert human tutors: Lessons for the design of computer-based tutors. In S. Lajoie & S. Derry (Eds.), *Computers as cognitive tools* (pp. 75–105). Hillsdale, NJ: Lawrence Erlbaum Associates.

Littlemore, J. (2001). Learner autonomy, self-instruction, and new technologies in language learning. In A. Chambers & G. Davies (Eds.), *ICT and language learning: A European perspective*. Lisse, NL: Swets & Zeitlinger.

Mostow, J., et al. (2001). An eight-month controlled evaluation of the 1999–2000 Reading Tutor. *Proceedings of Conference on Artificial Intelligence and Education (AI-ED 01)*.

Mostow, J., & Aist, G. S. (1997). When speech input is not an afterthought: A reading tutor that listens. *Proceedings of Workshop on Perceptual User Interfaces*, Banff, Canada. [Reprinted in *Proceedings of Conference on Automated Learning and Discovery (CONALD98)*, June 11–13, 1998, Carnegie Mellon University]

Mostow, J., & Aist, G. S. (1999a). Giving help and praise in a reading tutor with imperfect listening—because automated speech recognition means never being able to say you're certain. *CALICO Journal 16*(3), 407–424.

Mostow, J., & Aist, G. S. (1999b). Authoring new material in a reading tutor that listens. *Proceedings of the 16th National Conference on Artificial Intelligence (AAAI-99)*, 918–919, Orlando, FL.

Mostow, J., Beck, J,. & Bey, G. S. (2004). Can automated questions scaffold children's reading comprehension?. *Proceedings of the Seventh International Conference on Intelligent tutoring Systems (ITS-04)*, Maceio, Brazil.

Mostow, J., Roth, S., Hauptmann, A., & Kane, M. (1994). A prototype reading coach that listens. *Proceedings of the 12th National Conference on Artificial Intelligence (AAAI-94)*, Seattle (Recipient of AAAI-94 Outstanding Paper Award).

Niemiec, R. P., Sikorski, C., & Walberg, H. (1996). Learner-control effects: A review of reviews and a meta-analysis. *Journal of Educational Computing Research, 15*(2), 157–174.

Schnackenberg, H. L., & Hilliard, A. W. (1998). Learner ability and learner control: A 10 year literature review 1987–1997. *Proceedings of Selected Research and Development Presentations at the National Convention of the Association for Educational Communications and Technology (AECT)*, St. Louis, MO, February 18–22. [ERIC accession number ED423858].

Contributors

Gregory Aist is an Assistant Research Professor in the School of Computing and Informatics at Arizona State University. Previously, he held positions at the University of Rochester, the NASA (National Aeronautics and Space Administration) Ames Research Center, and the Massachusetts Institute of Technologies (MIT) Media Lab. He received his Ph.D. at Carnegie Mellon University as a National Science Foundation Graduate Fellow.

Agustín Álvarez-Marquina serves on the faculty of the Computer Science Department at the Polytechnic University of Madrid (Universidad Politécnica de Madrid) in Spain, where he also received a Ph.D. in computer science. His research interests include speech recognition and automated speaker identification.

Jesús Bernal-Bermúdez holds a Ph.D. in computer science and has been a professor in the Computer Engineering Department of the Polytechnic University of Madrid (Universidad Politécnica de Madrid), Spain, since 2000. He currently investigates multimedia signal processing systems.

Jared Bernstein serves as chief research scientist of Oordinate Corporation, which he co-founded in 1997. He has been active in speech technology for more than 25 years, focusing on applications in language education and in the design of instructional and prosthetic systems. He led the design of automated spoken language tests in several languages as well as automated tests of reading skill in English, work which has transitioned into practice through a range of products. Dr. Bernstein is consulting associate professor of linguistics at Stanford University, where he teaches phonetics, applied linguistics, and language testing.

Jesús Bobadilla-Sancho has been a professor in the Computer Engineering Department of the Polytechnic University of Madrid (Universidad Politécnica de Madrid), Spain, since 2000. With a Ph.D. in computer science, he conducts research in multimedia signal processing systems.

Harry Bratt is Senior Computer Scientist in the Speech Technology and Research (STAR) Laboratory at SRI International, Menlo Park, California.

His research interests extend across human-machine interaction, computer-assisted language learning, and spoken language systems, including the extraction and application of prosodic information. He has been engaged in research on speech technology for second language learning purposes for the past 10 years.

Jian Cheng is a senior research engineer at Ordinate Corporation and is responsible for all aspects of the research and development cycle for automated grading in Ordinate's spoken language and oral reading assessments. His expertise includes speech recognition, artificial intelligence, and natural language processing. He received his Ph.D. in information science from the University of Pittsburgh.

Ray Clifford is associate dean of the College of Humanities and directs the Center for Language Studies at Brigham Young University, Utah. Previously, he served as chancellor of the Defense Language Institute Foreign Language Center (DLIFLC) in Monterey, California, where he shepherded research projects to investigate technologies such as speech recognition and pronunciation scoring for language learning and opened collaborations with research organizations such as the Spoken Language Systems Group at Massachusetts Institute of Technologies. He has a Ph.D. in foreign language education from the University of Minnesota and has received several national honors as well as a Doctor of Letters, honoris causa, from Middlebury College in Vermont.

Jonathan Dalby is a professor in the Department of Audiology and Speech Sciences at Indiana University-Purdue University in Fort Wayne, Indiana. From 1992 to 2003 he was senior scientist at Communication Disorders Technology (www.comdistec.com) in Bloomington, Indiana, a company that won a Tibbetts Award in 2001 for small business innovative research. He was principal investigator on the HearSay and You-Said-It projects at Communication Disorders Technology and participated in the development of the Indiana Speech Training Aid (ISTRA) and other computer-based training systems that employ automatic speech recognition and pronunciation scoring technologies.

Rodolfo Delmonte is sssociate professor of computational linguistics at Ca' Foscari University in Venice, Italy. In addition to his work in computer-assisted language learning, he has developed a range of computational language resources for Italian. Formerly on the faculty of the University of Trieste, he participated in groundwork research in natural language processing to support Italian DECTalk (Digital Equipment Corporation). Recently, he has held visiting positions at the University of Texas, Dallas, and at the Center for Spoken Language Research (CSLR) at the University of Colorado. He has served on the scientific program committees of major international conferences in speech and text processing, such as the 2006 Conference on Language Resources and Evaluation (LREC).

Francis (Pete) Fisher is a senior electronics engineer in the Computational and Information Sciences Directorate at the US Army Research Laboratory in Adelphi, MD. With engineering degrees from Johns Hopkins University and the University of Maryland, he has led projects to adapt speech recognition for computer-human interfaces and for computer-mediated speech translation, as well as projects to develop robotic systems and handheld document translation and triage systems. His current work includes the development of a new form of radio for transmission of sensor data.

Neil Granoien specializes in post-secondary language learning, with more than 30 years of university experience in teaching and administration, focused on teacher training and curriculum development for second languages. Most recently, he served as vice chancellor of the Defense Language Institute Foreign Language Center (DLIFLC) in Monterey, California, where he launched initiatives to evaluate the use of automatic speech recognition and other technologies for language learning, teaming with Massachusetts Institute of Technologies Lincoln Lab and other research institutions. He recently retired from DLIFLC to pursue interests in learning technologies and the development of speech-to-speech translation systems.

Pedro Gómez-Vilda is professor in the informatics faculty at the Polytechnic University of Madrid (Universidad Politécnica de Madrid), Spain, where he heads the Group on Computer Science for Signal and Image Processing. With a doctorate in computer science, his research interests since the early 1980s have included automatic speaker identification and robust speech recognition. More recently, he has begun investigations in biomedical signal processing and genomic signal processing. He is a member of the IEEE, ISCA, and EURASIP.

V. Melissa Holland heads the Center for Language Technology Research in the Computational and Information Sciences Directorate of the U.S. Army Research Laboratory. She leads projects to develop and evaluate machine translation for text and speech. Previously at the U.S. Army Research Institute, she applied speech recognition and natural language processing to second language instruction. She also studied the usability of technical documents at the nonprofit American Institutes for Research. Her doctorate is in experimental psychology with a focus on human language processing.

Fenfang Hwu is associate professor of romance languages and literatures at the University of Cincinnati in Ohio. Her areas of expertise are computer assisted language learning, the effects of individual differences in CALL use, second language acquisition, and Hispanic linguistics. Active for more than 10 years in CALICO (Computer Assisted Language Instruction Consortium), she is a member of its journal review board. She has published in Spanish linguistics and computer assisted language learning. Her current research interests include CALL instructional design, individual differences in CALL design, and the use of tracking technologies in CALL.

Diane Kewley-Port is professor of speech and hearing sciences and professor of cognitive sciences at Indiana University in Bloomington, Indiana. She is a founder Communication Disorders Technology (www.comdistec.com), which won the Tibbetts Award for small business innovation research in 2001. She served as principal investigator for the development of the Indiana Speech Training Aid (ISTRA) and during the past 16 years has been involved in the development of many other computer-based training systems that apply speech technologies to help children and adults with speech, language, or hearing disorders.

Rafael Martínez-Olalla holds a Ph.D. in computer science and since 2003 has been on the faculty of the Computer Science Department at the Polytechnic University of Madrid (Universidad Politécnica de Madrid) in Spain. He conducts basic research in signal processing and robust speech recognition.

Garry Molholt is professor of linguistics at West Chester University, Pennsylvania, where he directs the English-as-a-Second-Language (ESL) Program and is graduate coordinator for the Teaching of ESL (TESL) Program. His interest in the visualization of speech patterns began at Rensselaer Polytechnic Institute, New York, in 1982 while helping international teaching assistants and professors communicate better with students. He has teamed with a commercial spectrogram developer in projects on accent reduction and he regularly collaborates with the Center for Technology Enhanced Language Learning of the United States Military Academy at West Point.

Jack Mostow is research professor at Carnegie Mellon University in robotics, machine learning, language technologies, and human–computer interaction. In 1992, he founded Project LISTEN (www.cs.cmu.edu/~listen) to develop a speech-interactive automated tutor that listens to children read aloud. Project LISTEN won the Outstanding Paper Award at the 1994 National Conference on Artificial Intelligence, a United States patent in 1998, inclusion in the National Science Foundation's "Nifty Fifty" projects in 2000, and the Allen Newell Medal of Research Excellence in 2003. He has held faculty positions at Stanford University, the University of Southern California Information Sciences Institute, and Rutgers University, served as an editor of Machine Learning Journal and IEEE Transactions on Software Engineering, and was keynote speaker at the 2004 meeting of the Association for Computational Linguistics.

Víctor Nieto-Lluis holds the position of professor in the Computer Science Department at the Polytechnic University of Madrid (Universidad

Politécnica de Madrid) in Spain. With degrees in mechanical engineering and computer science, he has worked in signal processing since the late 1970s and focuses his current research on micro-array speech processing and database recording.

Kristin Precoda is eirector of the Speech Technology and Research (STAR) Laboratory at SRI International in Menlo Park, California, where she leads the development of systems for speech-to-speech translation. With Ph.D. and M.S. degrees in electrical engineering, an M.S. degree in statistics, and an M.A. degree in linguistics, she has been active in speech and language technology work since 1983. Her interests include user-centered system design, speech perception, and the transition of systems from research to real-world use. She notes that she has studied seven languages the hard way.

Victoria Rodellar-Biarge holds the position of professor in the Computer Science Department at the Polytechnic University of Madrid (Universidad Politécnica de Madrid) in Spain. With a Ph.D. in computer science, she has since the 1980s investigated signal processing system software as well as supporting hardware.

Index

For Product Safety Concerns and Information please contact our EU
representative GPSR@taylorandfrancis.com Taylor & Francis Verlag GmbH,
Kaufingerstraße 24, 80331 München, Germany

Printed and bound by CPI Group (UK) Ltd, Croydon, CR0 4YY
11/04/2025
01843977-0003